BEING MY OWN BOSS

(A sequel to the bestseller book 'creating new jobs from the existing jobs')

EXPLICIT.   MOTIVATIONAL. PRACTICABLE. TOWARDS CREATING NEW ENTREPRENEURS AND NEW JOBS FROM THE EXISTING JOBS

AMUSA ABDULATEEF

Author of the bestsellers "**Jobs with zero capital**" and "**Creating new jobs from the existing jobs**"

Addin publishers

A division of:

ADDIN RESOURCES VENTURES

IBADAN NIGERIA

+234 80567 10944   +234 803215 5018

Latlib222@yahoo.com   addinrv@gmail.com

Visit www.amusa-abdulateef.com for our other books.

ISBN:1979866139

© No part of this book must be reproduced, stored in a retrieval system or transmitted by any means without the written permission of the author.

ACKNOWLEDGEMENT

The foremost appreciation goes to the Almighty Creator that creates all creation that inspires and guides me into the writing of this life changing work. As I always write and say 'I remain a pen being used to communicate to people'.

My second appreciation goes to my soul mate- **Kudirah Adunni Joy-nee Oladipupo**. She has been my safety net since the moment all the researches into the series of employments creation through identifying of opportunities from different dimensions they used to appear. And this effort has produced the **three volumes** of different titles namely '**Creating new jobs from the existing jobs**,' '**Being my own boss**' and '**Wastes to wealth jobs**'. Her jolly friend, owner of Adesol catering service in the person of **Mrs. Sheriffah Falade** really contributes meaningfully into the making of the visionary. My next appreciation goes to my sponsors while in schools in the persons of Mrs. Anike Abe and her hubby, Pastor Abe; Mrs. Tomilayo Laniya of Bloom group of schools, Mr. Olabayo Olafusi, Mrs. Modupe Felicia Adeleke of Nickdel group of schools, Mr. Abdulrazaq Busari-Olaoye, Mr.Iziaq Ademola Rauf-Olaoye of Zico Entertainment, Mr. Samuel Ayotade (Sayotal enterprises) and his wife Mrs. Sarah Abosede Awujoola, Alhaji Isiaq Adekunle Sanni and his wife Alhaja Rafat Idowu-Kunle Sanni, Chief Wale Ohu, my jolly friends like surveyor Abdulrahmon Abubakar, Olalekan Joel Awujoola, Principal System Analyst of Nigerian Defence Academy Kaduna, Isiaq Ademola Olaoye (of blessed memory) of Zico Entertainment, Tiamiyu Jimoh Abiodun, Education Officer of Nigeria International School, Cotonou, Oseni Jimoh Folayemi, ex-NULGE Chairman for Odigbo Local Government, Ondo State, Alhaji Musa Akande, Mr. Muideen Bukhari (Mubak Wood Technology), Mr. Abdulsalam bin Salam (Sasco), Mr. Solih Tajudeen, Ms. Ajoke Simbiat Oluwakemi, Ms. Joy Ayodeji, Mr. AbdulKabir Oladiti among others numerous to mention.

I shall not fail to recognize the moral, spiritual and financial supports of my in-laws in the persons of Alhaji. Bashir O. Adebisi and his wife Mrs. V.O.A Adebisi, Mr. Musiliyu Mustafa of Forest Research Institute of Nigeria, United Kingdom-based Mr. Tajudeen Babatunde Oladipupo, Alhaji Shuaib Adebisi, a baker of repute among others.

Lest I forget Mr. Abdulkabir Oladiti Olanrewaju, my website developer and director ICT arm of Addin Resources Ventures, the Director of OMIC technologies, Mr. Babatunde Olajide Yusuf, He is never forgotten in the making of this writer just as Mr. Yusuf Tunde, the Director of Teckmanit technology for their technical inputs as and when due. Only God could reward all the mentioned people accordingly. To all of them, I say, jazakumullahkhairan.

And may this be accepted as a form of worship like the previous works intended on turning round the lifestyle of people positively as this is <u>a great opportunity</u> to open the eyes of the readers to limitless ways by which jobs, gainful and secured jobs could be created. There must be creation and opening the eyes of potential entrepreneurs into opportunities to create lucrative ideas towards creating jobs to fix the millions who are employable but unemployed and therefore living below standard in stricken poverty. Good and secure jobs are major solutions to all the scourge of unemployment across the nations. Again, may Almighty accept this from me as a form of worship.

DEDICATION

The book is dedicated to my inestimable mum in monetary and spiritual value, **Haolat Aduke**, of blessed memory for her unflinching supports in the course of parenting and nurturing me towards my educational and spiritual fulfillments.

TABLE OF CONTENTS

ACKNOWLEDGEMENT

DEDICATION

AUTHOR SPEAKS

FACTS OF THE MATTER: LUCRATIVE JOBS ARE ALWAYS AVAILABLE PROVIDED....

CHAPTER ONE

1.1 ZERO-TOLERANCE TO UNEMPLOYMENT

1.2 APPETISERS

1.3 OPPORTUNITIES KNOCKING AT YOUR DOORSTEPS (1)

1.4 SIDE KICK

CHAPTER TWO

2.1 WHAT IS AN OPPORTUNITY?

2.2 THE FACTS ABOUT EMPLOYMENTS OPPORTUNITIES

2.3 NATURE OF EMPLOYMENT-WEALTH CREATION OPPORTUNITIES

CHAPTER THREE

3.1 OPPORTUNITIES KNOCKING AT THE DOORS (2)

3.2 LET US BE PRACTICAL

3.3 STEPS TO BECOME PRODUCERS AND SELLERS

CHAPTER FOUR

4.1 NEW JOBS OPPORTUNITIES FROM THE EXISTING JOBS OPPORTUNITIES (Supplement)

4.2 THE GAINS

PART TWO

How to start a business, where and when

REFERENCES

AD-COPY

AUTHOR SPEAKS

Our first book on the series after the forerunner popular book titled "**Jobs with zero capital vol. one** and the recent release in **volume Two**" dealt with how new entrepreneurs can be unearthed and what it takes to be entrepreneurs including how to create new jobs from the existing jobs' from the point of view of adding **new features** to make the existing businesses have a new look that would appeal to potential customers who are not initially interested in the products and services. Our further researches show that it is not only the existing business and jobs can catalyze the creation of new jobs and businesses. Opportunities are in all non-existing ones too. Employment **opportunities** could be expressly stated as in the author's and publisher's permission for the translation of their works in other major languages at a condition. This is to promote new authors and publishers with different imprints. Imagine the value chains from taking this opportunity. Many producers used to give open checks to willing sellers and distributors of their products inside paid advertisements. I have witnessed wrong marketing and distribution strategies that open up selling and redistribution jobs in a household material. '**Water guard**', a popular brand name in water treatment plant, was being displayed for selling at popular malls that were mostly patronized by the middle and high income and literate earners who lived in government reserved areas and serene settlements where all social facilities were at their beck and call. These targeted customers did not need the product as they lived in places where treated water was never their problem. My wife started buying, re-distributing and resold to people living in densely populated areas where water treatment was a must before use. To those of like mind, this opportunity cuts across all products and services. What are the products and services that could create avenues to start lucrative jobs and how would this evolve? The contents of this book from head to tail serve readers right as eyes opener to embrace identifiable employments opportunities. Several are opportunities to kick start new employments and therefore taking the idle ones out of the streets and secluded homes to create new ideas of jobs. These are got inside prints, digital and broadcast media. Contents from the broadcast media like radio, television, terrestrial and cable are enough to start lucrative jobs. Many have radio schools teaching pupils (audience) via combining teaching with entertainment; medical practitioners are running telemedicine; lawyers have law reports on electronic and print media. In the light of this, we have seen great opportunities in converting OPMs to start jobs. By the acronym OPMs, we mean 'other people's minds, materials (resources and assets), methods (technical know-how, innovations or intellectual resources), markets and machineries to commence a job. With these, it is so easy to generate millions of employments for the idle ones. Make optimum use of the personal digital assistant with you to fish out jobs. I have lost count of numbers of people who secured lucrative jobs, contracts and placements through **google** of internet. Unlimited opportunities are in the information vectors. You lack nothing, depriving you self-development and anticipated growth, except right information which is being churned out as you are reading this! Be internet and innovations conscious from being information and communication technology friendly to unveil right jobs and you escape being unemployed or underemployed. Can you? Yes, you can! It is very simple to identify employments opportunities as you read patiently and you move along with us in the expository material. Always put on your thinking cap and meditate over what you come across in the course. If you cannot think to solve problems of others, then think over how to solve your own problems. Mind you, thinking for others is the best solution to solve your own problem. Let us swiftly cite some ways of identifying opportunities to elucidate this fact. A filthy environment with open dumps and blocked drainages in a community and industrial layouts is a communal problem. Solving this could open up employments opportunities in the fumigating and refuse evacuation jobs for private companies at a good price under community-business partnership. Government could use Public Private Partnership (PPP) to ensure private wastes management that would engage in evacuation from house to house, office to office, market to market and the like wastes zones and then convert the recyclable into useful raw materials. Recycling of solid and other wastes open up wealth-employment generation. High breeding of vectors of diseases like the mosquitoes carrying plasmodium that leads to malaria infection is a common problem. Now, when residents bitterly complained about the evasion of the vectors of malaria (mosquitoes) during a particular season, I saw this as a great opportunity to engage drainage clearance and fumigator; provided efforts are made to enter into business (service) agreement with the inhabitants at a fees as the service charge. What about the unhygienic places in the parks and markets? Don't they need your service as the residents?

In a nutshell, just like the situations on ground at different places at different times could open up jobs opportunities, every tangible and visible product is a path to start up new jobs or better the existing ones to be positively engaged for those who can think, reflect and understand. My resources venture, which is into problem-solving of national and international issues that are mostly multi-dimensional, ventured into running school to school what we called '**Mathematics picnic**'. It was aimed at eliminating the usual fear for the subject by the pupils. In the picnic, we engage the pupils and the teachers on how to turn the subject pupils-and-teachers-friendly with practical illustrations on the methods of teaching and imparting the knowledge. There was a time we commenced discovering new writers from schools through our teen writing contests with the objective of producing one-day authors from all the literary genres. We can conclude that squeezing jobs out of services is unlimited for think tanks. Now, let us examine a common sample in products. A book, from the book market or reading environment can produce seminars and workshops to train people on different issues. Books on entrepreneurs could ignite the seminar trainers. Prose books could produce all formats of books, audio books, films and special documentaries. Radio contents and interview have inspired writers and entertainers. Think about what a product or service could provide in employments. Who are there that can unveil the new ideas? Are there people who can use their creativity to create new business ideas from the existing ideas? If there are these, then employment generation should be an easy task for the nations and nationals.

Nevertheless, in this second series of how to create new jobs from the existing jobs, we looked at real and unusual **opportunities** being created in different forms, kinds, sizes, measures and shapes by the existing jobs, institutions, academies, policies, places, events at different perspectives. At the flip side, we look at **opportunities** to create jobs from the non-existing of infrastructures and challenges. Studies show that the more the challenges, the more the employments- generation opportunities. If there is a boost in the markets such as snacks, property, books, films, songs, foods, beverages, costumes among others, the employments opportunities soar. The rise and growth in population and the high the tastes of the people, the more jobs **opportunities** for those who have brains to identify them. Someone whose interest is being his own boss must learn new skills always in order to add values to his interest. Many counsellors on different or choice areas of interests could get right guides from reading write-ups of columnists inside the newspapers and through listening to interviews of specialists. Get this stored at the right part of your sense (brains). Identifying new opportunities across boards is a lifetime learning process to start-up as self-boss. A younger brother came for counselling of a new business idea of his. He had interest in dry cleaning service from one of his three bedroom apartment since water is available in the fenced house. I advised him to go and learn the skills of dry cleaning service from those in practice. Through the continual learning, he would understand the type of water to use for certain cloth, the type of detergents and soaps, the perfume, the packaging before he should think of home service and delivery. Through the process of learning, he understands different fabrics by texture, the amount being charged per fabric, the rules for abandon of clothes by customers, the added values among others. Then, he asked how to have patronage. I told him bluntly that 'selling or marketing is the simplest of the art of production. If the quality of product or service being sold is of global or regional standard with right endorsement, the primary customers should be the main target of a starter before the general public as contained in details in one of my books (referencing to 'Winning huge sales and increasing clients' base). I told him about a faith-based publication that was looking for marketers when the faith-based institutions, schools and associations are at the publisher's beck and call. Those are the primary marketplaces and therein are the prospective customers. Sellers and distributors, by mistake, are stocking their products at places where they are not needed or came into the market at the wrong time or with the wrong quantity that would never meet the demands of customers. To my brother whose interest was in dry cleaning services, I bared my heart, 'For a dry cleaner of clothes, the corporate offices are one of the places to secure customers. Others are institutions and individuals whose time for dry cleaning have been occupied by events and other socio-economic ventures. I learnt the modern style of writing before I was able to produce two bestsellers. In short, towards being one's own boss, we must ensure that new skills are learnt. It is our final findings that show that new jobs can be created in multiples depending at the recognition of **opportunities** and also on the creativity of the entrepreneurs-producers and sellers'. Field researches show that jobs in existence could be the sources of generating new jobs at all times and places. This is not just from adding new features but on forward and backward integration. In the period of shortage of forex in a nation that runs monolithic economy, if the companies decide to invest locally on the local content instead of importing all their raw materials abroad, new employment **opportunities** are generated for the local producers including the value chains. I was at an office where a guy was hawking stains cleaner. I advised him to move up the ladder to add toilet and bathroom tubs cleaning service. Can you see that opportunities can be created by existing **opportunities**? With the contents and expository facts with unambiguous every day occurrences, one can say that there is no need for more publications on entrepreneurship books. Anyway, this is the second in the series. And the third in the series is titled '**wastes to wealth jobs**' where the author researched into how to identify 'wastes' and the wealth and employment opportunities creatable from their conversion. Inability to convert opportunities is seen as a waste too in this dispensation. The thin line between this book '**Being my own boss**' and '**Wastes to wealth jobs**' is that the first identify and unveil opportunities to start jobs while the latter deals with how to identify the underutilized materials that can be transformed into lucrative jobs and increase the wealth of the nation. The common thing is that both contents open eyes to opportunities to start-up. The three books are inevitable in all libraries for tutors, researchers and students not excluding agencies of government, private and charity-based institutions. I would like the readers to flow with me on how opportunities to start good jobs are created. A teacher was posted to the rural areas. He was admired by the parents of his pupils for his hard work and good morals. He sought for free fertile lands to farm after school hours and weekends. His first harvests of cassava and maize was the turning point of his life where he started to become a rich in the town. Yam and cassava flour is highly priced in one of the oil-producing states in Nigeria. I learnt about how to process cassava from the farms into flour. Imagine reading on the pages of newspapers about foreigners investing in recycling of solid wastes and packaging of cassava flours from the direct purchases from Farmville. This shows that the business opportunities are in the nation for the local which they did not see. I gave selling and distribution channels a thought. At last, I sought to use a trusted friend living in the commercial town for selling of the cassava flour. These are business **opportunities** any person can try. All variants of farm produce are there for suppliers in my shoe. The increase in the farm produce is a path towards the development and proliferation of small scale, medium and large scale manufacturers. In the rise and fall of prices are employment opportunities particularly the itinerant international traders engaging in importing and exporting. There are talents in different sports that can be harnessed by people and institutions to make legitimate money and by so doing creating jobs. Government directly employ or indirectly create employments opportunities at the instance of their programmes under each Ministry, Departments and Agencies (MDAs). For instance, the Anchors Borrowers Scheme of the apex bank in Nigeria is targeted at creating new farmers and boost farm produce for food security assurance to the nation. In the news I got information from the Bank of Industry on the soft loans scheme of the institution to capitalize the artisanal jobs. This is an **opportunity** for the artisans to boost their trade and make more money from expansion and employing of more hands. When I was talking with a foreign firm about selling my books as e-books under its label, I got information from the advertisement slots of a radio station about a company at my nose (some metres away) that would provide me all the services being sought for abroad. What an opportunity at my fingertip! The whistle-blower policy of the government to report the corrupt people and the illicit loots is an opportunity for whistle-blowers to earn certain percentage of the discovered amount. In one of my dual-purpose proposals to the government, paid whistle blowing job should be used for all crimes such as vandalization, hoarding, kidnapping among other social vices. This is one of the intelligence works from the government. In the electronic media, it takes a form of i-reporting for i-reporters which would create avenues for jobs for i-promotion, i-marketing and i-selling. Another is the home-gown feeding programme for the school children that would create employments for a great number of people aside boosting the farm productions. Many of the agencies used to give information and directives that would promote entrepreneurship. I could recall the establishments of foundations especially those tagged entrepreneurship foundation. Nigeria's **Tony Elumelu** entrepreneurs is from his foundation that is supporting new entrepreneurs to be their own bosses. What of other foundations in your nation? Many do not explore websites and blogs to identify employment opportunities. In the sites are placed what each owner needs in products and services. Millions of youths that are searching for jobs, do you make efforts to tap the opportunities created by the foundations, institutional and companies' websites? Do people see opportunities in the private establishments? All existing and non-existing establishments or institutions- private and public, charity-based or profit-oriented, all self-employed entrepreneurs, the partnership business and the joint stock companies, all existing and dearth of academies, all training institutes, existing and non-existing, all positions of authority and academic qualifications, all qualities and assets (potentials) including skills in man, institutions and places, all tourist places and festivals or events- faith-based, ethnic-focused, national or regional, open rooms for employment generation. I used to educate a friend who is a disk jockey to venture into recording and promoting of young and aged talents in poetry and related. There are several business owners that have potentials to diversify or add new jobs to their lines in order to create employments for others. A close guy who is so endowed on internet-based jobs was advised to start online publishing of books and related intellectual property of others. United Kingdom's Sir **Richard Bransons** and Nigeria's **Aliko Dangotes** of this world always come to my mind on how they built and still building (via expansion and divestment) their conglomerate of businesses. The more the naturally skilled artisans, intellectual property owners and talented sportsmen in different sports, the more the opportunities to create more jobs by the publishers and sports directors, scouts, managers, promoters and marketers. Those are the **raw materials** needed in manpower for the proliferation of different business institutions and more jobs for all the unskilled. A nation or town where academies and artisanal jobs training institutes are not available, let some people show interests and establish them for the production of artisans and the other manpower for the public. Failure to have adequate artisans, there is great tendency for capital flight as foreign artisans would repatriate their earnings to their nations. The more the institutes, the more quality of products and services that would be churned out for the public consumption. Is creation of better structures not a way to create new jobs? Many producers (farmers, proprietors, artisans, fabricators..) and designers need marketers to sell their products and promote their services. In the third volume in the series '**Wastes to wealth jobs**', we identify how people and business institutions can convert idle assets into revenue-employment generating resources. Several publications and programmes inside the print and electronic media contain employment opportunities. What about all the underutilized items at our beck and call? How many, among the idle ones, see these as opportunities to become their own bosses? At the period of shortage fuel supplies, an undergraduate invented solar-powered tricycle with local contents. Had the government of the supported the guy on mass production, numerous chains of jobs would have been created. The epileptic supplies of electricity create opportunities for the proliferation of the makers of solar power panel and installers, the manufacturers and sellers of solar inverters and the energy savers. All the lapses of governments, individuals, associations, institutions and the likes open rooms for employment generation. All the right steps of the listed also pave the way for lucrative employments. I used to monitor the paid advertisements on the electronic and the print media to identify employments opportunities. One can say that over 80% of the promotional contents are paths to start-up jobs. Had those looking for jobs meditated over the advertisement slots, they would be on their own. In addition, the events and exhibitions always unveil employment opportunities that can be tapped for millions to become their bosses and of others (employees).

I used to ask myself 'do the people protesting against the governments with such placards 'give us employments' really identify the limitless jobs being churned out by limitless opportunities? Left, right, up, down and centre, **opportunities** stark us in the face. The faculties endowed man is needed to be tasked to identify them. Opportunities may come straight away or may be in disguise. They could come from negative and positive sides. In different shades, shapes and sizes are

opportunities. This is the purpose this book is out to serve the readers and institutions.

In retrospect, the entrepreneurship books being churned out to nations is an added value to those in existence opening up opportunities to start lucrative jobs. And reading all the works with the intent to meditate and research in order to develop the contents shall reduce search for employment to zero if not below zero level. You have enjoyed '**Creating new jobs from the existing jobs**' and '**Jobs with zero capital Vol. One and Two**', enjoy this irresistible one focusing on how to meditate and identify real life opportunities. And you shall discover limitless employments-creating opportunities and how they are created **every day**. The contents have some similarities to the contents of the book '**Wastes to wealth jobs**' by the same author with different approaches!

In short, no man can exhaust the number of **opportunities** to start good jobs. No writer is capable to write about the opportunities in volumes. To an extent, we are able to show the readers how opportunities are figured out and the paths towards unearthing them for employment creation and wealth-making. Natural gifts in the use of senses matter to identify countless opportunities. At the end of reading the book, I would like to see millions of **employment opportunities** that have been created for self-reliant people and thereby having a landmark record of zero-level of unemployment in the nations. Ask me where you should look for the opportunities to generate jobs and spread the wealth; it is from producers and sellers. When producers, as defined in the work, produces, they need the sellers in order to make the production complete its cycle. All cannot be producers and all cannot be sellers of goods and services. In most cases, sellers, in whatever forms, are in multiples of the producers. In the view of this, we specially dedicate some sub-chapters for the art of producing and selling in the down-to-earth and simply explicit book. All opportunities to be successful in all facets of life cannot be done outside having adequate information. With gathering and access of information, opportunities are created. Problems are solved. Institutions grow and the government would work- **Author**.

FACTS OF THE MATTER: LUCRATIVE JOBS ARE ALWAYS AVAILABLE PROVIDED....

Knowledge is sought and endlessly sought for to solve all crises. Factually as regards employment generation and loss, surveillance cameras, alarms, scanners, intrusion detection among others have sent and still sending many away from security jobs just as Automated Teller Machines (ATMs) have reduced the number of banking operations hence the staff. Several ICT solutions in form of apps have reduced and kept reducing the number of employees in factories and offices. Despite this, several employment **opportunities** are daily and constantly created. When government claims to have generated certain thousands of jobs, do you believe? Are you ever aware? If you do not know, it is the anticipated number of people that key into their programmes that makes the basis of their claim. For instance, if a government provides soft loans and subsidized farm inputs on agricultural production for 500,000 farmers; it is assumed that at least a farmer-beneficiary would have employed two directly and three indirectly in sellers and transporters of their farm produce. From our own perspective, the provision of loans and other enabling environment for certain sector is an opportunity to become one's boss with the supports. It takes brilliant minds to identify the lucrative opportunities from all sources. Many **apps** create rooms for service **outsourcing** and render many of the staff into casual workers. GPRS technology has reduced the purchase of qiblah finders for millions of Muslims. Tourist guides service may not be needed again with the same technology. It is easy to run errands at the comfort of one's homes and offices with the apps on mobile gadgets for information and communication technology development.

Mechatronics have taken over jobs of roadside mechanics especially in today's world of electronic cars. Think of any electronic devices in your mobile phones, they are in your modern day electronic cars! Most of the apps to build the latest in all sectors are done, tested and sold online. It is not a mincemeat of words to say that we are in a new world of internet innovations creating countless online-based businesses depending on individual creativity and versatility. Online publishers and online libraries are becoming the rave of the moment at the peril of traditional publishing and conventional library. Online retailers in the markets are getting more popularity and fast replacing physical marketplaces and the proliferation of online retailers and sellers have added values to the emergence of several online businesses such as online makers and suppliers of products and booking for services. Digital and social media selling has become the rave of the moment. Nations could create several thousands of employment from the maximum use of the internet facilities. Imagine what a nation would generate in forex from selling of software that is written and developed from within at global market. Software is developed by number of programmers just as a large number of people work on books publishing. Imagine the surplus for the exports if the nation engages in commercialization via modern mechanization of agricultural practices and heavy investment on manufacturing and processing the farm produce.

The bigger the landmass of a nation, the bigger the space to create employments. The more the institutions in a nation, the more opportunities to expose the unemployed into employment **opportunities**. If it is a norm for a nation, individual, institution to compare notes through visitation to the established institutions for short term seminars, new farmers in arable and livestock shall be created not to talk of manufacturers and processing entrepreneurs. The huge the population especially the teeming youths, the higher the chance of generating new jobs for the virile youths from the bigger market. It always amaze yours sincerely for a nation with vast arable lands and very large percentage of youths to be under industrialized. The **opportunities** of big market has propelled the servicing, manufacturing and transactional activities in many nations. And by so doing, wealth shall be created and distributed to millions. People, places, nations and institutions transact via online more than physical shopping for their convenience and easy access to products and services of their choices. Virtual business activities are taken over the business world reducing the workforce.

Fears are gripping the electronic markets that smartphones may soon send many out of jobs when the phones become all-purpose to on and off gadgets. Jobs market keeps swelling as a result of advancing technological innovations. One factual thing is that as people are losing jobs by the technology advancements, new types of jobs are equally created by the increasing innovations by the day with the use of the same technology. There are limitless **opportunities** daily from internet as always appear in the outputs of search engines optimizations. It will only take an intelligent, creative and versatile mind that lost his or her job to the advancement to start fresh as his or her own boss. If someone lost jobs to machines, the same machines could still provide the three square meals, pay the bills and savings for a rainy day. Let me ask, can such learn on how to work on the machines if they develop inevitable technical faults or act as a link or seller for buyers? Such only needs to updates his technical skills and amass relevant knowledge in order to stay relevant in the industry.

There are different ways to start one's own job especially when national economy is down or in recession. In fact, new jobs are daily created during the period a nation is having flagging economy. Ask me how? A recession economy is a situation where different challenges are created such as food shortage which open eyes of new farmers of arable and livestock to start production to increase food production or feed the industries; everyone becomes participant in farming of different crops with fallow and idle lands even at their backyards. Those in small scale farming would increase production with the supports of the government who has just found food security as a priority. Another effect of recession is the dwindling sales and very low patronage of services of companies whose solution is for independent sellers to expand the sales tentacle with their blogs at a mutually agreed service charge; other challenges in a recession economy is the spiral inflation especially in a country where costs of production are determined by imports and the exports are bringing in lower forex periodically. In this situation whose solution is the massive investment and more participation of stakeholders in small, medium enterprises to increase their participation to cover more grounds. Many companies have to downsize or cut remuneration of their employees. Many who lost their jobs are therefore independent to start new jobs with the garnered skills and social resources at the last place of work.

In view of the above, the economic downturn is an eyes opener (opportunity) for people in the nation to cut expenses and learn new learnable skills that would enhance multi-steam sources of income. Every challenge creates opportunities to start a good job. Think hard. Look within. Seek expertise opinions. It is anticipated that for companies, under national economic downturn, to make maximum profits as anticipated, they must record huge sales constantly with more independent marketers and sellers. Why can't those who lost their jobs in the industries they understand what they produce for sale become their independent sales representatives on commission? It is a matter of interest and mutual agreement. Let me give an instance. If someone lost his job in the bank and he is able to have good relation with the bank. Such could become agent of the bank promoting the services and products for a good return as marketer on the basis of agreement and such can run POS money payment service to out-of-cash customers, individuals and institutions on agreeable charges. Someone, not a retiree from bank, but proficient in financial accounting, finance or money management, who has interest to loan out money can start with the use POS at a choice station, where he could get huge customers' patronage such as close to the shopping malls, cinema, fuel stations, hotels…, on an agreement to the clients who suddenly run out of cash. This is a mobile banking business that can be registered under the relevant regulators endorsed by government. I have met a close friend that is into this for his former employer. Many could use the ICT skills to sell the services and products of the firms of choice. One can become i-reporter and photographer to boost the archives of existing media stations. Losing a job is an opportunity to start better and more lucrative job if senses are tasked. Many in history who become wealthy and influential had passed through such circumstances when they lost job by interest or through company policy to stay afloat. They picked up from the rubbles, dusted their bodies, tasked their senses by having a list of opportunities towards identifying what and how to start afresh and become independent. Most started to pursue their interests. And interests are evolving. They could become <u>e-products creators and sellers</u>. People can become venture into e-commerce in view of the technological innovations that sent them out of jobs. Many, with advancing innovations, can start several creative e-services and e-products. When I say e-service, I mean acting the offline jobs for online booking. Restaurant operators could add mobile service through the infusion of online bookings for their supplies of foods and drinks. And with the use of internet technology innovations, no business would record low sales or patronage again and no one should be idle as opportunities on internet are limitless!

In short, opportunities are not time and place bound. They evolve every seconds of the day at every place from different events. One can give limitless instances. The relocation of businesses from a nation to another without franchising, merging or acquisition by other indigenous firms is an opportunity for another business to fill the vacuum. If agribusiness departs for other nation, it has created opportunity for another firm to start production. A closure of a service-based business is a permit to start similar service business. When a residential area lacks certain businesses, new opportunities to commence such have opened for those with interests. Imagine the number of **opportunities** at a nation where several companies relocate! What about the flooding of the markets with foreign imports? Is this not an opportunity for employment and developing of business interests? Of course, yes. The imports have brought in new technology and better devices that the local-based artisans could use as specimens to develop indigenous devices. New products and services is regarded as an indirect technology transfer to the importing nation for the think tanks within to produce the local substitutes. I could recall a friend residing at new residential site where rental services are not existing. I advised him to learn about the job from someone that is trustworthy to guide him on to procure the materials needed and how to manage the business. He seized the golden **opportunity** to start the chair, table, canopy, drums and cooking utensils rent to people and party makers. He started small with the little capital sent to him by a family member and not loans from financial institutions or venture capitalists. Keep thinking about how one can unearth **opportunities** to start business ideas hence jobs. Again and again, limitless are the ever evolving **opportunities**. What about a place where neither private nor public-owned-institutions like medical, education and others are lacking? Employments **opportunities** have being created for those who have interest. It is a matter of the level of reasoning and the application of the senses that would help to discover new grounds. Listen attentively to people around you; try to study them for what they desire or hate; try to read between the lines while reading prints and you would unveil opportunities to be self-employed at least. In fact, jobs **opportunities** are always created from identified jobs **opportunities**. These are major discourse in the book. Several **opportunities** are being created by the technological advancements support to develop jobs from different professional leanings. An example is a creative certified statistician who combined his statistics knowledge with information and communication and technology to roll out statistical data for football league in the nation. Many can operate similar websites for the recording of data of other sports and institutions. This would attract advertisements from businesses. This is the major focus of this work as a sequel to the **first volume** titled- 'Creating new jobs from the existing jobs'. They are sourced from **emerging opportunities** in torrents at all places, institutions, events... And opportunities are eternally created for those who have eyes to see, brains to think, hands to design, legs to move distance, ears to hear, reading to understand, and feeling organs to feel. One good thing about the business environment is the limitless opportunities that are created by the innovations and inventions. Opportunities would always create new **opportunities**. I could recall the school feeding programme of government open jobs opportunities for the food vendors, the food sellers and merchants, the transporters, the farmers and the suppliers. A friend told me that the children who are the beneficiaries are not insured and they must be insured by the government or the corporate institutions as the latter's corporate social responsibility (CSR) to the public where their business thrive. By this thinking, insurance has won good job-creating **opportunity** for idle ones. And another way to generate more funds for the sector to sustain industrial sector. On the other side, negative event could pave the way for new employment **opportunities**. In a state where the pupils are failing external examinations; there is need for the teachers' training seminars or workshops in collaboration with the government. Let someone go into research for the causes of the mass failure and fashion out how the teachers could live up to expectation in their jobs. Is this not an **opportunity** to become one's boss instead of chasing round scarce jobs? Unfortunately, idle people turn blind eyes into lapses in the society they live to start good business ideas. The poor disposal of refuse has become a source of the epidemic of communicable diseases. One wonders the reasons dumps are being 'wasted' for being neglected or underutilized to kick start revenue-employment generation. Not only human wastes being recycled is a way of having self-reliant people but there are several ways lucrative things are kept in the cooler unused, unvalued and hence neglected. We have done justice by the written of the **third volume** in the series titled "<u>wastes to wealth jobs</u>". In the unused and misused airtime on radio and television are opportunities for captivating programmes that can be aired to generate real advertisements. In the websites of companies and institutions are vacuum and what can be added to boost the site for more commercial gains. There are columns in the newspapers for columnists to boost the popularity of the print for anticipated commercial success. Both sides of an environment of a business creates opportunities for right thinking people to set up lucrative businesses. If the eyes are closed, minds should be open always. When a discovery is made, better discoveries should be in the pipeline from think tanks. The world has created rooms for imitation to equal or better an invention. If a car is four-wheeler and power steering, a good auto maker should think differently as the customers driving such cars would not mind replacing it with a better and more exotic cars in a few years. This is true with all the stuffs people, places and events need as basics and luxuries of life. With the level of information and communication technology (ICT), the time is soon when educational services, lectures, seminars, meetings would be done via web conference. E-tutorials have taken over classroom lectures. E-books and audio books are gradually taken over from the hardcover and paperback. Bookless libraries are taken the positions of the conventional libraries in the urban settlements and not the same in among the rural population. Already, mobile libraries, mobile malls, mobile eateries, mobile schools, and several mobile-enhanced services and trades are becoming the rave. Who says that there are no jobs for the unemployed? Opportunities, appear in different forms. Shapes and sizes. They are there for grab and effective use to live a quality life. By this, what do we mean? It is simply <u>tapping into</u>

carefully selected opportunities among the unlimited ones in all sectors by all the unemployed people across all sectors in all nations. I have seen a learned that convert street boys into sports star especially in football. Many destitute once walking the streets have been trained to become sales representatives. In the recent, a bread hawker was spotted and discovered by a scout for modelling and she has become a celebrated model signing big contracts for modelling for super designers across the globe. In what forms do **opportunities** come? How would they be identified at different times and places?

Let us refresh a bit. We should be aware that opportunities come in different forms, shapes and sizes. It could come in form of a gift, a trust or an inheritance. The conversion of these to start jobs is what we referred to as opportunities. Connecting to people that can impact lives is an opportunity to be self-reliant. Many have become what they are by the effective and quality use of the **opportunities** of meeting mentors. Scouts at stadiums and training pitches create opportunity for the players to get call-up to camps and therefore registered with renowned clubs. Everyone must find his right senses to tap the identified **opportunities** to be employers of labour even without spending a dime! Can you add complementary products to your stock? Add brushes and painting materials to your paint shops. Add building materials to your block making business. Join domestic needs to your provision shop. Turn your shop into a one-stop shop. This step could take different forms. It could be from forward or backward integration. I could recall how a close pal opened eyes of my better half, a professional estate manager, into how to start cleaning service business. My spouse is a popular and trusted by the colleagues who had offices in a complex. They summoned her to get them domestic servant on a part-time basis that would do the cleaning services (sweeping, clean the glass, washing the toilet) at a price as service charge. She called on a few persons who could do them. Before you say Jack Robinson, the woman was given the job for the 12 apartments in the complex by different occupants. Today, the woman had got too much cleaning jobs that she had to contract some out too. Imagine my wife whose estate management jobs comprise house cleaning service jobs for those who are leasing a property from them, she would have added another arm to her profession as the friend admonished. What my wife could not identify until the friend came to her life, many in her shoes are also regretting not doing.

A friend, hardware technician by professional training, upgrading experience and qualification, who has been jobless since the time he lost a job, an ICT job, demanded for what he could lay his hands on. Here was somebody that needed some motivation to start his owned technical business for dearth of fund. Such in his shoes lacks the methods to generate funds from nest eggs. He thought jobs are not available after years of fruitless search. Based on our research findings, I made it bare to him that the jobs that are readily available outweigh those looking for jobs especially those who are ready to sell other people's products or services. Such friend could move up the ladder to learn how to develop and run blog for promotion of contents. We are in a period when people who are internet-savvy and computer literate are making huge pay from blogging of different forms. Do you aware that we are in an era of video blogging? Think of distinct blogs for different areas of life and courses. Someone ask me how to have specialized blog. I asked him the area of his interest. His interest is in procurement. I told him to pick identified goods he could do a perfect job on. Here is someone that is into health related business. What would you suggest or prescribe for him? To me, I would suggest he develops interest in the procurement of medical laboratory equipment and drugs. If his blog has its contents developed around his professional area and he is able to draw traffics from the target customers across the world, he should be able to connect the sellers and buyers through the blog for agreed commission on procurements. This is added value in the instance of advanced ICT to professional leanings. At least, he must have a little understanding of programming while in school as elective course. The guy could develop full website for special purposes. And nest egg is simply procured from cutting of all bills and save from free gifts (cash) from errands and mobile services (quick jobs). It is high time the graduates who are jobless think of converting their talents, funs, hobbies, skills et al into lucrative jobs and abandon the search for the scarce white collar jobs.

Many could start a talent or skilled-oriented job based on the level of the effective use of their faculties. Dull events could create **opportunities** like the charge events. Empty stadium during matches gives an opportunity for thinkers to prepare how stadium could be filled up during matches. Several quality products that are not moving in the market have created opportunity for creative salesmen. An unpopular team could be made popular by sportsmen who are intelligent and professionals. Independent marketers, retrenched from the financial hubs, could generate clients for insurance and banking institutions with sound partnership agreement. We have discussed these under agency and outsourcing in the book- **Jobs with zero-capital vol. One'**. In one of our books titled **'Winning huge sales and increasing clients' base…'** there are several idly **opportunities** under the first sub-section of **chapter two** under the topic **'Just imagine-inevitability of customers'**. If people could proffer practicable solutions to those highlighted in each paragraph, there would be lucrative jobs created. Managers of tourist attraction centres and zoological gardens only need to create attractions to crowds. This could be packaged by independent professionals. Many unemployed youths need to learn from the biographies or historical profiles of people in order to know where to start. Popular Arsenal football club of **England Premiership League (EPL)**, Arsene Wenger, was an economist by professional training. Manuel Pellegrini, ex-coach of Manchester city football club is an Engineer by training. I advised him to throw aside his pride to go and learn a skill and never stop learning to boost the skill at interval, qualifications and work on the learnt skill of his or at best polish his talent to become something from nothing.

In retrospect, this is the right path for all unemployed graduates across the world. I gave my buddy some ways of creating lucrative jobs especially those that attract zero-capital especially on becoming agents for different established ventures. It is just creating **new features** for the **value chains** of identified sector of the economy. These are my words-Critical look at some structures, bodies, individuals in different sectors and segments and find the vacuum created as there is always a vacuum to be filled. Those are the **opportunities** for new entrepreneurs to creating new jobs from the existing businesses or jobs. Identify problems facing any interested individuals, business, institution or industry, and you create employment opportunities. Work out how to fill the vacuums or a selected vacuum. Fill the vacuums and you have engaged yourself positively. There are two main ways of getting self-employed. Think of becoming a producer, manufacturer, promoter et al or think of selling what has been produced as products or services.

On the other side, jobs may be scarce to come by since core capitalists target at making profits maximization from minimizing costs and therefore could decide to acquire machines that would reduce costs of production to maximize the profits. As introduced in the first paragraph, in the modern world where technological innovations have replaced and replacing several workers with machines, the number of employable people is reducing everyday by the owners of businesses even governments. Both, entrepreneurs and governments (institutions) do not want employees who would slug it out with them over improved remunerations and allowances. And the incessant strikes of employees over working relation issues render the capacity production ineffective. Instead, they all prefer devices and machines that would perform works of several workers, that would do a more perfect job than what the man-workers would do, that would never go on strike, that are easier to maintain and manage and that would never down tools despite working **24/7** throughout the year. Therefore, they choose to replace workers with Automated Teller Machines (ATM) cards (for dispensing and depositing funds), e-solutions software and electronic devices. On daily basis, domestic servants too are threatened by the arrival of machines, robotics and devices that have taken over their jobs. Banks that employ in tens for various departments have resolved to recruit a few experts managing the machines since jobs are no more done manually but with machines. Does bank who have automated teller machines that are for payment and deposit of money need the services of workers again?

In manufacturing sector too, labour-intensive jobs have now become machine-intensive job-that is, machines have rendered the recruitment of workers a thing of the past. Administrative works that could be done by ten are now done by two (in shift) as a result of the computerization innovations. Nations would also reduce the number of workers on their payroll with the advent of machines. Software innovations are daily reducing the men-services.

In fact, many producers could collapse all the links of selling their products through the effective use of internet facilities and software. The distributors, the independent marketers, the hawkers et al may soon be sent out of jobs with the latest technology from the use of internet facilities where they (manufacturers) sell directly to the final users. Does a nation need as much of road traffic wardens when there are effective traffic lights, scanners, intrusion detectors and Circuit Cable Television (CCTV) along the roads? Drones are reducing the number of security agents to be employed for the nations.

In retrospect and candidly speaking, jobs, at the outset of inventions, would be reducing in the employment market with the advancement in technologies in the making of devices and machines. Therefore, there is no way employments could be effectively created without mindset change of the millions of graduates being churned out of schools-formal and informal. I have heard of a pepper seller that decided to grind and preserve some for sale to ladies and housewives to remove the stress in the kitchen. This was against selling raw that was the vogue in the marketplaces. Vendors could sell the new papers with the most popular ones in order to make sales for the former. The broilers keeper could divert into frozen chickens instead of running the same type of market of selling live broilers. In all business, there is always a better way to start new jobs. The only way out to avoid the scourge of unemployment is for people to **identify real opportunities** created by the same devices that are around them and desire to become artisans who would also employ others instead of looking for unavailable jobs in the oversaturated labour market; situations, events and **unlimited opportunities** are periodically created by the day at different places, private institutions and MDAs, they should tap into them; and make efforts to start their own jobs with personalized meaning **'Being My Own Boss'**-Volume Two in the series after '**Creating new jobs from the existing jobs**'.

By **opportunities**, we mean the old and the new value added services and products in all sectors, policies, institutional objectives, community targets, manpower qualities and potentials, ethno-religion values among others. These value chains pave the way for creating new value added jobs from the existing jobs in the production of tangible goods and life-changing visible services. All along, we have cleared the air on the limitless opportunities from different perspectives. In the content of the book, we shall deal with the theme to the satisfaction of the readers. As a poser, bear this in mind: '<u>where are the employments opportunities to explore</u>? We have opened and would open eyes of readers into several ways to identify opportunities and there are several others as far as the value chains are concerned as being revealed in the book. Do not close your eyes and ears to the good and bad sides (wrongs) in the society you find yourself. Think to sort out opportunities. The incorruptible scriptures reveal that '<u>no creation is a waste</u>'. Those towns cum nations with food shortage (famine and starvation) need more farmers and the suppliers of food crops. The factories in the industrial layouts require the inputs from independent suppliers of raw materials and new technology with its innovations in machines. Sink commercial boreholes, with new drilling technology and latest machines to save time, funds and material resources, at arid region to start water business from production to distribution. Cities that have malnutrition issue need balanced diet suppliers and nutritionists for guides. Not all can be producers or farmers but all can be marketers or agents to the final users (manufacturers, processors, hoteliers, restaurateur…). Miners are producing for the designers and builders that would use the precious stones. And, to ease the tasks, let sellers be links as a form of employment. We are opening eyes and minds to opportunity-driven employments. **This has been the major focus of this book-**<u>how to identify emerging opportunities to create new jobs from the existing jobs</u>. There is eternal joy in being one's own boss from opening the senses up for all opportunities.

Dearest readers, clearing the way; do you know what? The inference of everything written is about creating **opportunities** from being producers or the sellers. <u>We produce unique products or create services for self and others to sell</u>. Many times, we fail to produce what is needed or fail to render the right services at the right place of needs; or those producing tangible goods and rendering certain services (basic or luxurious) are not adequate; or periodically, the consumers or clients desire new thing in features, quality. They need a better product or more quality and satisfactory services to enjoy quality life. These are the vacuums that are opening every day at every place by different market segments requiring think tanks in entrepreneurs or entrepreneurs-in-making. Those vacuums are where the opportunities and new opportunities reside for people who can unveil and package them for readily available customers.

In short, in producing and selling are the two inseparable ways to create employment and wealth creation **opportunities**. The material contains deeper knowledge on how to invent paths to either be a producer or a seller. Never hesitate to identify lucrative opportunities at your fingertips! Read each paragraph of the each chapter as someone looking for lucrative employments and you shall find several ideas from what you would learn chapter by chapter. Ensure you have a pen and paper beside you as you are reading each paragraph hence you can scribble down the employment opportunities from meditation over the contents in each. Without doubt, this book is for no other person than you! Read with full attention and get value for your money!! Never wait for robots and innovation send you out of jobs rather use the innovations to start lucrative jobs that are being created daily. Put your senses into task to see the jobs and start the jobs! Give all supports for your gifted child to be a self-boss from the young age. Make efforts too to be self-independent and turn your face off paid employment. Use choice opportunities around you to start a business idea. There is wisdom in the saying of revered **Abraham Lincoln** "If you want your future to be good, start creating it now". To create better future, available opportunities must be positively used at the right time and place with minimal inputs possible.

CHAPTER ONE

1.1 ZERO-TOLERANCE TO UNEMPLOYMENT

Do you ever know that all challenges and unused or abandoned things or assets are gateways to employment generation? I counselled a guy that the bad economic challenges in the nation are eyes openers to have multi-streams of income. He was told that market and marketing research must come before production of goods and provision of services. Do you know that employments **opportunities** are hawked at your presence every day? Of course, yes. Do you listen to broadcast stations for such **opportunities** you could benefit in attending free seminars? What about the hand bills being distributed in the newspaper vendor joints for you to key into the projects being hawked? Several times I have picked interest in handbills with several business opportunities. Recently, I picked handbills that contained how to plant, nurture and sell medicinal mushroom within one's home and with nest eggs. Prior this time, I did not know that there are medicinal mushroom. Inside the newspapers and online media are found **opportunities** to be picture-writer, freelance investigative writers and designers for blogs. Stroll the streets and offices including all institutions to discover opportunities to start-up viable business you have never dreamt of in life. A guy was at a seminar for education development in the state. In the course of the seminar, the attendees were challenged to forward viable projects that could resuscitate the dwindling quality of education in the state. This was an eye opener for him as he presented how the state could develop students from the elementary schools on how they can develop interest in agri-business from a 'plant and nurture tree crop around the premises of each school at no cost to the government except the inputs of the students learning while nurturing the tree crops selected for different zones. Discovering of employment opportunities is simple task. Visit a residential community where there is concentration of population. Ask for certain product or service. If you find a sizable number that confessed that such product or service is not available. Or the person rendering the service or selling the product has relocated or closed the business for another, a vacuum or an **opportunity** to start a job, has been created which must be filled by another person (entrepreneur). Even though, the interested entrepreneur must also do his or her homework to unveil why the business was not located there or why the shop was closed. The product or service must be the one that the target consumers and clients must yearn for with no ethno-religion disputes. The product or service must read 'we have been looking for this again' or 'we long for the product or service' and not that 'we do not bargain for this' or 'who dare permit this business in our midst?'. To start with, the rising unemployment is every challenge that opens new doors to chains of employments. How? By tapping and converting identifiable **opportunities** at one's fingertips. Let us cite a few instances. There are companies that have stocks to empty. These require independent sellers. Many are distributors of inverters to power homes and millions do not know the existence. Can you serve as good link between the distributors and the prospective buyers? Epidemics may be deadly to lives but the finders of solutions in curative drugs have been employed. What about those who engage in sensitization of the public through the production of documentaries, films and publicize through conventional and online media (print in books, magazines, on electronic like blogs, social media handle, website...)? Our studies show that most unemployed have '**I don't care attitude**' to the contents in books and other medium of broadcasting employments. In the economics and entrepreneurship books are jobs for most unemployed roaming the streets. In the books of all professionals in different courses of studies are jobs for the millions idle-handed in the streets. I developed interest in recycling of solid wastes after surfing some books studying the gains for recycling the solid recyclable waste to improve the socio-economic state of the nation and the wellbeing of the inhabitants. I saw recycling of the wastes as a call to improve the quality of life and adding to the aesthetics of the business environment for investors and the residents. Many who are into soap and detergent making got their information and guides from books from professionals. Extra efforts through attending workshops and seminars add value to what they read inside print. Visitation to manufacturing places help a great deal for many others to become their own boss. In the prospectus and roadmaps from the public (Governments at all tier) and private sectors are employment opportunities for discovery. One of our referential entrepreneurship books '**Wastes to wealth jobs**' focused on how to convert 'wastes' into wealth and lucrative jobs. Let me take some instances on how to create new jobs. A young couple rented a three bedroom apartment instead of a self-contained. What do you think the other rooms and the facilities within could be used for? Think of business ideas such couple should go and learn and start doing within. Let me give some. They could start dry cleaning service, confectionery and fruit juice making business, fashion designing, snailery and livestock among others in vegetable, herbal and ornamental flower plants farming. They could start commercial business like typing or typesetting-related businesses. I have seen housewife who converted the garage to sell grocery for the neighbours. What about those who have other skills or interest in baby-sitting, crèche, nursery school, adult class, counselling or post-school home and services. Limitless are the opportunities of business for such occupying such apartment especially at the urban areas in the metropolitan states. Numerous of these are in the book 'Wastes to wealth jobs' in the street with school-age child-hawkers though a form of child abuse, but they could be converted into more productive use by those who have the brains and the heart of love if they could not finance their education or accommodate them.

Convert the street hawking into employment by conversion of the child-hawkers into corporate hawkers who hawk with mobile gadgets like smartphones, laptops and their social media handles. Many on the streets and the traders in the markets and workmen working in offices could embrace digital technology to boost patronage. (Read details in of our books '**Winning huge sales and increasing clients' base**'). How would it be for scouts of talents in different areas of life to start scouting for them and transform them into limelight? These efforts are paths to create self-employments and spread the wealth of the nation. In the first book from our stable is solution to the idle ones who are facing the paucity of capital to start. In the materials are methods to start business ideas without capital. What does it take a child to convert the idle backyard of his parent house to start orchard or livestock of cattle specie? What would it cost many who owned smartphones and can afford data with their nest eggs to start digital selling jobs? Limitless are the chains of employment opportunities that require zero capital but skills and efforts plus idle assets. Our second work dealt with how new jobs can be created from different applicable strategies. Had the unemployed read and study hard tomes of choice areas or courses in books, magazines and newspapers, not to talk of other means of communication of business ideas, no one should be protesting for no jobs. Jobs are daily created and readily available <u>for those who can see</u>, <u>those who can hear</u>, <u>those who can feel the pulse</u>, <u>those who can meditate</u>, <u>those who have interest to create new things</u>, <u>those who can reflect on issues, features and objects</u>, <u>those who can move from a place to another</u> and <u>those who have interest to traverse the lands, water and the rest spheres</u>. I wonder if the idle ones really understand the unequal opportunities to start good jobs in the internet. This reminds me of a condition of need I found myself at a time. Instead of travelling to places where the vital information is needed, I browsed internet and got them without moving an inch. I am aware of friends who have converted their social media handles into their own websites and blogs where their products and services are promoted, marketed sold thereby making money from their new found jobs. In the build-up of this work, it is stated that every challenge or crisis is an eyes opener to start new jobs. **Malnutrition,** although, in nations is **a problem** but paving the ways for employment generation as opportunities for the producers, distributors and sellers of the balanced diet foods. Recently, as a result of sky rocketing prices of foods, many have started to engage in processing at small scale. Yours sincerely was into cassava flour processing for consumers. There was a confirmed report of Indians and Chinese buying cassava from the farms for purposely for processing into cassava flour or any other industrial use. All producers and marketers of foodstuff and the balanced diet would earn huge in the nation suffering from famine, minor or major not to talk of wars. Imagine what profits the suppliers to the prisons, the internally displaced people's camps and strategic places that urgently needed the food supplies would make from the venture. Piracy of goods have encouraged me to write books on how to tackle piracy headlong and stem the spiral effects on the consumers and the economy. It is amazing finding people who could not keep memoirs and diaries to be released in publications and documentaries later. I educated some guys about the limitless opportunities to start-up lucrative jobs. Visit the internet, type selected lists of jobs from different nations. Copy them in your flash drive or computer for critical study. You shall find agents that you can work with abroad on a basis of commission over those you scout for as an agency for recruitments for employers within and abroad. You can retract the vacancies in the print and electronic, compute them, make thorough findings to understand the requirements and about those persons for the jobs and by these information, you can start employee recruitment agency work. You can start visa business with all the information sourced by this in addition to the study of tourists-attraction places in the world for the clients to make choices of. I have seen many who used to be friends with creative designers and end up selling their designers within and abroad. When someone is close to a factory or institute, he or she should be able to learn the skill. It is a great opportunity to learn new skills to start good jobs. It is my belief that all visits, attendance to seminars, workshops, institutions and the like create **opportunities** to start good jobs. What stops a teacher to start writing on books from his experience of teaching a particular subject? Adding writing to teaching is an opportunity to boost the income and earn respect and popularity aside adding values to education and professional leaning. In my findings, no shop is absolutely one-stop shop. There is **opportunity** for proprietors of specialized **one-stop shops** that are major in a particular produce. Let there be one-stop shop for livestock produce. More business owners should have one-stop shop for print materials. Creating departments in a shop does not make one-stop shop as each department may not have good percentage of the goods needed by the prospective customers. Pay impromptu visits at different times to many popular malls within your axis for confirmation. One thing or the other must be missing. Make efforts to fill the vacuum and by so doing, employment is generated. The information to start-up would be got from visiting places. In many cases, the talent and skill in a child is enough to sustain all the family members if such is rightly nurtured. It is odd to see the formal education as the all-in-all. Many talents and skills can be nurtured through the skills and capacity acquisition centres and relevant academies. Locate them and enroll your talented or skilled ward. Support your wards with the right tools, moral supports and finances to create future employers of employees and wealth creators 'Traverse through the earth..' and learn as the incorruptible book teaches mankind. I was able to write informative book on drug abuse to teach the young and adults about how to identify the adulterated drugs and counterfeited products and their sellers. Imagine the numbers of books that could be written on the same issue for the readily available markets in schools, libraries, bookshops, researchers etc. If writer cannot exist what to write about; then the producers of films and research-based documentaries cannot exhaust what to produce in films and documentaries for public consumption on commercial basis. Have you ever thought of the waves of life? Do you ever know that one can be one's boss from teens? Study your children. What interests do they have? Discover them. For instance, engage your kids on how to rear domestic pets from young age and make saves for them as they earn from the sales. Talk and encourage them to start a good job hence they develop interests right from young age.

In retrospect, expose them to academies and skills acquisition centres from the little age. A good seed could bring forth hundreds. A working teenage earning from the job he had started at a young age could sustain the family. Do you reflect on the creatures in your ambience? What about the beauty in each creation? Do you ever meditate over the alternation of day and night? What comes to your mind from the reflections and the change in weather conditions each day or the climatic conditions over a period of thirty five years according to the climatologists? Do you know that programming is a natural course as one of the lessons man learnt from the Creator? To the monotheists, programming is predestination. Do you ever give the measurements of all things a thought for a while? Have you ever transformed what you read from the Divine scriptures into a physical objects and actions? If you are able to try to find answers to the posers, then you would agree that it is very easy to imitate and creating ideas that would create new jobs or even extracting new jobs opportunities from the existing jobs.

In view of the above, if the parents, the governments, your educational institutions and others cannot sponsor you to such places to learn, make yourself available to academies, institutions and offices where additional skills and talents are sourced to add values to yours. Pay visit to agricultural institutes to learn about new (modern) agricultural-based innovations to start a good job from numerous chains of farm opportunities. A number of students that stay in a farm where all productions and processing are done for some months would come back with practicable feasibility reports that would win the hearts of the financial institutions.

Let me give more lucid illustrations. The scriptures taught us that mankind, apart from the first man created from the soil, is a product of the mixture of the sperms from men and the eggs in the ovaries of women that develop in the womb. This is the origin of laboratory experimentation especially of test-tube babies. The product of the mating of male and female brings forth child that shares their traits in first or second filial generations. (See details in one of our published books titled '**MAN**). This is how grafting and budding in agricultural practice produce in the sector to bring forth good and right harvest. The programming of the worlds and the creatures therein is what the internet-savvy brains use in the production of software for different usage. Do you know that many problems today are solvable with software? And software writing and production is like books writing and publishing. There are limitless ways to develop software for different functions and applications for all sectors. Private and public institutions with different objectives require software (applications) for installation on their systems to ensure and enhance productivity. Just as books require editing and new editions, software developers and writers must come out with better software every day.

In the world of recurring challenges, new software is required for all facets of live. My inference is that **opportunities** to be engaging in jobs are created in all aspects. During the day at a part of the world when some at the other sides are having darkness, people eke for livelihood working to earn for their living. Those at the other sides are expected to be resting or sleeping. Every problem facing a man, a nation, a place creates opportunities to make good jobs. Every dull moment in a place calls for spices. And the provision of spices has become a job for several people.

Austerity measures, in parts of Europe, not to talk of most nations in Africa, suffering from economic recession, seem not working to stem the tide of the scourge of unemployment. Working out the solutions presented by the socio-economic think tanks of the government must be one that spread the wealth of the nation through creation of new jobs across the nooks and corners of the nations. The economic downturn is a challenge and the challenge would always create new **opportunities**. It is right to label economic crises in a nation, profit loss in a company, embezzlement in an institution, non-performing of a staff in a company, low productivity of an institution, and all forms of negativity as blessings for they create new **opportunities** to create jobs. If a nation does not have insecurity problem, what is the essence of recruitment into the law enforcement agencies and creating of new ones with special tasks? If the nation is free from disasters, what jobs are there for the emergency agency crews? What is the wisdom behind building blocks of classrooms if education is not a social project with the aim of transforming the people into literates? Why the establishment of the primary, secondary and tertiary health care institutions if not for the health needs of people? And with the investment on the social projects, jobs are created for thousands on contract basis? A nation has to collate relevant data to identify the urgent needs of the people for employment to be generated. A nation that has housing and social infrastructural deficit needs massive investment in the built sector and by so doing **opportunities** for jobs are created especially in the involvement of the private construction companies in consortium under public private partnership. Refusal to grant entry visas to nationals from certain nation could ignite employment creativity in the people. This visa refusal is a halt or setback to brain drain to the nation. If they work in synergy, opportunities to develop their nations would be created. The challenges faced by the United States in the second world war led to the bringing together of brains which resulted in the production of bombs. We went into research on how the nation could boost economic growth. Each time economy of a nation is in the woods, it struggles or tries to wriggle out of the crises. Through the process, concerted efforts are made with relevant ideas from think tanks to solve the identified problems.

Therefore, solving problems, challenges and the likes are the best way to open the lids from employment **opportunities**. Nigeria's economic recession open eyes into identifying new employment opportunities. It is so as the nation sees reasons for diversification of economy into agriculture and mining instead of solely depending on the oil sector. In short, the crises serve as eyes opener to unveil new opportunities that are either underutilized in the time of plenty or never utilized for ignoring as non-issues. Nigeria's stuff of economic recession is one where dollar scarcity is biting harder on the importation of raw materials and parts not to talk of drugs, fuels and foods. The major phenomenon is the spiral inflation. Though all these are negative indicators showing an economy heading to total collapse. By all standards, windows of opportunities have been created for the wise. In short, the evils of the flagging economy is an eyes opener to unveil other sources of generating exports to earn forex. Some of these areas we discovered as opportunities are the books we write and publish, the films and documentaries we produce within, the arts and cultural festivals that can be packaged for tourism promotion, the traditional wears and foods, the local herbs for different diseases. It is onus on the government to move away from monolithic economy into diversified economy. Another window of **opportunities** is the massive investment on agricultural practices at the nooks and corners of the nation to have food security and more raw materials to support the agro-allied industries. What do you expect of schools that surround their structures with cash crops like palm trees? The trees would generate employment and revenues for the schools and the nations in a few years.

By this effort, there would be lower demands for dollar and the nation shall generate billions of dollars from selling of the listed intellectual property and the branded products and services of artisans within. Such nation is expected to invest massively on the basic services such as education, health, security and other social services in order to reduce the demand for dollar to travel out before such quality services are got. The diversification of economy would be incomplete without resuscitating the moribund industries such as the textile factories, the paper mills, the steel industries and promotion of sports and professional-based academies. Intervention funds that are properly distributed would serve the nation better to be free from grip of economic recession. Our findings show that a nation can generate millions of jobs at a swap from the creation of national e-market places from training youths on digital selling. This is an opener to opportunities for employment creation. Recession is blowing revenue-employment opportunities across the nations for think tanks to develop. To a lay man, the major spiral effect is the increasing unemployment and underemployment. In some nations, without exemption, it has turned to xenophobic crises. It is unfortunate that the nations fail to create several **opportunities** towards generating palpable employment for the increasing teeming jobless across the length and breadth.

Nations could seize the **opportunities** of large percentage of idle youths to increase agricultural production to feed the mouths in nutritious foods and drinks as well as the agro-allied industries with raw materials. The nation with such crisis only need to create enabling environment for the youths to embrace farming in large scale. Imagine a youth-farmer that is given a new car and a self-contained house with running expenses whose overall estimated costs are repaid at 10% of the annual harvest, free access to farm inputs like the machines, the seeds among others, that is registered with national health insurance scheme, that has his farm and person insured with choice insurance firm, whose one member of the family enjoys scholarship for each year of farming and has his produce purchase by the government-owned produce boards at prevailing market prices. Would it take the nation eternity to create direct jobs for several thousand of the youths from finding solutions to the identified problems or challenges? What about supporting those who engage in the value added chains too with adequate grants and other incentives like free space in mini industrial layouts, facility and relevant machine to work with under an agreement on repayment at a very low rate? Imagine what the 'problem' of economic recession has created in employment opportunities and food security. A nation that is able to feed its citizens and industries is a developing economy. Such would have growing GDP and GNI that would have direct impact on the standard of living.

We have also illustrated several ways to generate millions of jobs in the **third volume** in the series titled "wastes to wealth jobs" in different ways using different approaches to identify opportunities which idle people could tap in order to become their own bosses. The contents and provisions in the national constitution create rooms for employment generation. It would take someone who has the **brains** to have the **working senses** to create the desired opportunities. I used to think about using other people's facilities to get myself engaged. I had 'sold the message' of my materials gratis through the working blogs of fellow colleagues in order to create huge awareness ahead of official release of my works. The blogs and sites brand my intellectual property and vice versa. The attempts boosted the blogs and the websites too as the traffic increased geometrically. Look at the opportunities for both parties. What does it take me to use other people's blogs and websites to sell my materials? Agreement on business working relation is only needed as catalyst. The blogs and sites have created opportunities and they are opportunities too. One can imagine the number of secure and lucrative jobs in thousands that could be created if the railway transportation is privatized like the land transportation and air systems. Imagine the number of direct and indirect employment opportunities that could be created from seaways privatization and several other monopolized companies of the government. One cannot predict accurately the number of employment opportunities which are creatable from concession of expensive and long term projects or jobs and public private partnership. Every activity points to an opportunity to create jobs and spread the wealth. In **Nigeria**, taxes are placed on certain goods in order to generate revenues as a result of fall in the crude oil price in the world market. The increased number of prohibition list, that would have forex access, from the apex bank has open avenues for the local manufacturers of the products to increase employment for the populace. Devaluation of currency is done and this measure is enough to lead to jobs loss in all sectors of the economy. The borrowings of the investment banks on the markets to increase the lending rates to the small business in Europe are also not working to make the unemployed people be gainfully employed. The State-aided jobs in **France** by the former president of France, **Francois Hollande** administration are not performing (Wikipedia: 2013). Loss of jobs keeps increasing across the nations. On the good side, e-commerce could create jobs for millions at a swap. Imagine the promotion and marketing of registered goods and services of individuals, corporate institutions and the likes in a nation. It has created avenues for those who do not produce products or provide any service to market and promote for shared commission as gains for their efforts.

Nations and administrations at all tiers need no fear. They only need to create platforms to open the eyes of their nationals to opportunities to start their own jobs. Nations should open new sectors. Administrations, through their quality think-tanks who should work for public policies formulation and implementation, should create opportunities through exploration of the bills and institutional corporate objectives and structures. Candidly, with the existing structures that could create investments opportunities in all the continents namely **Europe**, **Australia**, most part of **Asia**, **Africa** and **America-North and South**, there is no need for government jobs to mop up the unemployed roaming the streets by short term empowerments and monthly stipends to the millions of unemployed nationals. The latter effort is a greater financial burden on the national treasury. They should rather provide <u>practicable and adequate enhancements</u> for the individuals on the streets in search of jobs to be self-employed or creators of new jobs from exposure to opportunities. The underdeveloped and developing nations in Africa and Asia that are having the problem of social infrastructures, lapses and inconsistent economic and political policies have created millions of jobs by the lapses. The entrepreneurship book 'wastes to wealth jobs' and other books on jobs creation by the same author contain the bail outs. There is no possible gain in tackling the scourge of unemployment from the establishment of capacity acquisitions centres and all other forms of economic empowerments being invested on. Most of the economic empowerment in form of distribution of machines like grounding machines, tailoring machine, hairdressing equipment...to artisans; Cash as grants or non-refundable loans are given to traders and others to engage in petty trading thereby turning the nation into buying and selling nation instead of encouraging production; some are given motorcycles, tricycles for transportation is creating more hardship as the level of poverty keeps increasing. This is so as the number of partakers in such jobs has been increased and the sharing income in the transportation is decreasing as more are empowered to enter the business. In short, the so-called economic empowerment is like feeding a man for a day by giving him a fish instead of teaching him how to fish and hence feed him forever.

In other way round, it is fuelling the fire of abject poverty in the nation through ignorance or for selfish reasons. Teaching the millions of the idlers on how to create jobs would do the magic. Breeding new entrepreneurs in the primary sectors (agriculture, mining, education, health..) of the economy would have developed the secondary (manufacturing, processing...) and tertiary (servicing of the human and the non-human factors in all the sectors) sectors in servicing businesses. This effort would increase the production of raw materials to feed the industries and feed the citizens. It is simply done from **creation of viable ideas (opportunities)** by the socio-economic think tanks with nationalistic views. And ideas are limitless in developing and nurturing for employment creation. There are limitless chances or opportunities knocking our doors, staring us at our faces every day and at all times and climes to create budding entrepreneurs. These are **ideas** that could be created. Turn the potential contributors who have vast business **ideas** experience into new captains of industries. Instill confidence in them. Support them with right incentives and avoid all forms of disincentives.

This is creating enabling environment in the business environment to stabilize the operating costs for viability of businesses. They should be made (encouraged) to lead the pack of those loitering the streets. It takes 30% or less in each of the sectors to create jobs for the 70% unemployed in form of relevant or complementary services. What do we mean? Let those in the production (primary sector) namely agricultural sector, mining sector and educational sector be 30% and these would create enough (adequately) to engage the rest 70% in form of services. List all the sectors and the sub-sectors of the economy. Group the areas to find or create jobs **opportunities** into social and economic services. By legislation, the 30% in the primary sector would be created through turning the professionals from the products of the institutions into the producers. All top or executive officers in all the target primary sectors and sub-sectors who have garnered at least ten years of work experience should be retired from the sectors to lead the packs of new entrepreneurs that are fresher as mentors, senior partners and consultants in businesses of choice. As aforesaid, they are turned into new captains of industries overnight.

In a nation of twenty millions unemployed youths, it takes 200 senior staff members who have garnered huge work experience from different departments in different sectors of economy to mentor or be senior partners to new breed entrepreneurs of about 200. The total would create not less than **500** jobs (direct and indirect) from each of the sectors. Most of the jobs are selling-based for retailers, hawkers, distributors, wholesalers among other value added services. Let us take an instance of a publisher. Publishers could create jobs for several thousand within and outside the shores as more authors who are adequately remunerated in royalty keeps increasing through attractive publishing packages. I found a big opportunity to publish my books free on some sites online with royalty attached. How many people are scouting for the related **opportunities** online? A good partnership with the film makers would turn many stories in books into blockbuster films. From the **opportunities** created by the release of the bestselling books and blockbuster films, researchers are tasked hence proliferated in numbers. By this, jobs are created for research assistants, office staff and domestic workers. Back to the publishing section, aside the printing or publishing crews, there are jobs for librarians (conventional and online), bookstores owners, book hawkers and other sellers. This is not added to those who are from ICT, graphics, transportation and financing sections. All these are the assumed sum of the staff for online and offline arms of the publication. Mathematically, a total of **200** by **200** by **500** (**20million**) have been created in a swap! To get the five hundred workers, it is addition of the offices, factory workers plus the indirect independent workers in the streets selling or retailing the products for a good fee. It took the vast experience of <u>Fola Tajudeen Adeola</u> and his late partner, **Aderinokun**, from different chartered accounting firms to establish one of the most profitable and reputable banks in Nigeria and overseas, Guaranty Trust Bank in 1990. Imagine engaging professionals who have professional experiences that span at least ten years in the creation of specialized jobs in the nations. Can some professionals gather to create specialized commercial banks such as artisan banks, farmers' bank etc? This is an **opportunity** at your door step, grab it! With the involvement of export-import banks in the nations, excess products are sold and relevant raw materials and technologies through innovated machines are purchasable into the nation. Through this effort, jobs are created for millions. <u>Break the monopolies</u> being enjoyed by a few industrialists, **opportunists** and professional bodies, <u>by strict compliance to legislation</u>, to enhance proliferation of industries, high level of productivity in all the sectors and sub-sectors resulting into the creation of **opportunities** or avenues for millions to create new jobs. Competitions in the market and all sectors (and sub-sectors) would enhance quality products and services. In short, to create jobs for the millions on the streets, **it takes those in** <u>**the top positions of existing businesses**</u> and no others from the limitless **value chains** depending on the entrepreneurial natural creativity!

For the promotion of new breed entrepreneurs who lacked the working experiences from institutions but having the sole desire to be their own bosses; Segment them, by different classes or specializations of skills, talents from among the list of the unemployed listed per region or location. With the involvement of the experienced people (some consultants recruited from those within the sectors), the industries would have positive contributors. Create relevant workshops, seminars on creating new breed entrepreneurs and not the dependents who search for jobs. Those who are searching for jobs need experienced mentors to guide them into becoming self-employers or full entrepreneurs from deep meditation over the value chains. This, meditation over value chains, is where **employment-opportunities** are invented and created. The confidence and the guidelines from the shared experience would do the magic. And the nation reaps the gains in the save of costs of stemming the tides of the scourge of unemployment in the nations.

Every member in a family is a potential, direct and indirect creator of employments. Parents and guardians including matron, teachers, specialized tutors and counsellors at schools should catch them young. Studies show that three out of ten married women are full-time housewives by religion, culture, retirement, redundancy, divorce, personal choice and death. These (full time housewives) are potential entrepreneurs that could create jobs for not less than 30% of the unemployed roaming the streets. Let us take a few illustrations. A woman with culinary skill, in many ethnic and continental meals, could employ millions if she could run a special **blog** for recipes. Many who follow the blog could drive traffics to the blog and all make money from the internet activities. Such could prepare the recipes for the entrepreneurs in hospitality business and boarders and cooks in boarding schools. Many spinsters patronize such site to develop their own culinary skills too in order to meet up being caring and dutiful housewives and mothers at matrimonial homes. A good example is found in the northern Nigeria where the husbands are predominantly famers and shepherds and the fulltime housewives are the processors or manufacturers of products. The raw materials for industries are processed by them for sale to the industries within the comforts of their homes. The famers who are groundnut farmers are cock sure of the ability of the women at home to process the nuts into groundnut cake locally called 'kulikuli' and extract groundnut oil for commercial purpose. What the children and the youths are selling in the markets are products from homes. One could imagine the number of sellers of local beverages like Kulli kulli, 'masara', maize cake called 'maza', 'kunnu', soyamilk, 'zobo' and 'fura de nunu'. It takes a government that has economic vision to invest on the farmers through provision of grants (financial empowerment) and relevant farm equipment and instructions to enhance large scale productions in farms (of crop and animal). Each family of the farmers in the communities is capable to create jobs for many street lads staying idle and becoming nuisance to the streets if well remunerated and packaged.

The noblest man ever in the history of mankind was reportedly to have said that 'beneath the feet of the mothers lies the bliss of the children'. The target children are the future of any nation. For them to be successful here and there, mothers have to play greater roles. The mothers nurture the baby to adulthood from homes. On the other hand, mothers can package good standard of living for the youths outside the homes especially in the area of jobs creation. Women at home have enough time to plan ahead of time. There are facilities that are at their beck and call. With all these in place, it is easier for the folk to create lucrative jobs for the unemployed people in the nation. An ex-prime minister, a female, was also reported to have said: "woman who can run the home would run the nation". Many women industrialists could turn all the facilities at their beck and call into commercial ventures to create lucrative jobs for those roaming the streets. Some are turned off by gender discriminations in the private and public offices and therefore prefer to be their own bosses. The sole proprietors among the folk who are allergic to work under people and institutions could employ at least a family member and selves aside the hawkers, sales agents, distributors and others for their products and services aesthetically packaged from home.

Based on the available facilities at home, it is possible for each of the home-grown industrialists among the women to venture into different ventures and run them successfully. These could bridge the vacuum for not less than 20% of the unemployed populace. Let us be practical. The twenty-three million unemployed people in Europe could be adequately provided with lucrative employments at the instance of the limitless **opportunities** created by the digital technology revolution across the continents.

The contents in the two-volume books "Jobs with zero-capital" could create jobs for not less than five millions from just **50,000** creators or interested trail blazers if each of them employs **100** people directly and indirectly. In actual fact, if the online-based jobs are added, the number of jobs that would be created is in millions though many could be on sales commission basis. To yours sincerely, independent persons earn more than the staff under contracts if they can plan their time and put in more to all employers needed their services. The content would be more relevant in environment where there is shortage of capital from financial houses or the poor nations where there is no provision at all. The enabling environment in each nation would however determine the quick success of the jobs therein.

The volume one of this book "Creating new jobs from the existing jobs" could effectively open the eyes of the potential entrepreneurs among those roaming the streets to millions of jobs creatable. This, "**Being My Own Boss**", a sequel to the above named book, so far has added greater impacts in the employment generation from limitless **opportunities** across nations. Note the word 'limitless' just as needs and wants, we made references to the two books simply to open up the **opportunities** as gains from reading such materials to become self-employed or even entrepreneurs. In reading books, watching television, listening to radio, watching films and documentaries, visiting public places, touring distances, attending public lectures, listening to interviews, listen to analyses, participating on social media, attending seminars and the likes are paths to create new opportunities to start lucrative jobs. In short, opportunities are created every day. Only the right thinking person who is not suffering from personal ego, self-esteem, pride and so on blind to such **opportunities** grab and make the maximum use of them. It contains simple features to enhance creating new jobs without stress from the existing jobs. I read a newspaper advert of a renowned paint company verbatim "Irresistible Business Offer; Be Your Own Boss; Become a………… (Company's name) **franchise partner** for an **opportunity** to earn great returns on your investment (The Punch, April 22:2015:57) in paid advertisements are seminars, searching for distributors, agents, depots, warehouses aside vacant positions for different qualifications. All these create chances to become self-employed at least. Let us look at highly probable gain in the enriched seminars. If **55,000 youths** are mobilized across the nation to be participants of different artisanal seminars (based on choices) and such were adequately motivated by the facilitators and sponsors across the nations; assuming all of them are adequately supported with resources to work with; if all the number eventually take up some of the jobs therein, and **100** jobs are created directly and indirectly. A sum of <u>five million, five hundred thousand jobs</u> have been created. Sincerely speaking, the advanced nations have the capability of creating the equal numbers of jobs that are available in the nations if the content is totally digested and implemented. What is the big deal? List the existing jobs, create or design some new features that could turn them new. Take these few instances. Turn the books into audio-visual books. Turn the media into wholly specialized stations. Turn the stationary business or services into mobile businesses or services. Create new products as tastes change. Get the content right and there is no need having insomnia over unemployment!

The housewives, full time or part time, are potential employers of labour in thousands. In a nation where we have retired but skilled women of about **50,000** in figure, each of them could create jobs for sellers, instructors and others that would not be less than **100** directly and indirectly. This also amounts to <u>five million jobs</u> creation. More of the doable jobs are in the book '<u>Housewives are prospective entrepreneurs</u>' by the same author. This shows that family business can be created through the submission of lucrative ideas by the member of the family. Many big companies like **Lever Brothers** (**Unilever**) and **Cadbury** are **family businesses**. <u>Ideas can be created locally from different events and needs</u> in all nations. <u>Lucrative business ideas (opportunities) can be created from the existing ideas</u> that are thriving and popular in the nation. Sometimes, they could be developed from the foreign idea. Imagine the presence and the commercial success of social media entrepreneurs that is paving the way for bloggers across nations. And who are the creators of viable ideas opening eyes and other senses into lucrative employment opportunities? They are individuals, institutions and governments. It could be from grapevine sources, gossips, hot spots, and from different kinds of personality. I could remember a man who became a supplier of snails to hotels based on what he heard while on transit. Many thrillers in films are events, scenes, talks, stories that took place in the markets, homes, offices, places of interests et al. Just imagine the number of thespians and other acting and production crew aside makers and sellers of costumes, electronics…, television rights, cinema houses… that would be gainfully employed from such idea sourced from those places. Are you assimilating and meditating over the content? This is the main theme of this work.

In retrospect, from the previous narration, over twenty-five million jobs have been created. Somebody itched to know- 'how would a nation mobilize **50,000** established names to serve as mentors or senior partners? Would this number be too much in a nation?' Let us answer these arithmetically:

Assuming a nation is divided into **5** regions. The number of the sectors and sub-sectors identified are **20**. Under each of the sectors listed are **100** different jobs opportunities for direct and indirect workers. And our target creators of jobs from retired by legislation who have garnered working experience in different fields at between ten and above years in all establishments under each of the sectors are **200,000**. Divide the **200,000** by the multiplications of the regions, the sectors and jobs opportunities. We have **20** as the needed jobs creators or the real entrepreneurs per region! The so-called economic powers have less than **100** entrepreneurs who are creative socio-economic thinkers that turned the economy round for millions to enjoy. Turn this Mathematics into practice!

When we say **sectors**, we mean those under the social and economic categories of sectors. Under the social sectors are the constructions of social infrastructures, educational institutions, research stations, provision of security services, medical services and regulation of the services by legislation under the watch of the administrative services by those at the echelon of power including their value chains that would add new values to lives. The economic services create jobs **opportunities** for millions through the public private partnership arrangement of all businesses that would better the quality of standard of living. Such include the hospital services, food security services, financial services, manufacturing services among others. Under each of the mentioned services, the primary need of the people is largely meant from the activities of those in the agricultural sector. This sector, which feeds the industries (textile, processing, manufacturing ...) is purported to be the largest creator of jobs (**opportunities**) years ago unlike now when the online jobs from internet services have taken over. In the former, several thousands of jobs are doable from added value chains.

Truth be told, under agricultural sector alone, there are not less than fifty practices that could employ others who are potential employees. Nations who looks towards agro-based jobs are living in the past. From records, amazon.com, an online company, has employed over 65,000 as at the second quarter of 2012 according to Wikipedia. There are <u>limitless</u> **online jobs** that are crying for unemployed people to turn to. Just expose them into internet and electronic gadgets in the information and communication technology by their uses and operations. Equip interested with laptop and free data for some months after certified trainings. Many could package ethno-religion caller-tunes for sale starting from freebies to attract them. Live streaming is another way to promote persons, products, places, events and services. Package via branding them vice versa. '<u>Buy one and get one free</u>' (BOGOF) strategy could land you in money and freedom from unemployment and underemployment. Specialized caller-tunes that would promote companies shall be paid for by the management. Imagine devising caller-tunes that promote the products and services of popular telecoms and financial institutions. What about the freelancing and outsourcing jobs that are done online with mobile electronic gadgets and the inputs of the skills on information and communication technology? People, institutions and businesses that are in need of the products and the services. **Opportunities** of jobs on the internet are limitless. One can turn his increasing number of connections and followership in the social media handle to sell (promote) products and services for companies at a price. Boost your resume and upgrade your resources in bio details to attract patrons of your specialized social media handle. Come out with new captivating contents every day to retain the crowds visiting your blog or social media handle. You could become face of many businesses for good pay. 'Freebies' could be the starting point. Learn from the social media entrepreneurs who employ freebies to generate traffic of fans following their sites. Let the bloggers use freebies to increase popularity and the number of 'likes'. Use your skill, love money and nest eggs to produce samples of what you have to boost the trademarks of desire companies or institutions. And the management shall handsomely reward you. It is like the fashion designers producing unique customized uniforms with different fabrics of variants of designs and colours for target business institutions. And to recoup the capital invested by the state, start deducting the cost at the beginning of the fourth month. Each of these businesses would be employing people on the need basis and as divestment and expansion are taking place. If you turn your traditional publishing business into online business like the Print-On-Demand publishers, you would employ and engage several people from different professional leanings across the continents. If you engage in online marketing, your employees may triple what a farmer can employ in a year within a few months. A study of the tertiary schools showed that several beverages existed but not all variants from different grains and fruits. The grains and fruits create opportunities to create variants of beverages for the consumers at every places and events. I was thinking about soya milk when I discovered someone was producing soya-maize. I asked myself, what stop brewers to produce such combination of soya beans and nuts; soya milk plus apple or any other fruits. The combinations of the nutritious liquids from fruits, seeds and grains would increase the number of beverages for different classes of consumers at all places. And the number of firms increases the employment **opportunities** from the value chains.

The online activities always create **opportunities** to sell what is brewed locally and for all nature of convectional jobs even the politicians are soliciting for electorates' votes through online engines! Today, we have online radio, online television, online advertisers, online entertainers, online service providers that have idle airtime and spaces to sell among other services. All these could generate more jobs if they adopt specialization as contained in the first volume. Let us look at the mining sector-artisanal or corporate. Individuals who obtain license to mine would create jobs for marketers and users. Corporate miners would create greater employment **opportunities** for professionals as they operate in a bigger way. Government could create the **opportunities** for both in order to generate employment **opportunities**.

Imagine mining sector of solid and liquid mineral resources; imagine the vast estate and tourism business and the number of workers this could create directly and indirectly. What about the individuals? Only the 'poor' defined by acronym as "**P**assing **O**ver **O**pportunities **R**epeatedly" by a renowned writer and author, **Usiere Uko** may not find opportunities to create something (jobs) from all the events, objects, situations… around him. Those, be it a person or group of persons, an institution or institutions, an agency or agencies, an organization or organizations, a government or governments, a faith or multiple of faiths, a party or the parties.., who need helping hands create room for **opportunities**. It is a fact that no one among the listed that does not need one help or the other. Shortage of staple foods in a town is an **opportunity** for suppliers of the consumable products. In a natural disaster prone nation, **opportunities** of selling relevant materials are created for the makers and suppliers.

Think of this, some businesses, individuals, institutions, distributors, manufacturers.. are supplying foods, clothing, drugs and other relief materials to the internal displaced persons camps across the nations of the world. Some deal with the refugee camps not to talk of the inmate in prisons serving terms. Some are employed to attend to their health needs occasionally, some are there to render cleaning, counselling and education services as inevitable needs for an agreed price. If you have distinct skills to sell to the camps, contact the right institutions overseeing the affairs there. Many Non-Governmental Organizations (NGOs) started in the charity-based jobs. Many orphanages home got started to cater for the orphans. They get financial and material supports from government agencies, corporate institutions, faith organizations, voluntary and social clubs and rich individuals to pay the staff, to sustain and maintain the business. Students who are failing examinations create employment **opportunities** for after-school coaching classes or extramural classes. These directly create rooms for professional tutors, new books and educational materials publishers, authors and printers. The sick on the sick beds have created avenues to create several effective drugs for commercial purpose. Read the minds of the people around you; study what they lack or could add values to their lives and living conditions; study their mood; show empathy to their situation; carefully listen to or meditate over their complaints and you would identify limitless **opportunities** that would solve their needs. And this is the path to tread in order to create employment and becoming your own boss or even boss for others!

In this world of internet and information and communication technology, many can start several limitless online businesses for different products and services depending on passion which helps to be more versatile and creative to make the business a success. Take your breadth. Think of businesses that are competitive online. Just consider the needs of people, places and institutions. I was not astonished to see slimming belts for the obese at good prices online. Artists are selling their works online. Professionals are selling their services online. Many sites are online to create platforms for products and service providers. Some are selling used books, used wears, used electronics-phones, laptops, televisions, radios, used car, used furniture. Many could become i-reporters or news writers. Several services could be rendered for good prices online. Have you heard of online tutors? What about online radio and magazines? Many journalists could come together to start specialized online newspapers and magazines.

Limitless are ways to creating new jobs from generating new value chains from all existing businesses in all sectors. Create selling hub in the media of all forms. Serve as a link between merchants and customers. Place ads on newspapers and electronic media. Tell your prospective customers the kinds and other features of the products you are hawking to the public. Become writers' scouts. Write to heads or managements of schools. Reach out to heads of departments. Give out selected topics on burning issues for them to write about. Support them with tokens and relevant materials to work with. With a good memorandum of understanding, you have engaged self and others. This is applicable for all other intellectual property. Videos-on-demand, documents on demand, books on demand, prints (of textiles, wears, magazines, documentaries, researches ...**on demand**, accessories on demands, foods on demand, drugs on demand, Proffer solutions to all challenges and several challenges crop up every day for thinkers and creative minds. The need for improvement on revenue-employment generation in states in Nigeria brought about different findings from our research-focused office to meet the needs of the state in introducing such jobs like recycling of wastes materials especially the solids into final products that have economic values such as recycling tyres, plastic bottles into oil, rubber into rubber pellets, and liquid wastes in black oil into usable engine oils. If domestic solid wastes are recycled by different people to create jobs, what about the hospital wastes, chemical wastes and other sources of recyclable wastes? (REF: **Wastes to wealth jobs**)

The research showed that evacuation is incomplete until they are recycled. Both the process could fetch the states billions of naira. Individuals who had the recycling skill can start with public private partnership (PPP). Sometimes, one can do it as small and medium scale enterprises where locally fabricated crushers are procured to produce pellets for sale. One can imagine the number this effort can create from the idle minds among the virile youths. The scavengers can be converted into sorters and cleaners (laundry professionals) of the stipulated materials. In another clime, sorters are not needed on dumps but working streets by streets for government agency on environment to help sorting out of wastes dump on wastes bins or dumps along each streets before the evacuators come for the wastes. In order to collect the right amount as wastes disposal levy with 100% accuracy, e-waste billing is introduced where all enumerated houses, shops, offices and institutions in the covered areas are given alerted the moment their periodical service charge is paid at the collection centre and wastes disposal zones. The installed software in the system would alert the payers the confirming the date, the names and the streets by number of the payers and the officers it was paid to. By this, the collecting officers from place to place preferably ward to ward shall be fully engaged.

A study into the practicable solutions to the paucity of internally generated revenues to the government showed that the state can generate billions from tapping into the gains from digital economy. We introduced state-owned e-portal to the representatives of the Ministry of Finance and economic planning. Through the portal, all trades and businesses under the MDAs shall be enjoined to register to boost their promotion to general public within and outside the shores. The subscription-based ads for the products and services shall generate billions per annum by all estimations. The issues of drop in adverts by the advertisers brought us the chance of working with the associations of professional advertisers. We introduce turning their e-billboards into reading tablets at strategic locations like the school campuses and hostels. In fact, this would fetch more ads and forex to the agencies and their hosts. Our research ventures, an economic think-tank, whose objective is to fashion out practicable solutions to challenges came up with digital football sense to boost football development in a way that the sports would attract investors to the nation. We introduce the use of apps in marketing, administration, coaching, security and ticketing, live watching on mobile and electronic gadgets among others. The state that accepted this had its IGR improved within a short space of time.

A paint industry intention to make huge sale added a value to the sales of paints. It employ painters who would paint offices, houses, institutions et al that purchase certain number of paints for free. Sub-professionals of artisans can effectively key into this kind of initiative. Imagine an association of bricklayers who commence a repair for good discount for classified structures. Tyre-making industry can sell the products with free tyre fixing and wheel balancing through employment of vulcanizers into a new department in the sales outlets. We shall use first-hand experience on how individuals can generate more value added jobs. All other makers of products can take a cue and thereby create new jobs. The service providers can also pick example in the product-making firms to improve the level of patronage and employment generation. Let us pick some examples. A bank can employ new depositor-capture strategies through the newly inducted marketers. Marketers can be allowed to source for unique business proposals, instead of cash-deposits, from different classes of people and institutions for partnership. I could recall some proposals we sent to some convectional banks over financing developing on online printing business under partnership agreements. This, if scaled through, would provide jobs for thousands. When I saw the beauty and gains in creating interest for listeners having aware that many are good listeners but do not have flair for reading. I saw a good business in this. I recommend getting readers who would read to listeners on radio and television with the supports of the brands as sponsors. One can imagine reading for students on e-reading mobile tablets or digital billboards at strategic locations. A time would come when students, tutors, elderly, politicians, entrepreneurs, professionals would adopt mobile reading books-a more developed audio-books. In addition, what about creating visual books where lines are dramatized for the users? Creative dancers, singers, visual artists … would be great **opportunity** to create new jobs and markets.

What do you use your products or service to promote? What about the uses of your personal assets and time? Do you know that you can use your mobile phone and laptop for promotional purposes? Just create a blog with your nest egg and start promotional works. Do you know that you can convert your motorcycle for distribution of products? Start cutting your costs to have nest eggs; enroll as a distributor to the newspapers; employ hawkers and put them at strategic locations where mass movement of people; and in a month, you would see what you would generate after payment of bills. Also, you can become distributor of essential and luxurious products for the residents in the government reserve areas among others. Do you know that you can use popular products to promote product or service to promote service? Many companies are recording huge sales from using the strategy of selling theirs with others. Imagine the sellers of data with free phones. Free auto scan could boost patronage of auto-repairs and sales of parts. Producers and sellers are to be alive responsibilities by being creative. Let us take writing again. Is it written to promote a research finding? Is it written to promote culture, sports, events, administration, ideology or what? This is an area that is not fully explored to create new jobs by different professionals. Imagine writing and publishing specialized books to sell courses or professional leanings and findings, personalities, institutions, events, festivals, products among others. Imagine producing albums to purely advertise products and services just as titles of books are engraved on T-shirts or the logos and trademarks of institutions, football clubs, agencies, government projects and policies… are embossed on the wears-body and foot wears. All this would create several new jobs for millions aside improving popularity and sales from unprecedented patronage of goods and services by old and new customers. Through the publishing of specialized books in different formats in print and electronic versions, specialized bookshops like medical bookstores, technical bookshops, administrative bookstores and similarly the specialized libraries for users even the proliferation of space-based bookstores for billions of online shoppers!

Many states in the nation are facing two-pronged problems namely revenue and employment generation. After thorough research, we roll out series of ways people can be employed. One of those are new jobs that can be created from digital revolution called digital economy where e-portal for the state would have stations at each of the local governments. Many digital business as summarized in a section of this book are new jobs in many nations though old stuff in advanced ones. For the latter, the jobs can be repackaged with additional and unique features to creating new jobs from the existing jobs. Do you know that promotion of the artisanal products and service on the national e-market platform? I saw food crises in the nation as a way to start good businesses for those with thinking caps. What do I mean? Many perishable farm produce in the rural areas are there for the local 'importers'. Start as retailers and move up to become wholesalers. Supply what you 'import' from farms to modern shops and shopping malls instead of popular ancient markets. Cogitate over all sectors in the national economy. Browse their functions and responsibilities. Pick out the areas of opportunities for people and institutions. And several jobs can be created. Many citizens do not know that institutions used to have different opportunities to create employments. Many financial institutions are specially created to add values to the specialized businesses. Countless are the instances.

In Nigeria, Bank of industry (BOI) provides financial supports for different listed jobs from different sectors. How many of the unemployed that are informed enough to key into the objectives of the bank to be self-employed? Bank of Agriculture (BOA) finances agricultural-based jobs with their value chains. Work on such business activities of such banks like bank for social infrastructures and their major beneficiaries. If the beneficiaries could discover the professional or institutional responsibilities, then millions of jobs shall be created. I recently overheard of an interview with a Minister and I was able to create new jobs from their deficiencies. The areas such ministry has not covered in its history pave the way for the new jobs with huge values that are creatable. The Nigeria's honourable Minister of Communications during an interview session called for proposals for the transformation of the postal service towards generating more revenues to the coffers of the nation. The outset of androids and smartphones using internet services has reduced the patronage of the postal service as millions are not writing again. They send messages through email and picture-messages with optimum services. We delved into how to generate letter writing business from the huge millions who are still unlettered from the nation. By this, the agency would be generating revenue and even employ large number of people. The content of the proposal sent to the office of the Minister has the following as headline:

TURNING NIPOST INTO A MODEL AND REVENUE-EMPLOYMENT GENERATION AGENCY

Our findings analyses confirm the use of different approach towards modernizing the tasks of the agency to compete favourably with the courier services and the financial institutions across the nation. Studies show that many convectional banks have around five million depositors or customers. And most clients have at least two bank accounts. The depositors are mostly the city-dwellers and literate people. Millions of non-depositors are in the city and rural areas. These give the opportunity for the NIPOST that has offices and annexes across the nation to come up with products and services to ease communication and spread the wealth as a delivery link between the prospective senders and receivers of cash in form of e-transactions and e-delivery under the themes-**Nipost e-cash**, **Nipost cargoes** and **Nipost e-mailing services**.

Alas! The proposal never see the light of the day!

BRAINSTORM

a) Identify some new jobs creatable from **opportunities** from what you have read so far. Domicile the jobs.
b) Create new employment **opportunities** from the above in 'a'. Identify the possible threats or challenges to the new opportunities.
c) Prepare feasibility studies for the new employments created from 'b'.

Now, we generate new jobs ideas from the services and products of the postal agency. What comes to your mind? Never say 'I can't', 'you can'. Close the book for a while. Pick your pen and a sheet of paper. Identify with an agency of government, list what the agency stands for by objectives through proper understanding of the mission and vision, wait a bit; think of new things that can add values to the objectives to better the products and the services. Scribble them down. Let me use another agency. Under the Ministry of Education is books and intellectual property agency. One can turn the agency into employment-revenue generating agency through the introduction of specialized online library to the agency where all the recommended texts, theses from schools and researches are uploaded and promoted to the outside world. People who are internet-savvy can become affiliate sellers of the works on the site for good commission. Think for them. Think for the institutions- private or public-owned. Use the samples above for other ministries, departments and agencies to churn out **employment opportunities**.

1.2 **APPETISERS**

> "Opportunity is found in all challenges
> Everyone encounters opportunities every day
> Without doubt, in difficulties are opportunities
> In various shapes and sizes they come
> It could be as social crises to be fixed
> As economic recession to be put back on track
> Frail institutions and lacked social Services to be rendered
> Political issues to be resolved
> And lasting solutions to be procured
> By finding the solutions, hero is made, legacy is created"

We will continually create new jobs through conversion of identified opportunities. Individuals and institutions used to make mistakes in interpretations on **opportunities** based on our level of shared intelligence and natural wisdom. <u>There is no limit to opportunities since challenges (problems) never cease to exist</u>. And according to the noblest mentor, problems that pave the ways for opportunities lie side by side with the solutions. In his lip 'God does not create a problem without its solutions very close to it. A challenge faced by a people, an institution, a government, a corporate body, an association creates avenue for new jobs to be created. <u>Every free vacuum is an open opportunity to create both employments and wealth</u>. Every shortage of staff and equipment has open windows of employment **opportunities**. Every under-performing in an institution is a path to create new employment. Every drop in sales of companies open ways for independent sellers and distributors just as economic downturn in the nation is a big eyes opener for massive creation of employment in all sector to spread the wealth instead of accumulation with a few people and institutions in control. Let me cite a few more instances. Products and services that lack huge promotion have created rooms for proliferation of online and offline independent advertisers in the print, electronic and digital media sectors; marketers, retailers and salespersons. The starvation and hungry people have created rooms for agro-allied businesses. Those who are in the manufacturing and processing sectors must have their hands full. The rapid expansion of houses and streets has created employment creating opportunities for the proprietors and proprietress of schools, suppliers of educational materials, artisans, publishers and printers. Nation that is economic crises especially in the building of social infrastructures has created operating space for the investors to create both employment and wealth for the nation. Man is enormously naturally endowed with five senses even six to identify opportunities created by places, people, events and institutions. Each **opportunity** creates rooms to create lucrative jobs. The needs of people, to spice up places, to add aesthetic values to institutions, homes, offices.. are enough to create thousands of jobs. We need God's wisdom to get things rightly interpreted and develop lucrative viable ideas from the limitless number of quality **opportunities** around us. It is a mistake on our part taken **opportunity** or **an idea** we come by for a mere '**waste**'. Everything around us open eyes to opportunities to create employments and wealth. Challenges facing institutions, people and places breed opportunities to be positively engaged with lucrative jobs. Factories who are not making sales need independent salesmen. Schools that are not adequately equipped need makers and suppliers of the educational materials and resources. Only the think-tanks can see and use the real **opportunities**. Someone who has tertiary school education has been offered opportunity. Someone who visited places may have gained opportunities to nurture his innate skill. **Kodjo**, a pretty damsel, in her early twenties, was a natural thespian who never knew her potentials until she accompanied her sister, a professional thespian, to a film location. The person to take the role failed to meet up and she was persuaded to take up the script. She performed excellently well that she was chosen for the role. Since then, she has taken up the job as a profession. Today, she has produced block buster films.

A popular figure in the nation recently threw up a party at a public place. The gate was thrown open for everybody. This gave **opportunities** to different artisans especially social functions aesthetics-related jobs in entertainment. Outsourcing jobs, a policy to empower the registered artisans compiled in a national database shall encourage others to learn a skill of choice from the artisans. There were jobs opportunities for photographers, artists, comedians, drummers, dance-drama, souvenirs sellers, the beverages and drinks' sellers et al to make brisk sales and patronages. Someone who never attends formal schools but informal schools has been given **opportunity**. Those who fall to the category of the former become professionals doing office jobs. Those people in the latter category end up becoming artisans of repute. People who reside in the city are living with **opportunities** to be creative and become self-boss. Those who are rural dwellers are living and sleeping with natural resources that are invaluable. Everything, positive or negative, creates **opportunities** to become one's boss. Allowed in print and publishing business is the sales-on-return strategy of selling. Vendor (of print materials) is always a zero-capital job. Newspaper firms favour hawkers called vendors (even the chain distributors) by supplying free (no advance payment). Pick a newspaper. Inside the pages are news, columnists' write-ups, opinions, events, entertainment, sports reports, breaking world news, advertisements... Each of these creates rooms for opportunities to create jobs. Pick up a product. What do you think you can earn from promoting it? Do you have the resources to make some money from the manufacturers or the major (customized) sellers? I admonished a story writer in a newspaper company to turn his works into scripts for film makers or books for publishers. Imagine the number of employments that would be created. I equally commended efforts of a woman who wrote to expose the idle ones into jobs they can do. Such can introduce them into employment seminars or consultancy under her watch. Fashion designers only need to read and share intelligence on the use of materials and create new styles at all times for all times. It depends on the level of the thinkers. Losing a lucrative job does not point to the end of the world. Nay, your life is not shattered. A fall is calling for a rise.

In fact, it opens the brains and eyes to several other employment **opportunities** from searching in media outlets-print, broadcast and electronic media. Walk around the streets. What do you think of the needs of the people you meet and the places you visit? What about the structures and the institutions within the ambience? What lacks the business empires you come across? What about the business and residential places? In all the streets are residential buildings, business offices, institutions (schools, medical, hospitality..), recreation places, markets and business districts… All of them would continue to lack certain things or the others. Schools need new enrollees. Insurance firms need clients buying different insurance premiums. Companies with dwindling sales need sales boosters in independent salesmen. Governments who lack finance to implement capital projects need the brains and intellectual minds of the consultants and the private financiers under public private partnership (PPP). This reminds me of several proposals written to the state government on how to shore up their internally generated revenues without increasing running expenses with simple zero-cost ideas. Every challenge or problem facing different people, places, institutions, objects, creatures… are eye openers to **opportunities** to create lucrative jobs. Think about them and you have got opportunities to become your own boss. Work out something for sports arena. Take football for instance. There are footballers for different departments of any competitive game, the football agents or scouts, the footballers trainers, coaches, administrators, managers, medical team, analysts, psychologists, costumiers, supporters… even the stadiums where they play always create rooms for employment **opportunities**. Can you design souvenirs for the teams? What about souvenirs for talented players? Those should create avenues to start up a lucrative job! Anyway, where are the working experiences you have garnered in the course of working at your last or former places of work? The experience garnered and the exposure of such is enough to kick start a new job. All what you read about in biographies is adequate to bring the best jobs out of you. The advertisements you read about in the newspapers or listening to on air or watch in your television sets are paths to start a good job. Reflect on what you read! Don't just read for fun. Read to study new paths to unveil new jobs. In the latter part of this work is how to unearth jobs from news, adverts slots and several features in the print media. Inside books are information that can turn you into self-employment. On information board are right places to have new crops of entrepreneurs. When I listen to radio programs or television broadcast, I look into employment **opportunities**. Have you done any of this?

Ask, always ask yourself, what positive jobs can I create from what I heard, saw or felt? Many course contents, core, elective or general, in your major course of study can create employment **opportunities**. My wealth of experience and the courses of study helped a great deal to write several books on jobs and sales creation. Moving with a friend that is a professional in an artisanal job is an **opportunity** for you to learn such skill. Never waste your precious time. You could be the next thing in the job. Many graduates today never really learnt what is popularizing them from any particular person. We have seen popular singer who used to be band member of a popular artiste.

I met **John** (pseudonym) at a newspaper vendor joint. He was a free reader but an unemployed graduate for over ten years. Funnily, he was still hopefully searching for jobs despite the grey hairs on his head. I interacted with him one day. I discovered that good readers are always good critics and may be poor writers. Some only read for the fun of it. Good readers are those who read to research into issues to have knowledge of how things are or should be rightly done. Most never know that reading add values to knowledge and improves wisdom. And both are inputs to have a good script. I advised him to summon courage to start writing on issues. He itched to know the nature of issues to write about. I told him to start collecting materials from he has been reading on prevalent issue that needs practicable solutions. I told him that that was the position I took to write on jobs creation which had produced two published books. He was advised "Make the best use of your reading volumes of newspapers every day gratis at the vendor joint. Your experience and knowledge have been increased over the years. Practice the theory. You can write on different issues with facts. Engage in writing and turn writing into a profession. Recall that writers of scripts always end up becoming thespians just as songs promoters and managers rise to become star singers of chart topping songs. Check history of the award-winning singers, thespians and bestselling authors. And this will pay your bills. I was an attendant to a free seminar of an herbal drug selling company. In the seminar, I realized like others that I was interested in partaking that one could start distributing business of the products to stores just like newspaper, magazines, journals and books distribution business. What do you expect of such who paid heavily to attend seminars, workshops? Fairs, exhibitions, seminars, workshops, training institutes ...attended create **opportunities** to start lucrative jobs. It is a waste of hard-earned fund watching football or any sport in competitions without rolling out jobs **opportunities**. If you visit a stadium just like a beach or park, go there with your artistic minds, interests, creative skills, tools and materials to make some artworks and paints for the celebrities; move in with a good recording phone or portable gadget as a freelancer. Ball joggling and soccer artistry skills would be a source of income for the talents. What about talented artists? If good artists are at stadium during live matches drawing live or with paintings of the popular coaches, evergreen players, match commissioners, big guns watching at the VIP section and other dignitaries even star players, such would record huge sales. Several skills and tense moments that are worth remembering could be recorded for commercial production to sell later. I could recall when I could not get enough from my works. I decided to work with some ICT partners to create e-reading billboard at campuses; the e-reading board is an advancement of the e-reading apps in mobile tablets; later the e-reading platforms for a price becomes a segment in my website for the readers across climes. Imagine what we make monthly from this venture. We sent proposals to the schools who are offering entrepreneurial courses to sell the ideas of our books on jobs creation through their server office to the workstations. It worked! Do you see reason in what we did? We used others existing facilities to promote and sell our works for a negotiable fees. Grow a business by combining ideas. Share your business intention with trustworthy partner who has role to play. Create the script for the person and a business is started. Forming a partner is an easy task. Schedule a meeting. Rub minds together. Discuss your business ideas to the level of understanding of a lay man. Develop a mutually beneficial agreement. The script contains the inputs of each partner. The shares of gains and losses must be carefully and clearly scripted. When to start and when to end among other sensitive things must be prepared by a legal practitioner.

Never see all the facilities around you as a mere waste or idle. Think about how you can transform them into commercial-based materials; ruminate over what you can use them for in a positive way towards generating employments and lucrative jobs. When a thing is left idle; it remains purposeless whereas it has created another opportunity to make wealth out of it. Such is renewable, re-usable, recyclables and could be reduced with some efforts that would have been paying salaries or wages for doers. Therefore, zero-demand, of a 'waste' in an ambience, does not amount to a useless waste elsewhere. Zero-demand does not stamp a product or service as a waste. We complain of no jobs as we fail at our capacities to make optimal use of the opportunities in opportunities at our fingertips. <u>With limitless **opportunities, ideas** are created to engage in lucrative employments</u>. <u>Opportunity</u> is the free gift of nature that must be discovered!

Man does not need to do certain things, even if they are in the vogue, before he engages in something that would give him instant success. This is what we referred to as grabbing the **opportunity** when it comes before others. Work on the ideas. Work out on how to make the dream idea into a product or service. Many successful internet-based businesses started from mere blogging. Blogging jobs are usually one-man business in the advanced nation where the owner designs his in the comfort of his residence. Based on the latest innovations and the relevance of blogs for business growth and social activities, blog has been employer of many contributors as correspondents of videos, pictures, animation and news. What is blogged could be a simple game; interest in socialization; hobby among others. The devices are the personal laptops and other few electronic devices within the homes. The use of brains, software production, information and communication skills, and natural intelligence make creativity in such blog sites and this determines popularity. Those in the advanced economies could easily launch the sites into internet since the cost is affordable. The interest of the owner to trade the idea with venture capitalists or turning it into big businesses. Billionaire **Bill Gates** does not need to finish his course at Harvard before he opted out to grab the **opportunity** or use the idea which paved the way for Microsoft incorporation. **Mark Zuckerberg** 'dropped' out of Harvard too after he had discovered what could make him great in life and the popular social site **Facebook** is created. Many who are tech-entrepreneurs today start with the blogs for its low cost of production compare with more capital-intensive and more technical website. Blogs, just like products, have no limit. Creating new blog is a function of the creator by his level of creativity and ingenuity. A good communicator, editor and writer whose added value is thorough research could run as many blogs as possible. **Bill Gate** built his business on the platform of computer already in existence to build his software. **Zuckerberg** seized the **opportunity** of the available internet facilities probably in the provided incubation centre and consistent economic (science and technology) policies that enhance investors and celebrate brilliance (the right platform) in his era to build his own digital business. Businesses of social values are created with natural ideas as they rose to become social media entrepreneurs of repute with internet technology. Apps are created daily by numerous ICT firms. Take note, they are never dullards but of exceptional breeds and blessings to this generation. They are good exemplary characters and role models for others across the globe. Both (and those in their shoes) enjoy working social infrastructures, consistent economic policies, technological advancement and political stability to make good their inventions. It is up to people that have the wherewithal to buy technologies from technical students and local people to set businesses up for jobs **opportunities** from **ideas**. The traditionally-sourced technologies could be transformed into global product to create numerous employments-creation **opportunities** for generation lasting thriving **ideas**. The **Bill Gates** and co of this world makes the best use of the right factors in the nation to create the niche for themselves. All the stated factors are opportunities at their disposals. There are several jobs opportunities from where the likes of Bill Gates, Mark Zuckerbergs, Steve Jobs temporarily stop. They buy technologies to establish their marks. The technology could be ordinary game purchased online for as little as five or ten dollars. It is developed and packaged in the comfort of the buyers' homes, set and edited in the home studio and placed for sale to millions. This is a good example of one-man job that could turn the doer into overnight millionaire. As aforementioned, if the buyer decides to trade the idea, the venture capitalists are invited in and the production takes a commercial or corporate form to employ thousands. Twitter, facebook, google that bought Backrub and so on started this way to lay examples for others. This is how a local business is transformed into a global enterprise. One can use similar platform and professional experience to create something new. In the developing nations where the internet facilities are costly, they could be subscribed from the developed nations for a good price. This means that what is done in the advanced nations could be imitated by the skilled nationals effectively in the third world nations. The use of the right platforms could serve as foundation to other opportunities for creative more tech-entrepreneurs in all economies. Technologies can be brought from any visitor online to reduce the cost of transportation. Visit the search engine created by google and others to locate lucrative jobs placed online every hour. **Adams**, a friend who studied Fire Safety Engineering at Dublin, secured lucrative jobs through the search engine at far away United Arab Emirates. Through many social sites like linkedin, several jobs **opportunities** are opened to searchers. Many skills and arts are developed from visiting sites and these can be transformed into lucrative jobs opportunities. As aforementioned, the working social physical infrastructures in the advanced nations pave the way for jobs opportunities in such nation.

Conversely, in many poor nations where all the infrastructures and superstructures are not available or defective, that (the inadequacy) also creates several other opportunities to create jobs and wealth for distribution for those who can reflect and meditate. Recently, all the yardsticks to measure the state of economy show that the economy is broke. States need money outside the dwindling monthly allocations from the federation account. We commenced research on how states can generate revenue internally from certain services. Our research showed that each of the least populated states can generate not less than two billion per month from just two sectors- infrastructural and environmental services. The opportunity to engage in such research was from the bad state of the economy. Each time a problem is identified, then, several practicable solutions proffered are jobs-creation oriented. It is high time the heirs of the celebrated authors re-packaged the best sellers into audio-books and drama books. It is the era of book to film or book to poetry. Bookless libraries are the new trend. My team decided to make our monies from selling licensed book-containing compact discs to central server base in the schools where e-libraries are established. The e-libraries facilities could be used for e-seminars, video-conferencing, computer-based tests, e-learning, e-advertising and several uses with the internet connections or internet-enhanced facilities. Imagine the business opportunities and lucrative employment ideas created from the infrastructures. What a million worth idea! Who is the doubting Thomas who still says employments are difficult to be created? Such may be bereft of ideas. And ideas are created at every place and time with different infrastructures. Coming back to books; such books (their contents) could be transliterated into major languages of the world.

Imagine the jobs being created for many people of different nations speaking different languages. Re-mix the poetry works; re-write the block buster films to suit the moment; flavor the chart-topping songs to educate and champion different causes. Produce all of these in different languages. This is another great avenue to create jobs for people by them. Manage the social miscreants in the streets through rehabilitation and skills discovery programmes as a way to create jobs opportunities from developed ideas. Discover the talented ones as independent scouts for academies. Establish entrepreneurial academies to nurture fresh prospective entrepreneurs. Many successful singers and thespians in Nigeria in spite of the challenges pursued their skills and talents instead of wasting precious time chasing certificates or working under companies earning peanuts as remunerations.

There are others who never seize the opportunities that come their ways. They do not reflect on the opportunity to be at the best of their careers. They end up become wretched people. Learn the technical languages of all products and services. Learn from the singing birds. Learn dancing from dancing insects. Learn diving from whales. Learn swimming from the fish in the ocean. Learn adaptation from animals in cocoons and shell. Many things are at our fingertips to learn from. It is not for idle creatures are created. Learn through meditation the workability of services. Learn from service providers. Learn from peer group. Take a model in models and mentors to teach you new things. Learn through the 'abandoned' intellectual materials in the archives. Browse the newspapers to learn about existing advertised jobs **opportunities**. Several secrets of buying and selling are in prints, learn to understand them. Learn from the wisdom of celebrated professionals to add more values to your knowledge. In doing this, jobs opportunities are created in millions. Learn from internet facilities. Never see a thing as perfect except the works of God, The Creator. In whatever a man does are lapses. Fix the vacuum to create for yourself (and others) good jobs. This is how <u>lucrative **idea**</u> is created. Many things are yet to be in the search engines. Design after research to create your own search engine.

Many a business needs rivals to be up and doing. Challenge the monopolies and create your brand. I told a partner that government should also invest in e-marketplace like the **amazon.coms** of this world to enhance competition of quality services and e-products at lower prices. By this, more independent digital sellers and software makers for the site. Breaking monopolies is a road to generation of jobs. It could be an insurmountable task, start now with right, gradual consistent and consecutive steps. They could be the only **opportunity** to make your mark abroad. Never think as a local person, see yourself as a potential international brand in making. Keep learning new dialects. Learn at least one in a year. The more you understand and speak, the greater your chance to create jobs for self and others. Many successful business gurus in this world would have increased their presence everywhere in the world but for lack of this. And in this act, you become an international business owner. Understand many dialects could turn you to become executive officers for international organizations, embassies and multinational companies. Imagine the reverence the company or nation would have for your office. And your brand as a worker or as an entrepreneur would grow beyond your scope and generation. If you have the **opportunity** to enroll in a language village or moving with other tribes, seize the **opportunity** to learn the language. The noblest among us was reported to have said '*he who learns other people's language is free from their cunning ways*'. Keep learning '**hows**' and '**whats**'. That is the secret of doing things. Teach what you learn to improve your fountain of knowledge. What you teach improve the skills you possess. And you could end up becoming a consultant in the field. Keep learning about towns and nations. Learn about the people and their values. In this are the useful opportunities to make it big within a short time.

Never be satisfied with stagnancy. Traverse the crust within and beyond. Discover many lands of different people and cultures. 'Traverse the earth and learn…' as the twenty-three year long revealed scriptures reveal. Africa was discovered by seas explorers in the names of **Mungo Parks** and **Lander brothers** just as many Caribbean nations and islands. And the discoveries expose the opportunities to create wealth for people within and outside. Remember that many who seek for green pastures overseas end up making their legitimate money from they had learnt and the skills they had acquired. If you fail to learn, many opportunities would by-pass you. In any shop you find yourself, learn the tricks or the secrets of buying and selling. In any class you are, learn within.

What could transform you into the top of a career is learnt through grapevine source. In the story of old was a migrant from **Makkah** that found himself in **Madinah** by fate. His host intended to share his own belongings into equal halves for him to pick a share. The man rejected this offer. Instead, he preferred to learn the art of buying and selling. He knew the situation could be different from what it was used to be in his former place. Therefore, he demanded from his host verbatim 'Take me to the market in the city and teach me the secrets of buying and selling. I am okay with this'. In the history of mankind, the man became one of the richest men. He was able to accomplish the greatness simply because he never started a trade without learning the art of buying and selling. Learning is therefore a great opportunity. And it is eternal from womb to tomb as the noblest guided the mankind, male and female in his teachings and sayings. He who is tired of learning, they say, is tired of life. Somebody might itch to know where to learn. Is it in the convectional schools? No, not at all! Man learns from all places, formal and informal places, in print or broadcast and sometimes through grapevine sources be it in the private or public, from individuals and groups of people, regardless the sex, the age, the level of perceived education, working experience, ethnic or religion inclinations, ideological school such belong and the environment such is found, from all creatures outside mankind even from products and services including events, situations, activities in the mobile and immobile facilities. What is learnt in the scriptures make reverend fathers out of men. Many become spiritual mentors and role models from what acting what is revealed in the divine scriptures-the manuals of life here and beyond. Counsel for good returns or write mentoring books in volumes for buyers. Imagine the **opportunities** before the priests. Many a creature is defined as unique in the scripts. Breed the quail in a large scale and get the bucks. Plant the olive trees and create your wealth. Go into bee-keeping and reap the gains. Many a job is a natural job for doers. Discover them from reading the scripts. The forbidden animals are the ones forbidden; rearing the rest and using the parts are good jobs **opportunities** for the readers and believers. Imagine the gains in rearing grass cutters for commercial purpose. Imagine the gains from breeding quails in commercial quantity. Imagine the gains from all the contents in the bees produce for commercial quantity. All the parts in cattle are not waste. Imagine what animal husbandry producer could make from the jobs. Several opportunities for jobs creation are inside the scripts you read. Not just the holy books but in several other books. All books are written from inspiration to guide the readers serve as a great **opportunity** to pick lucrative jobs of interests!

Grapevine information has turned many into the class of the rich. I was a living witness to what made two friends to hit it big at the prime time of their lives. The first man, by chance, found himself in an operating room where phone boxes were being repaired by a technician. He studied how the man did the job within some minutes. He went back home to put what he learnt into practice. He got it right. He tried some other phone boxes and got positive answers. He thought of getting connections to the right clients. His target was the government of the day. He bared his mind to a friend who had the connections. Business agreement was entered. They got contracts from governors of three states to repair all their boxes in all the ministries and agencies. And the proceeds from the contract became the source of their wealth. Had he failed to learn from the technician, he would have lost the opportunity of making money and fame. Many pauper and aged parents never attempt to download the life experience and historical facts about the components of their environment to the heads of their children due to their ignorance. Doing so would have created opportunities that could open way for the children. Many of such children would have become celebrated writers and film makers creating several relevant jobs for the entertaining industry. Many would have developed interest in pharmaceutical business. Imagine the number of jobs opportunities that would have been created by the children for people and the effects on the nation in wealth distribution.

Many never expose their children into positive aspects of life that the children could use to make their mark in the sands of time. The worst part is the failure to teach the children the mother tongue. Wherever they (the children) find themselves, they would have become jobs creators for indigenous people if they understand the languages. How would it have been if a soccer talent takes along his male children to the training pitch in order to learn from his skills? In the developed climes, successful parents expose the secrets to their children in order to develop their own interest in such vocation. Some prepare motivating grounds for the children to develop their skills or talents. Through watching of soccer especially of the artistry of the legend in soccer on television, Diego Amando Maradona, then of Napoli Football Club and **Lionel Andrea Messi** of popular Barcelona football club developed his interest for football as a sport. Today, it is the sport that is giving him the laurels, reverence, the fame and the wealth to support his native Argentina, family and friends.

Many in the poor nations are backward because they want their own children to discover innate talents themselves. In advanced nations, parents take their talented children to relevant academies where their talents can be perfectly nurtured. Those parents prefer the academies to educational institutions. This is the difference. Let the other nations establish academies and license private owners to key into the business. Providing the facilities is creating the **opportunities** for the users. Creating effective social infrastructures and adequate security are enough to create **opportunities** to the people by the administration. Enhancing business operating environment would create chance to ensure quality no matter the quantity. It also opens room for meeting sales target for the company. If the right learning environment is provided in schools, limitless number of manpower would have been churned out of schools. Would there be need for the employment of expatriates? Of course no! Again, traverse through the earth and learn wisdom as the incorruptible scripture reveals.

On the earth are limitless opportunities for you to explore and exploit. In the cafes learnt the style and content of blogs. Create your own if you have got the skills. Create something bigger and unique to attract the traffics. It is high time multilingual blogs got created. It is time for specialized blogs for specialized disciplines are becoming the order of the day. Create graphic- illustration only blogs and instant response blogs. Sports lovers are in dire need of sports blogs with no dilution. Specialized bloggers could make money from popular football clubs or choice sports. Create blogs to celebrate legends-towns, nations, individuals. Imagine the number of jobs opportunities at the fingertips of the creators. Never mind the competition in the market. It brings the best out of all participants in the improvement of creativity and natural intelligence of the investors. And the product is quality as choices for the clients or consumers. Imagine the distribution of wealth of the nation to the nationals!

"*Close the shop if the business is no more paying the dues*"- someone admonished a business owner. A good piece advice but yet another opportunity created from the vacuum. Only a creative entrepreneur could discover this. To the former, enough is the earth to relocate your business. To the latter, a great opportunity has been created from filling the vacuum to locate his own. Exploring the earth is searching for greener pastures and this is in fulfillment to the command of the Creator. The more the travelling, the more the traveller appreciates the works of the Creator, the better his conviction to submit to Him. This is a way of searching for better opportunity to survive the hardship. Good farmer abandons a land after its usage. Abandonment is to allow the fallow land to regain its lost fertility after years of cultivation on it. Move your shops as the residential areas spread. The right economic policies and stable political system are the baits to the investors, local and international.

In such nation, investment opportunities have been created and there would be proliferation of industries. In any nation where there is proliferation of industries, there would not be unemployment and the wealth of the nation will be well distributed. Getting closer to the target buyers is enough (an opportunity) to sell-out the product with minimum cost. MTN came to Nigeria, a far bigger market, after making the name (brand) in South Africa. It was never a surprise when a guy said 'We are moving elsewhere'. The business was moved to another place of greater opportunity. The former address has been used up by the business. It was no more a fertile ground for the business to grow in leaps and bounds. On the other side, the vacated place is a good ground for the same business under new management or for another business that has complementary value. A maxim rightly says '*a man's food is another man's poison*'.

Another great opportunity is resuscitating the dead or dying business. The business that relocates has created a level of goodwill for the same business. If new owner of similar business enters with different techniques or market strategies to win (attract) customers, then the opportunity has been effectively grabbed! Opportunities are created in different ways. A nation that is no more conducive for a business is a fertile ground for another business. This is the same within the cities or towns in the nation. Lack of gainful jobs prompts many socio-economic researchers and consultants into writing books on jobs creation. The constant loss of jobs has led into several publications on how best to retain your work. Epidemics have been the major cause of unending medical researches. And this effort is creating money and fame to the partaker specialists.

In many poor nations with several difficulties exist jobs opportunities in thousands. Creating wealth from conversion of what they are wasting could create jobs for the millions-direct and indirect (Read 'Wastes to wealth jobs' by the author). Apply the **three R's** and start creating the jobs and distribute the wealth. By the **R's**, I mean **reduce**, **recycle** and **resold**. Re-use in order to reduce. Re-mould in order to re-package for re-selling. What is reduced is changing the type of packaging. Recycling is to elongate the lifespan of the material and to resell is to make extra money from other users who see them as raw materials for their first products. The problem of capital is solved by employing the tactics in the titles –Jobs with zero-capital by the author. And the last step is to start learning to act where the advanced nations and great entrepreneurs began. **Create ideas** from their thriving ideas to create lucrative employments. There are chains of great individual entrepreneurs in different fields such as education, hospitality, publishing among others. There are thriving family businesses that were and are products from great ideas of a few of them. Do not just be satisfied with an idea; develop new ideas as the events call for their emergence. Many successful people are into several businesses. This simply shows that they have developed many ideas and convert them into money-making ventures. It is not absurd to be told that they are authors, publishers, researchers, public speakers, politicians,... as well as industrialists.

In order to create room for ideas and their development, qualified human resources must be created from qualitative schools. Improve the promotion of the primary jobs and the industries have been given the lift. Tap the **opportunities** created by the good climatic conditions to **create ideas-creating jobs** from the farms and forests for all institutions. Develop by encouraging the natural arts and skills of your people to create jobs opportunities for millions. Learn from the colour combinations of birds of different species, you the artists. Learn from the behaviours of animals on land and the seas to create fun and amusement for a fee. Meditate over what you see and hear as you stroll across the lands.

Meditate over you hear over the radio and television. Practical jobs opportunities are always in all that you see or hear, watch out. Explore the natural resources around and within to create room for proliferation of several sectors in industries. Imitate the technologies from the imported products and services abroad to kick start yours. Improve your tourism business from developing ancient artifacts in museum, develop the parks, games villages, repackage your cultural values and heritage to attract tourists, entertainment and sports attract tourists across the global village and your people would get lucrative jobs in thousands.

Sell all the information about the nation through internet facilities and you have pulled the crowds to your business. The more the visitors, the more the increase in the number of new business idealists, the more the investments and wealth distribution in the nations and the more the jobs opportunities! Knowingly that needs are unlimited as time and climes change. The greater the growth rate or population distributions, the more the needs and the more the business ideas for creative entrepreneurs and think-tanks!

Therefore the nature of jobs, especially the products and services, changes with time and clime to suit the needs of the target consumers or clients. Let this factual statement stick to your mind, <u>the more the investors, the more the jobs opportunities for many idlers within</u>!

Develop all the primary sectors of the economy to attract the secondary producers and several chains of sellers and distributors. Some acres of fertile of schools and agricultural institutes could feed the whole nation if commercially and profitably utilized. Some flocks of cattle can turn a nation into self-sufficiency in food and even export excess to earn foreign currencies. Many advanced economies in the world are wise for that. Invest in learning environment and encourage writing and jobs are created for thousands in publishing and film making. Invest in agriculture and agro-allied industries grow in thousands for jobs opportunities. Without raw materials from farms or the precious minerals and creatures from soil and seas, no industry would thrive.

A poor nation in the landlocked territory without seas could develop dry ports. This attracts many investors in different sectors such as leisure and accommodation, financial and insurance services, medical services, security services, transportation and logistics, courier and outsourcing jobs among others. Attract them with several freebies and consistent economic policies under stable political system. Invest in social infrastructures and Information and Communication Technology to gain the rush for stay in the nation. Build industrial parks with relevant estates for investors. Create markets and the right transaction environment that attract buyers. Build relaxation parks and aesthetics environment for foreigners and local investors. Encourage them with attractive incentives.

Zero-account attracted customers to open accounts with Guaranty Trust Bank in Nigeria. Today, the bank is a major force to reckon with in the financial industry. Develop the education sector to a high standard that meet the global standard and the manpower being churned out of schools would turn the nation into knowledge-based economy like **Japan**. Let that be enough for the poor nations in this world. The advanced nations have no right to cry wolf when there is none. <u>Creating new jobs and services from the existing jobs and services</u> is what they should do. Let them **develop ideas** from the existing products and services. And **jobs opportunities** are created for millions. If there are one thousand classes of existing jobs, at least another one thousand could be easily created. Just change the feature of the jobs by introducing something new and by so doing new jobs have been created for the roaming unemployed (but employable) in the streets. What is permanent in life is change.

Business moves stations for different motives. Man moves for different purposes. Wherever a business leaves, another similar must grow but with different or better management pursuing different mission. A man vacates a position to create chance for another person. Closing a shop (office) creates **opportunities** (ideas) for the emergence of new shops (offices). Closing a business creates way for new business. Many businesses are living the third world nations at the time when some are starting to invest billions. At the time government monopoly on certain business ends, the private investors are licensed by the same government to avoid creating vacuum. The rate of entry and exit may be different. The project for the future by government or individuals (persons, associations or institutes) creates numerous opportunities for jobs creation for those who could read into the future. This reminds me of a government plan to create dry ports at certain location in some states. The proposed work would need private investors' ingenuity to create businesses around the ports such as hotels, restaurants, logistic services, courier services, transportation or distribution services and parks, parking space, gardens, car wash, auto-parts shops among other jobs. We live in a transient world even the world is transitory by nature. Such is life and that is life. A static life is a rigid life and a moving life is a flexible life. Stagnant water is filled with filths and always has bad odour unlike a flowing sea.

Opportunities of creating ideas could start at any point in time. One can develop interested employment opportunities after listening to a song or watching a film;

after the drama session, after attendance of a training or events; after participation in a workshop or seminar; during or after the sporting session or contests, after visiting a place, a people, a worship place, an office or institution among several other windows. They are like a phase of life. Ideas would grow if the originators desire. In fact, one can say that **opportunity** (or an idea) cannot be isolated from living. They are always together. Wherever there is existence of a living creature, there are numerous **opportunities**. I know a young graduate that was into breeding albino rats for commercial purpose while still in school. The business was successful. Suddenly, he decided to close up the farm, the big earning idea, for academic pursuits. Can you see the difference between graduates of different climes? The former would grow the opportunities (ideas) while the latter never give them a hoot. The former become successful and the latter are the lowest rung of the ladder.

In all the cases, the existed platforms are the opportunities that created ways to create lucrative ideas and translate them into brands. **Steve Jobs** and his co-partner develop the electronic devices to aid businesses and social engineering. The existing and cheap internet facilities and the advancement in the Information and Communication Technology (ICT) enhanced e-solutions (software) remain good and relevant platform. The combination of several technologies (already in existence) brings about the manufacturing of electronic devices that gave them the brand '**apple incorporation**' and the wealth.

Sit down. Have a stroll. Think. Think deeply. Reflect to discover opportunities. And these inspire ideas to create employments and free the nation from the scourge of unemployment. Combine internet facilities plus photography with videography with art aesthetics plus broad band for radio station and television and some other relevant memories to store data in the making of mobile set. What is discovered? The smart-phones! Think about the platforms already in existence that could help you grow your invention(s). Never get deterred by the inefficient social infrastructures. The epileptic supply of electricity almost disrupts my works in research and typesetting of the works. But, I seized the opportunity of the few hours of supply to do my work. If you cannot think of new inventions, think about the celebrities of the existing inventions.

What they need, you can produce. And a need is usually universal and a never-go-out-of-demand things. Meditate. This is telling you that all are consumers even if they are producers of some other items. And that paves the way for opportunities to make legitimate bucks from their earnings. Nothing should deprive you of the success if you have discovered certain things that could give you a brand. If you fail to use it at the right time, another person would take your right position. I am aware of a man who lost his job for some years. He grabbed the opportunity of his 'sabbatical leave' to re-discover his writing skills. He engaged his time (opportunity) to write collections of short stories which won him the best short story writer in a national contest.

A friend who had almost a two-decade experience with different auto companies was encouraged to scribble down all the technical knowledge and skills he had acquired over the years. Learning all the skills is a lifetime opportunity. Serving in different departments in several companies is a huge opportunity. Having adequate time to scribble down the experience to teach and mentor others through the content is another invaluable opportunity. He started the compilations. After going through the work, I had the belief that the book would be a best seller after its release. Everything around us gives way to opportunities. Living as a human being under whose all other creatures submit and work for is an opportunity bestowed on mankind by the Creator. What we eat, what we breathe, what we clothe ourselves with, where we live or put our heads...are opportunities. Many like us never have them. Professing the Creator in recognition for the natural endowments is a great opportunity when we are still living. It will be extremely late to realize the Omnipotent of the Almighty in the grave- a place of no return! Man shall account for all the opportunities paving the way for lucrative ideas in the next world just as accountability is major for check and balances here on the planet-earth. It will be too late for someone whose head has been cut off to cry for leniency.

Just like the calendar, priceless **opportunity** is an irreversible fleeting night and day. Just like your age that keeps increasing by the day, it can never be reversed. The baby cum old man can never return to the babyhood state. Once a bridge is passed, it is by-gone. Ability to possess all the working senses is an opportunity. Many are blind. Many are deaf. Many have lost their memory. Many cannot use their limbs. Speaking a dialect or more is a great **opportunity**. Identifying objects and their uses at different times is a rare opportunity. Providing for the convenience of the people regardless of their profile is an opportunity to the makers and the sellers. Nevertheless, many of these **opportunities** (ideas-prone) are used negatively by many people. If opportunities are used positively, then there would not be commotions on the crust-earth. Suffice the proper application of the quotes of the noblest among the creatures which says as reported: *"Value five things before five things- your health before sickness, your wealth before indigence, your youth before old age, your leisure before occupation and your life before death"*. In all the cases are opportunities that would pave the way for lucrative business ideas. A wealthy should have invested his wealth of resources on the right businesses to add more values to the wealth. The healthy should have make efforts to work with black hairs instead of postponing the evils day when he would have to strive with the grey hairs….. An opportunity lost or dumped idea would end up be a great regret for the loser. On the other way, an opportunity explored is a gateway to numerous value chains in new lucrative jobs.

Many true nationalists seized the first term opportunity of being in power to transform their nations. **Julius Nyerere** of Tanzania, **Nelson Mandela** of South Africa had the chance of ruling their nations for many terms as permitted by their constitutions, but they bowed out when the ovation was loudest. They have their names engraved in the minds of their people. History of People's Republic of **China** is not complete without the mentioning of **Chairman Mao**. **Jerry Rawlings** is unforgettable in the nation of Ghana. Trace the history of different nations and defunct empires. The aforementioned personalities made the best use of the opportunity (being in power) that came their way. They indirectly teach others in their shoes that a single term in office is enough **opportunity** to turn round the state of the nation. Learn to know how those people in the era used their opportunities. Many dream about the opportunities in different shapes, colours and sizes. Those who dream for them plan ahead. 'If I become the head of State or the President or in an exalted position, this is what I will do to better the lives of the citizens and the nation'. When they get there, they perform. It is a matter of firm resolution. Sometimes, power corrupts some to become despots. The former used the opportunity positively just as the **Nelson Mandelas** of this world. The latter used the **opportunity** negatively as they become hostile to their former resolution if the opportunity comes their ways. Those are the dictators of this world. A revolutionist turned around the fortunes of Singapore to become one of the richest nations and host to millions of tourists across the globe. Some military boys determined to sanitize the corrupt political system, when they get there, they imposed themselves on people as civilian presidents. Examples are many in Africa. They plunder the wealth of the nation. Many become richer than their nations. Instead of investing the looted wealth, they kept them in foreign accounts where no one even among their heirs and heiress would inherit after their sudden deaths. Watch out for your own **opportunity**. It is like the air. When it comes, think of its positive use. Then, use it wisely. If use negatively, your names enter the black books of history. Mind you, when it goes, it would not return again for use. Those at the helms, you have the **opportunity** to transform the nations and the living standard of your citizens and foreigners living within. You have **opportunity** to have good neighbours by being an accommodating neighbor to them. If your administration is hostile to neighbours, your nationals would suffer for it. If you rule by iron hands, posterity would speak evil about you. What would you choose?

Opportunity is always alive at everywhere and it is grabbed and used by choice of individuals or group. Every natural asset (faculties, limbs, lifespan, language, ethnic values...) in man and acquired assets like certificates, awards, recognitions, socio-economic values and all creatures around man is an opportunity that could pave way to greater opportunities.

Events create rooms for limitless employment creation **opportunities**. I could remember that epidemic led to the discoveries in medical and pharmaceutical history. If there is no such ugly event in the history of mankind, where would such profession get developed? The need to clothe people, the need to eat balanced diet and drinking nutritious beverages pave the way for all processing industries. The need for financial security for business owners creates the **opportunities** for the financial institutions and jobs for the workers there. The yearning for electronic devices that would enable high productivity creates employment **opportunities** for the employees (of different classes) in the digital-based businesses. Study the electronic mechanism in all the latest devices and you find all the earliest technological inventions. Take a critical look at the aforementioned technology again as an instance; what does a smart-phone contain? The smart-phones contain clock or timing technology, calculator technology, typesetting technology, recording technology, media technology, storage facility, and graphic artistry among others. The combination of different electronic methods and systems with their own creativity create bigger **opportunities** for the likes of Steve jobs, Mark Zuckerbergs, Bill Gates among others. They found the right platforms in operating under a right and conducive business environment with right incentives at adequately equipped incubation centres. They are exposed to all the technologies before their time. Through the grabbing of the opportunities, millions across the world are reaping from the value chains of their information and communication technology-based jobs. Meanwhile, new opportunities are extractable from the ICT sector promoted by the successful **tech-preneurs**. Cudgel your brains at the locality (nation) you inhabit. The ICT sector needs new software for the hardware. By the word 'new software', we mean constantly upgraded software with better features that make the work easier and better. This shows that no professional should stop self-development. They must seek for knowledge and new skills till death in order not to be out of recognition hence business. The social media and digital entrepreneurs need more to add to their media business activities. Learn to discover opportunities from opportunities and you are on the path of creating lucrative jobs! You can produce something better, build your confidence and think differently. Look for the vacuum in those technologies or add something unique to create new invention to be patented against your name for seventy years!

I could recall a senior lawyer who rose from grass to grace. He used to be at the courts to solicit for clients that had no legal representatives under pro bono legal service. His appearances and presentation before the judges were enough for him to get referrals from the judge and the old colleagues in the learned profession. Through the referrals, he rose to become owner of big law chamber in the city and at the moment one of the senior advocates. What is learnt from the above is simple-<u>sell your skills at the right markets where there are scouts or shoppers or the target buyers of your ware or skills</u>. (Get a copy of the book '**Winning huge sales and increasing clients base...**"for detailed explanation on selling from www.amusa-abdulateef.com)

In this book so far, our major focus has been the use of limitless opportunities from idle but available assets, identifiable strengths, skills, capacity, threats and weak-points. And these could pave the effective ways to lucrative ideas being wasted in the creation of good standards of living through the creation of gainful jobs for the idlers in the nations. The identifiable opportunities are sure fire to open doors for them. People cry wolf when an **opportunity** to create viable ideas slips away. It is after someone who is in position to effect a change leaves the stage that they cry wolf. (Hiss) crocodile tears, they shed! This is needless as the opportunity and potential ideas-creating chance has gone probably for good. Numerous are opportunities in this work for dear readers.

In retrospect, the time being spent to cry over spilt milk is a wasted time that must have been converted to think of another opportunity creatable from the lost opportunity. What do I mean? If a passenger missed the train, he must brace up to catch up with the bus at the park if he cannot afford a flight or transport on sea. There is no way all modes of transportation would be missed. The worst is to trek to the next station, bus stop, park, port where you find alternatives. In a nation that is having epileptic electricity supply as a result of vandals to the gas pipelines. Such should employ all the available alternatives like coal, water, solar and wind even if the nuclear energy is too expensive for the nation. There is always a way out of a challenge. A road opens where one ends. Open your ears. Read between the lines and open your hearts to learn the wisdom. Not just a wisdom in a thing but different wisdom to create something new in employments. Having no shop or office to practice what you have as skill is not a barrier to be on your own. Start from mobile service. Use your mobile information and communication devices like androids and mini-laptops. Always target to practice your trade where passersby or the people are concentrated. A big one satisfied customer or client is enough at outset. Through a satisfied client, you enjoy recommendation from such and the number of clients (patronage) would swell. You don't need all the machines before you start a lucrative job. Your ability to use all machines would earn you lucrative jobs. We have learnt about people who were good in the use of all parts of their bodies to dance and sing and this earned them acting jobs. I became computer literate through the personal use of computer at a friend's home after some minutes tutorial from an apprentice. I learnt how to ride bicycle at a tender age. Reading is a habit that adds values to the brains of readers. It is a hobby whose overall gains would add value to all facets of life. You cannot just be wasting time at owner's corner in pleasure driving when you have the chance to learn driving skill. Learn at least one new thing per day. In a year, you might have acquired 365 things. Do that for learning a skill per month and you have twelve different skills in a year. Each of the skill could create gainful job for you and others. Again, in each of what you learnt-language, skill, art.. are huge jobs **opportunities**, explore your topmost of your selected choices.

Sharing these **opportunities** is very dear to my heart as a form of worship to eliminate the scourge of unemployment across the nations. Just to spice you up; share from the experience of this young publisher. He started with seed capital with home-office. He could not afford to acquire printing machines, full time staff, typesetting machine, internet facilities, including the delivery or distributing vans. What did he do? He got his publishable information from internet service paid for by part of the capital. He got the material prepared for publishing by some newspaper workers, feature readers, columnists, proofreaders, and erudite editors on a part-time basis, published in the neighboring printing press and delivered the newspapers through the delivery channels of the other firms to target destinations. Can we call this a one-man business? Of course, it is alike! In all the cases, he had made the optimal use of all the opportunities based on his connections at his beck and call to produce his product periodically. Such opportunities could only come from his good personality. I knew of a man who was jobless for many years after graduation. He was at a bean cake maker shop where he read an advert in an unsold (used) newspaper. He applied for the job therein and was called for interview sessions. Today, he is a manager in the multinational petrol chemical firm.

Many nations enjoy proliferation of industries as a result of political stability, stable economic policies, availability of raw materials, human capital resources and demography factors. All the factors create opportunities for the businesses to thrive. In other cases, devaluation of national currency that could turn many entrepreneurs off a nation serves the opportunity for many investors in some areas to establish their businesses. In some cases, the incessant industrial dispute is a turn off to investors.

Therefore, there is no opportunity for the business to grow in such nation. Strong financial institutions like the banks, the insurance firms and incentives are the opportunities created by the administration to attract business investors. Sometimes, one can turn oneself into style consultant. Let such invest in designer wears of his choice from his own creativity. Get a good designer. Design it on a very good fabric. Make visit to selected occasions where celebrities visit and you would get admirers. Turn yourself into a socialite. Let it be on your must-do list. Some of the admirers would/could 'employ' as their style consultant. The opportunity is the use of other people's brains and creativity in designing to sell your product. Assuming you are a well-connected person to the seat of power and you have friends who are experts in interior decors. Get the contracts from your connections and employ the brains and creativity of your interior décor friends. Haven't you gainfully employed yourself and others with the opportunity provided by your connection which catalyzes viable **ideas**?

Many lecturers in tertiary institutions become authors and consultants overnight from the theses given to their students to work on. They compiled the analyses to become the original owner of the intellectual property. Social researches on the path to attain greater or additional qualifications of the lecturers in schools are traced to the contributions of the students. We have seen lecturers that got solutions to their theses from schools where they were students from their own students. They gave the problems to the students as theses to work upon. What did they use? It is the opportunity of having errand and submissive students under them which translated into viable business idea cum product and services! The students explore libraries where they browse books in order to find solutions for their lecturers. In some cases, the students are the libraries, encyclopedia and the fountain where knowledge is derived by the tutors. The idea that transformed into products today could be sourced from informal places.

Many poets and graphic artists have been discovered and nurtured by scouts in the ghettos and slums. Some started from being freelancers. And the freelance jobs create opportunity to meet their promoters. I know of a friend selling his technical knowledge on electronic cars on radio. There are those selling their stuff through the columns they have in the newspapers and free subscription online media. Connect yourself to the world with the skill or knowledge that you are known with. Failure to do so is losing the natural opportunity to hit it big. If you cannot go practical, start from being virtual tutors. Sell online the techniques and skills to improve you brand. Many a housewife would have become employers of employees' right from the comforts of their homes. Alas, they fail to use the opportunities of the home facilities at their beck and call. Many drop-outs, after discovery themselves, have become successful with the builders and mentors. The latter seized the opportunity of converting the wasting social nuisance in human shape into substance. These values are in animals, birds and plants too. Let some people create jobs opportunities out of them.

Many an artifact from the colonized nations contributed to the developments in the colonialists territories. Inspiration of writers could be from the social attitudes of the creatures like plants, birds, animals and the aquatic creatures. Someone who studied them but could not come out with something as benefits has wasted the opportunity of being at the scene of events. Imagine the list of lucrative business ideas that would have been developed! Many a film maker of high repute gets his/her block buster films through the grapevine sources. In the same vein, the renowned singers with chart-topping songs get songs from the dark spots and ghettos. Many writers seize different types of dictionary online and off line to develop their writing skills. They make the best use of the search engines to explore internets for their works. It is a great opportunity for the existence of the reference materials at one's beck and call. With this numerous jobs opportunities are created especially in the advanced world in technology. This writer is a beneficiary.

I once had interaction with a buyer of some stories from me. The guy was a sales executive of a renowned publishing firm. I seized the opportunity of the mobile facility at his disposal to sell my own commercially printed books. The materials were given to him at mouthwatering prices. I made my target sales and he made his own profits! Think about the opportunities around you or your business. Tap the opportunity before another person grabs it at your nose! Failure to perform a role at one's best capacity at a time would end up being an opportunity lost. A philosopher was reported to have said *"Whatever I am capable to do now, I shall do it as I may never pass the bridge again"*. It lives within individuals as natural endowment or asset. It is in all places, institutions, in human resources and offices in the nations. Many of the people in the nations are ignorant of these limitless opportunities. It could be created just like history by situations, events, individuals, animate and inanimate creatures, corporate organizations, institutions, associations, nations, climatic conditions and governments. Had individuals make optimal use of the opportunities within and around them, no one should be left poor of resources on land, inside the streams and the air. Think about water businesses; work on air businesses or what could add values to the air businesses like aviation to create employments. Again, it is a matter of tasking one's thinking faculty. Think about the essential and luxurious needs of the target customers in each.

In this case, there would never be hue and cry over the scourge of unemployment. The social miscreants that are refined based on their natural talents or skills by career builders create an opportunity put into good use. Conversion of many reserves and museums into tourist centres creates different jobs opportunities for people. Millions of tourists are visiting France, Egypt, Singapore, China and many nations in the world and by this, the host nations are creating numerous jobs opportunities. Imagine the volumes of goods that could be purchased by pilgrims in the annual pilgrimages to Makkah, Madinah, Jerusalem, Taj Mahal and the Vatican City. **Opportunities** in all the nations are enough to create lucrative and secured jobs in excess of needs. It takes a wise to identify many 'hidden' opportunities. The number of graduates from different institutions is enough opportunity to create new entrepreneurs. They only need financial and material supports. Imagine the number of people that would be self-employed or given appointments by the businesses if adequately supported. One is not surprised about this when many glaring **opportunities** are left unexplored or 'unexploited'. I got expose to reading newspapers and magazines at early period of my life. I developed analyses of every news reported and later developed the ability to create jobs opportunities from every piece of news in prints. I could create lucrative jobs from classified advertisements inside the papers back to back. It is very easy to read the lips of people in interviews. This is a skill that could be developed by all and sundry. A challenge of a fellow about how to start jobs without capital paved the way for the researches and the publication of the two volumes of 'Jobs with zero-capital. A lecture, by a PHD lecturer taking us 'entrepreneurial development course, when I was a tertiary student catalyzed the written of creating new jobs from the existing jobs. I am convinced that sectors can be created from the present sectors to create jobs opportunities.

Many are able to get scholarships by chance. Many secured lucrative jobs by seizing the available opportunity at their fingertips then. There is a general consensus that there is a thin line between life and death. The thin line is the opportunity. Many secured very high positions in offices just because they had acquired certain skill by chance. The time wasted by colleagues was made the best use of by them which catapulted them to the envious status in the offices. Sluggishness, nonchalant attitudes, ignorance, time factor and several other factors within and outside could debar many from achieving set goals and therefore waste the opportunities.

Meanwhile, the opportunities are natural or sometimes created artificially for the wise people to make resources out of them. It comes in different forms, sizes, shapes (designs) and colours. It could be either a problem or a challenge. It takes a wise to identify **opportunities** at all places and time. While tuitions fee based schools are all around, let some creative educationists start operating tuition-less schools. If three months authors are being produced from publishing houses, let there be one-day authors of unique books in all genres. Turn the books-filled libraries into bookless libraries and turn the business commercial on different specializations. Sometimes, like the precious stones in wraps, they are hidden and never visible to the naked eyes. In addition, like the popular film "Titans", films can be set and acted in a premises even within a room. This is displaying the creativity and versatility of the set designers!

Opportunities come in neutral ways. Man uses it either positively or negatively. Imagine man in the name of advertising mating with pets, mimic animals, walk naked in the midst of gatherings or those exposing their beautiful figure to attract buyers to a product or those in deadly sports in the name of entertainment. The created ones by individuals especially the entrepreneurs could take forward or backward integrations.

The administration of different institutions could create specialized institutions from institutions in existence. Imagine the creation of specialized radio and television stations from the universal radio station in existence. Imagine having such specialized radio and television stations like soccer, advertisement, entertainment, sports, fashion and the same is done with television and cable sectors. Imagine the number of direct and indirect jobs opportunities that would have been created. If the publishers create specialized newspapers, magazines and tabloids especially the online arm in addition to the traditional publishing- numerous jobs would have been created. In short, opportunities could come in any form. Inability of a government to provide adequately for the need of its citizens has created business opportunities for private business owners who can identify the needs to thrive provided such needs are invested upon. I could remember that the lapses in the finance of education and health sectors in many poor nations create room for the opportunity for the proliferation of different service providers outside the shores especially the private health facilities providers. A fashion designer, dealing in 'cut and sow' complained of low patronage. He was advised to think about forward integration in his fashion venture where he would buy materials of different fabrics in bulk and design them for unisex comprising children and adult wears. With this, he started running boutique where his designers were placed for buyers of finished designers. Incessant all-time high statistics of drop-outs especially among the school-age pupils due to inability of their indigent parents or guardians to pay tuition fees is an opportunity to establish and run quality tuition-free schools. Free health care facilities by institutions and individuals is another avenue to generate jobs and boost national productivity. It would take someone who can think out of the box to create these free institutions. We went into research to help the indigent masses on how their wards could enjoy quality education without payment tuitions. The contents serve as irresistible guides for the proprietors on to run school without paying tuitions. The discoveries and the way to achieve this feat led to the writing of a book titled 'How to run tuition-free school' (Get a copy from www.amusa-abdulateef.com). We have churned out several ways schools can be generating funds from selling intellectual property through the establishment of e-reading billboards across the tertiary institutions and running online library to earn forex. . It is the duty of man to grab it when it comes and in whatever form. I decided to publish some of my titles that could be accepted abroad simply because it gives me a great opportunity to become a credible and international author.

Excess products in warehouses create an opportunity for distributors or sales executives to sell as private sellers and make money. The improvement and advancement in the Information and Communication Technology (ICT) in Europe and part of Asia has transformed the business environments into a developed one. It is not ridiculous when research shows the number of employees on the payroll of online retailers like alibris.co.uk, **Jeff Bezos**' amazon.com, alibaba.com, barnes and noble among others. This is what we called the appropriately used opportunity by the tech-entrepreneurs. Failure to meet the market demand of certain product or service has created a vacuum. There is need for new producers to come in and supply the needs. The winding down of business (opportunity) through different signs of market failure is enough to guide many socio-economic solution-centred researchers to make their marks. Billionaire **Ross Perot** started his creation of wealth from the opportunity created by his last employers while he was their salesman. The producers from several industries created the **opportunities** for the salesmen. Writers create opportunities for publishers and film producers cum promoters, the independent marketers their employees across their offices within the nation and across the shores. Those who are into different ways of publishing, film making and the marketers need software that would ease the burdens and solve the challenges of the success of their choice professions. Software producers cannot do without the inputs of the internet providers who create the clouds for hosting of domains and the needed inputs. This is where the hardware and other forms of engineers are provided lucrative jobs. One can easily conclude that a job sparks the proliferation of other jobs. Researching in all facets of life would always create jobs **opportunities** for many technical, scientific, technological, processing, manufacturing and service companies to proliferate. The technical need of the customers that was not met was taken up by the likes of Ross Perot, Warren Buffet and they had the success story as role models and good examples or mentors to the entrepreneurial world. I am aware of many booksellers in this nation who capitalized on their familiarity with the buyers to start their own publishing outfits. They publish what they need and use their bookstores and relevant facilities at their disposals to sell to them. Today, they have success story to tell listeners. They are supplier of juicy stories to thespians and electronic crews to act and earn big money. Their books have created jobs for thousands in private and public libraries. The failure of government to put the right pegs on the right holes create many Non-Governmental Organizations (NGOs) that are making legitimate perks from taking up what government left undone.

Let us take a few more instances. Failure of government to provide quality education and medical services has led many private practitioners in the businesses. Today, they are successful. The lapse in security has paved the way for many security-based firms for all institutions-finance, politics et al. imagine the opportunities. An administration that fails to utilize the gains from the sales of its natural resources to develop all the sectors of the economy would fail to grow in all its facets of life. Selling above the budget price creates excess financial resources and hence a great opportunity to develop the sectors for the overall benefits of the nation. A nation that is so much endowed with good climatic conditions and fertile soil should tap the **opportunity** to open up the nation starting from agricultural economy to guaranty food and raw materials security. Harvest rainfalls and convert rivers or brooks into dams to irrigate the farms during the sunny period. Harvest the floods to power the electricity generation dams. Harvest snowfalls to preserve edibles. Do the sunbath to preserve the skin. Research into forests products (greenery) and produce drugs for different diseases. Resources within the seas are three times the ones on land, tap them and create jobs opportunities. Precious stones in the seas, medicinal flora and fauna in the seas are some of the resources waiting to be tapped positively. Ask the miners of precious stones, they understand their traces and races. Learn the contents of different creatures to create jobs opportunities. Learn to understand the tastes of water to know more about the creatures within. All these could create right jobs for many in thousands. Businesses could sell-out their product if online and off-line technology. Failure to tap the resources in different forms is missing the opportunity. There are a lot of such opportunities in all nations that could be tapped for maximum use. They are only awaiting those who are so endowed intellectually to discover them and brought them into realities. Imagine a reader that has this written in a book verbatim!

1.3 OPPORTUNITY KNOCKING AT YOUR DOORSTEP

Again, by **opportunities**, limitless are the definitions to the author and the think tanks. In simple narratives, we mean eye openers to create or develop lucrative ideas towards creating jobs from production of products and provision of services. Two inseparable opportunities always go hand in hand. These are production and servicing. It is either one is a producer or the seller. And employments **opportunities** are in the making or recycling never-go-out-of-demand services or products such as nylon packs as wrappers, gift wrappers and finished goods packs, from recyclable materials. Let a willing producer give all unused material dump at locations work on how to recycle them. Producers are the initiators. Not just the recyclable materials at dump sites but the recyclable stories and histories. There are events that are past which need to be re-presented or re-packaged for the new generation. What about the extinct languages and dialects? What about the norms and ethics of people of different races? Just as evergreen songs are remixed, new packaged intellectual resources of the past age need for new look. Give them fresh look via fresh package that suits the modernity and employs crews. Have you ever thought of these? This opens employment **opportunities**. They are like scouts scouting for who to produce or package. The latter could come in the form of advertisement, promotion, or active in selling (converting tangible goods or whistleblowing of a service to earn money. As a promoter, especially in this internet technology world, one can convert one's blog, one's email address, one's social media handle among others to promote a product or service at an agreed charge. At the time I could not officially release my website and blog, I had to partner with a fellow who was running popular blogs in order to be forerunner creating public awareness for my website and blog later. I have witnessed a telecom that procured compilation of digital and audio books, probably the versions of the books are given gratis or those procured for a price from the authors, publishers or producers. Sincerely yours, not all companies have versatile and creative think tanks towards attaining the set objectives, think for them with extraordinary package that they could procure or sponsor. Many companies and institutions need customized wears for their staff that would attract more patronage; some need to change their logos or trademarks before better offers in contracts could visit them; many school, sports clubs, institutions need to be re-branded to command their market share. Institutions are facing different challenges that have been there for years. Research into the practicable solutions, as a worthy job, and this would fetch you both fame and money. Many streets and parks lack modern comfort stations. Can you team up with right building company to start the building at right places? Work for them as an independent think tank. Numerous of my proposals to bail out the states and the nation sent to the right offices were lauded from the contents of their acknowledgements. A good package of contents for the companies could be another source of employment opportunity. A good example is a project called 'who wants to be a millionaire?' packaged for a telecom giant. People can package **distinct reality shows** targeting at selling a business to the psyche of the customers in the regional, national or global market places. Package quiz contests for pupils in different institutions. Let the target sponsor see reasons for bankrolling the project. Instead of discussing politics and economies on the road sides with the vendors and free readers; instead of public analyses of the events in the world of sports at public places... take this as an **opportunity** to package such for media stations and get sponsors from the sectors of choice. It is a job creating **opportunity**. Innovations that create new machines and technological tools are gateways to start new jobs. They are right devices and tools (items) to modernize several artisanal jobs. Have you ever given this a thought?

By this, new employments have been created for the crews. Readers should bear this in mind. It is not expected that the word '**opportunity**' should be searched for. Every event opens eyes and minds to numerous **opportunities**. However, whenever you see the word 'opportunities', think about statement below as explanations or illustrations to fashion out jobs to be created thereof. Limitless are these for creative minds. The following is posted in the **second volume** of the book 'Jobs with zero capital'. Quoting verbatim "Are you a seasoned seminar/workshop organizer or a distributor/sales agent or executive who has the market potentials of selling this unique product in millions? Virtual tutors and seminar organizers also have the chance to enter business agreement. Seminars, workshops and symposia are schools where new jobs are created by old and new potential entrepreneurs.

Taking the above into another level, let's look into employment-revenue earning opportunities for virtual businesses. Virtual tutor produces the content, in different languages for different languages, in audio and audio-visual modes for people (target clients) to enjoy. Contact this writer for organizing of all or one of the titles on jobs creation from our stable for audience for a good price and much to be shared from the author's discount in your country. Are you a talented multi-linguist that is into jobs seminars? Do you have the facility and the resources to turn this work into audio book, documentary and others? Can you transliterate any of our works on jobs creation into foreign major languages or dialects like Chinese, Arabic, French, Malay and others beside English Language? Then, you are a stone throw to get the patent rights on condition for a good fee. Do you have the social connection to launch this product or one of our books on jobs creation? This is a real and rare opportunity for you to become a multi-millionaire!"

If the other writers and producers do not provide you the avenues and the permission to do the above, consult them speak to their hearts and brains to win them to your desires. Broadcast their gains too and jobs would be created!

Looking for jobs or placement? Looking for connection to make breakthrough in business? Looking for ways to reach the top? Searching a way to catch up with those ahead of you? What you need is information. It is not those in air business like the information and communication sector or the airliners, but every ambitious should must try to seek useful information, track the information to the source and then work on how to make the best use of the information. Sincerely, information builds cities and crown the kings, leaders in all forms at all places vice versa. Walk into companies, offices, institutions… of your choice with your certificates and demand what area could fit for you. Just compose yourself and dress smartly. As you dressed you shall be addressed.

Have you ever thought deeply over the posters on walls, about the contents and message of handbills, the languages of those who advertise products and services on the media; the interviews from professional expertise on issues among others. They convey invaluable messages that can spur creation of lucrative jobs. Do you ever give the black and white on the print media? All the information provides rooms for creating employments. What about the mission and vision of the institutions? Give all you read in prints and listen to on broadcast media and employments are creatable.

That is a great **opportunity** at the doorstep of the readers of prints, writings on walls, graphics, visual artworks even mind and body language readers across the nations. It is a big idea to employ you with fat returns. Imagine thinking for the 'blind' (illiterate but wealthy and influential) entrepreneurs. Even a blind that is creative entrepreneur would need **Braille version** and the **audio-books** of all self-help books and reference materials. Is this not another opportunity banging the doors of the producers? Many could, with the title, even develop some other ways of making their own legitimate money if they are so unique and creative! Many national dialects are going extinct simply because the owners have relegated them to the back. They feel ashamed of their own natural gifts.

Meanwhile, in the language lives the civilization, sciences, technologies and many invaluable of the ethnic groups. If there are people with the interest of translating the book into their different dialects, imagine the number of people that would be taken away from the streets roaming in search of scarce jobs! This is a great opportunity to engage your people positively with the content of the book! Grab it. Employ it.

Learn more. This writer seized the opportunity of some typesetting facilities in an office to typeset and work on all editing works of all the voluminous works. If he has to pay the cost, it runs into several thousands of naira in hundreds. This is using other people's material by implication. Many employable graduates and of vocational qualifications out there have these opportunities at their beck and call, but they did not use them to get started. When would they get the capital to start-up? This simply shows that opportunity is more valuable in monetary value. It is invaluable to users. When it comes, seize it for instant use. I have seen people with driving skills that become owners of commercial vehicles after starting with idle vehicles of their parents, family members and friends rotting away in the garage. With simple agreements, they worked with the vehicles where they made enough money to buy their own.

Many intuitive lads have become pacesetters for their peers from making wastes out of what the parents dump in the premises. They collect and sort the dump for recyclers. Some used to sell the wares of their parents at their absence in shops. The little gains they made started the capital where they took off their own business too. What some learnt indirectly had catapulted them into becoming employers of labour. They started from being self-employed! One can rightly says that dumping grounds create opportunities for evacuators, sorters and recyclers of different kinds of wastes particularly solid wastes that are convertible into useful materials for new production. The same is applicable to the cleaning of water and the lands affected by oil spillage. If solid and liquid wastes are challenges to the nation, business institutions and individuals; they are opportunities to generate revenue and lucrative employments for the populace. Imagine the earning from engaging in private wastes disposal for business institutions; imagine being laundry service providers for homes and offices; what about cleaning services for target clients? Imagine how much in income that recycling of solid and liquid wastes (like oil spillage) can generate for the nation if more hands are into the recycling of different items.

The change in environmental conditions due to climate change is creating jobs opportunities for people especially those roaming the streets in search of employment. Billions of dollars donated and earmarked by the nations are to create cleansing jobs for land, seas and the air. Thinkers should devise ways to rid the world of the negative effects of climate change. Such could develop interest in tree nursery for government, individuals, organizations and institutions to buy. Gradual extinction of language should spur many jobless linguistic graduates or those with natural talents in speaking different languages into compiling works on the languages. Produce dictionaries for such languages. Publish materials teaching the proverbs, grammar, literatures of such languages and you are gainfully employed. Take this, if you are not employed before the age of thirty; then work things out to be self-employed. **Seize the opportunities,** seize all available opportunities without time-wasting. Another may use the opportunity if you are procrastinate. Create or develop lucrative ideas flowing like stream and gushing out the ground like the spring at your doorstep to be your own boss! Left, right, up and down are opportunities for you to tap. Pick up work on your choices. **Opportunities** are daily and periodically created by all creatures. They are limitless. And they are all up for grabs for all. A dwindling business is crying for sales. Let there arise independent sales agents, hawkers and franchisers. An advertised tool is looking for sellers and distributors. Popular figures need aesthetics that befit their status. Political and economic leaders need private socio-thinkers, consultants and researchers. An empty stadium during competition needs fans that would cheer the team into quality match and the victory. Who can attract the crowds and make money? In short, I am truly convinced that opportunities knocking on doors are echoed again to be limitless. It is a fact that **opportunity** changes with situational changes. The brilliant and creative Jewish and other communities in America develop different businesses to create positive impacts on the economy of the world power. Those in the diaspora have what to contribute to the host nation in creating new business **opportunities** particularly in an environment whose wages and salaries have been properly regulated in a way that both the employees and employers are not cheated. They should not live as parasites on the host. Let the indigenous people from other nations create indigenous businesses. Let there be it indigenous eateries, indigenous newspaper like the first French 'courier de l'Amerique' first published in America in 1784. By so doing, the languages are being promoted and celebrated. The cultures, traditions (history), values are being indirectly sold just as the nation for tourists. Most underdeveloped nations should have restructured their education policy in a way that the pupils of primary and secondary schools would be taught science and technology in their indigenous languages in order to create more interest in the churning out of interested graduates from the courses for the national development. With this, several new jobs would be created for the indigenous teachers and the likes.

And lastly, jobs opportunities are created for people. When policies change, opportunity changes; When climatic condition changes; opportunity changes; When the market conditions change, opportunity changes; when the demand changes, opportunity changes; when the tastes and fashion in vogue change, opportunity change; when man changes environment or affiliations, opportunity changes…..

Therefore, **opportunity** is not a permanent state. It is a recurring decimal. It varies from one man to another, one location to another location, one nation to another nation and at different situations and time. Just as the procreation of man, lucrative opportunities are created every day at every time in places and nations for different people of different profiles!

With the above appetizers, readers would no doubt find the work irresistible. It is your scripture. Knocking **opportunities** to grab your own jobs is at your doorstep. If you ignore the **opportunities**, you have wasted the chance to kick start your own business!

1.4 SIDE KICK

A: What renders the increasing number of graduates that are unemployed in the nation?

B: Not this nation alone but it is a global challenge. Meanwhile let me ask; are they from the right academic environment? If they are from such, then they do not need to seek for job as they are potential boss but if they are not from the right learning environment, may I ask you too 'are they employable?'

A: Let me start from the last question. I think they are employable because they could not be graduates if they did not pass through the courses averagely

B: I suspect that most of the graduates are not employable even for employing themselves by themselves!

A: Do you mean that they cannot employ themselves? Are you saying that they cannot be on their own practicing what they learn for years at the four walls of classrooms?

B: I maintain my standpoint. They nurse the fear as they are half-baked. I don't see the reason why a graduate cannot engage in one of the courses of study that he had learnt at school even an historian could become script writer for film makers and a librarian could run mobile library or book seller where he shops for the books needed by the clients and supply them at their locations for a negotiable price (service charge).

A: Then, they are wasted human resources and a danger to the future of the nation. They are human liabilities. Are they not?

B: *Of course yes, they are. I wonder what could have caused this rot in the system*

A: I suspect the incessant strikes of the lecturers and non-teaching staff of the institutions

B: *A reasonable students should capitalize on the striking periods to develop skills in his fields of specialization or learn a new skill*

A: You are absolutely right. As that would have making them employable or becoming their own bosses later

B: *It is no surprise that only a few quality and competent who is not affected by the age would secure employment at the end of the day*

A: Most of them might even end up becoming contract or casual staff in this era of costs-cutting by industries

B: *That is an absurdity and underemployment. How can casual worker and the contract staff provide the best like the bonafide workers? Why don't the legislators and the executive fight on their behalf to eradicate the issue of contract staff and casualization of workers? They have no job security in that development.*

A: Those who would sponsor the bill or pass the bill into law are the owners of the companies that employ staff under the contract and casual staff in order to avoid a lot of benefits for them such as gratuity, pension, medical, housing, holidaying, transportation, travelling, hazard and other allowances. If they do not own the companies, their close relations, family members, political and business friends and spiritual leaders own them! So, do you think they will be nationalistic in the abolition of contract, casual and domestic staff?

B *(nods):* *Then, the contract staff that is worth his onion should use the company as a stepping stone where experience is garnered towards becoming his own Chief Executive Officer.*

A: Of course, Yes! I pity the casual workers more than the contract staff. At least contract staff could negotiate their benefits or remuneration. I pray those contract staff that is worth their onion should negotiate for a big price hence they can start preparing for their disengagement as soon as possible to be their own employers (at least). Contract job has no job security a major path for underemployment; possesses no severance package and any other social benefits so doer (s) should set plan for his exit from the day of entrance (appointment).

B: You see. It is a fact that not all graduates can be employed by either public or limited number of private corporate institutions. Therefore, there is dire need for new budding entrepreneurs to join the private owners of business. They would also employ part of the idlers.

A: I accept your viewpoint. Students in schools are like fingerlings in the pool of water. In their midst are potential jobs creators for those who do not have the liver to be bosses. The latter could contribute with their quality intelligence to making the business of the owners work. But, the potential creators of businesses are not in the right environment to start their business ideals

B: The first thing is to show them the hidden opportunities they can build their potentials on, encourage them on how to run the business idea effectively. In fact, all the problems facing the nations are open opportunities. Let them create solutions for the problems to get employed. I do not see any perfect business environment on earth. What draws back a business makes another business to progress. Let us encourage new entrepreneurs to be bosses from several 'hidden' opportunities and ideas-creating jobs.

A: Fortunately, the target budding entrepreneur should not see starting a business as a mountain to climb. In fact, dearth of capital paves the way for starting from zero capital jobs such as selling services and skills in motion to earn nest eggs to start-up. The dearth of needs could be a problem or challenge to the nation, providing the need is an idea creating employment opportunity. When you are facing a problem of choice among many talents or skills, start with the least or one that can give you the first (instant) recognition and popularity. If such is still a big thing, break it down into phases and start from the scratch. This has been the focus of this book. Keep reading!!!

STEPS TO CREATE IDEAS AND EMPLOYMENT OPPORTUNITIES

Major cause facing the virile and ambitious youths who are employable is their inability to task their senses in the identification of opportunities at the tips of their noses towards creating ideas to nurture. One of my innate hobbies is writing and this triggers the research instinct within me to have internationally acceptable book materials. I started from a one-page poetry. I developed the skill into becoming a writer of several hundreds of pages bestselling book on different issues of global importance today. I studied the kinds of book my people here and there used to patronize and read. I got some models in writing and found out that the style of writing the course books not to talk of the religion books has gone motivational with the use of first-hand experiences of different people. It is working for me. In the amazon best seller ranked book "**creating new jobs from the existing jobs**', we referred selling as an art. Truly, it is an innate thing. Not every is endowed to sell. Those who are celebrated or top-rated sellers usually have certain features other sellers do not have. One needs to learn from the top-sellers. Get closer to the award-winning sellers to tap some of the inherent skills not taught in schools but in practice. Each time I see the depots with the words 'approved distributor' or 'Accredited customers or agents", I know they would need people who can hawk for them or those who have shops at densely populated places to empty the warehouse. With limitless products and services in the markets, opportunities to become sellers are there for the idle ones. Ideas are limitless to create. Dynamic ideas could be created at every moment and places (institutions, sectors) at all times from different situations and events. Had ideas been created, new entrepreneurs would have been created from a few that would employ millions directly and indirectly. This is a simple task. Creating lucrative jobs from the existing jobs to become one's boss is fashioning out of **infinite new ideas or use your ingenuity to create added value chains**. Ideas beget ideas just as needs beget needs. And limitless ideas are created, in the light of the above, there are **steps** to take:

STEP ONE

Generating **opportunities** (flourishing and viable ideas) are infinite and definite. Opportunity creates rooms for opportunities by the level of the senses of users. It has no limitation but it is a matter of intelligence of the prospective idealists. First of all, apply your sound faculties; think of limitless God-given opportunities. These include your natural skills that make you unique from others such as ability to act, write, report, dance, drum, read, weave, entertain…; inborn arts; inherent skills from your parents-paternal or maternal sides. In short, a prospective business inventor should apply all the **invaluable faculties** freely endowed him or her by God to fashion out lucrative ideas. One can imitate idea but re-package such to suit the target users' interests. Several foreign documentaries have been translated into local dialects. Several books have been acted and still being acted as stage plays for audience within and outside the shores for good prices. Several songs have been re-mixed. Old products are turning into new products by additional ideas to add more values to the work. In short, creating ideas is something inexhaustible.

Think of problems and relevant practicable solutions in all institutions, places, people and environment among others. Problems are limitless wants and needs which vary from man to man, animal to animal, environment to environment, nation to nation, institution to institution... No product or service is perfect. Every good product that has generic value has a defect. Find it. Such defect could be poor aesthetics, poor branding, poor packaging, poor forms of promotion or advertisement, poor network in distribution among several others. Every well-organized event could be better packaged if there are certain inputs. Think about the unique inputs. There is always room for improvements (on physical goods and services) by different socio-economic think-tanks. No places of events or activities are perfect that do not need additional aesthetics. Let us look at the communication electronics. Systems have problems in virus and just as internet connections and inputs are faced with the problems of the hackers. Work on software that could be effective as anti-virus and anti-hackers for different programs. Learn also from this attitude of the author. I taught of global problems from the list of **M**illennium **D**evelopment **G**oals (**MDGs**). The major one I was capable of working on was jobs creation. In the book market are several hundreds of books on employment creation. And this should never hinder new writers to contribute which I did with my own unique research-based manuscripts. In short, for a problem, there are chances of thousands of solutions. Malaria is attacked with hundreds of drugs from different pharmaceutical industries. A problem usually creates chances to proffer several solutions from different ideas. I believed if jobs are created or the ideas of creating jobs are made known to people, several other problems are solved. Those who are gainfully employed would be able to afford all the needs-eat nutritious foods, live in decent houses, live a good standard of life, pay the medical bills, send their children to good schools, take good care of their family members and other things. Maternal mortality becomes a thing of the past. All forms of abuses and human trafficking and social injustice are nailed to the coffin. And several others global problems are rested permanently. In short, I commenced research into solutions of the unemployment and underemployment problems and <u>the research has produced eight manuscripts</u>. Imagine the numbers of jobs that have been produced from the publishing of the books across the world. Imagine what can be gained as income from royalties on the books. Think being a problem solver. This is viable idea would create numerous products and services and a good path of making and distributing wealth. For individuals, they (problems) could be needs-basic, social, esteemed.. of different or segmented target users at different target places where they are largely located. A good business idea cum product thrives (a commercial success) where there are buyers in abundance.

Think existing and probable non-existing products and services that would add greater values to life. Many buy exotic products but could not maintain them. Can you maintain such devices like black berry, androids, iphones, systems.. expensive exotic, custom-built cars and machines? Then, you are on the way of starting a service. What do the segmented buyers buy from your observation? Think on the demographics (based on different criteria such as ethnic, affiliation, occupation, faith, nationality..) and their dynamic tastes and trend in fashion. Every product is meant to be sold. Every product needs to be branded and packaging. Every product needs to be promoted and distributed. The income from sales must be rightly invested. All these would create ideas for other services. Let us look at a product-book. Books can be converted into films, documentaries, internet documentaries and stage plays in different dialects for different types of audience. Publishing of books seeks the arts of brand makers, patent maker, copy writers, graphic artists, pagers and several other services. Not all books have all what it takes to be a global book, identify them and communicate the publishers to secure lucrative job!

Think existing facilities and assets around useful to create new ones or use them for your new business idea to thrive. Existing facilities include the open markets, abandoned sporting facilities like stadia, gym, swimming pool, tennis courts... shopping malls, repute sellers and distributors, institutions, bodies, internet facilities and their products, research findings, enabling policies, land resources et al. all the 21st century tech-entrepreneurs especially the social media business men and women use the internet facilities and the electronic devices to do their jobs; business owners are making more income (profits) with the use of massive promotions and advertisements with the use existing internet-enhanced devices. The online retailers, major and minor, use the facilities to make billions in income; many are into blogging jobs from their homes as a result of their access to internet facilities. Many singers use the facilities in their places of worships to commence their operation. Conducive environment found in the dormitory at **Harvard** helped **Mark Zuckerberg** to develop his facebook…. Search for markets (via browsing internets to study the right places) where your products or services could have large patronage. I decided to sell my books to bigger audience through the use of cyber cafes and the institutions' e-libraries to run my intended e-reading business. Through this, buyers are aware of the books and make orders. One, I am able to make money from the reading fees and still selling my books later in print and in digital form. Imagine what it would have cost me to establish my own e-library for such service. I could also recall that a friend started his auto-service business idea in an existing facility provided by a fuel station. All the online retailers use the internet facilities to sell for the manufacturers. They are independent sellers helping to grow the sales of the producers. The amazon.com, barnes and nobles, ebay.com, rakuten.com … of this world are using the existing internet facilities to do their jobs. Someone would always create certain facilities. Think about creating viable business ideas with the use of the facilities for commercial purposes. Existing markets for certain produce or items could be partly used for the marketing and promotion of other items. Existing sporting venues could become venues to sell sports-wears and kits, seminars for youths or visitors, entertaining the audience. Selling of sports souvenirs and gifts is one of them. Limitless are the jobs and services that could be done there. Think of complementary goods and inevitable services. Do not wait till you get adequate finance to start up, think on idle facilities that are in existence at your beck and call. At the same time, think of the non-existing facility; my venture saw that many schools do not have certain e-reading halls and we created some at strategic location where we can get the readers for a fee. Most cities do not have mobile bookstores. Create unique ones for different segments of target customers. Sell your books from serialization of the content in the media stations- print or electronic; that is, turn the stations into your bookshops as the only places where the books are got! If you can provide them, that move has become a new business idea. Create selling points as they are parts of non-existing platforms. Expect commercial success if the idea is implemented!

Think over existing services through critical thinking about events, situations, clime and time of people in different facets of life such as education, health, hospitality.. that are in dire need of repackaging or more selling points. Create them and start making your money and fame. Take some instances. All events are in need of private photographers, video-graphers, comedians, costumiers that can add aesthetics to the events. Schools are in need of mobile libraries, independent e-libraries and research institutes.

Think on existing leisure activities in sports, entertainment,… that are inevitably used or patronized by buyers by demographic distribution at different climes and times. Create something new.

Think of new features, components, ingredients.. that could add better values and produce new jobs. Move up of the contents in the first volume in the series- creating new jobs from the existing jobs'.

Think about norms and values of people of different ethnics, faiths, ideologies, institutions.. and from these, opportunities to create viable ideas become manifest

Think over preferences and priorities based on status and demographic distribution. Study them by status, gender, age-groups, location, affiliation, academic qualifications, hobbies, interests, income distribution, mobility, faith among others

Think and make efforts to discover the right business environment where certain products and services could get adequate patronage if you have the traits of selling running in your blood. Take the path of **Jeff Bezo** of amazon.com fame. The latter is an online retailer selling different products and keep discovering new markets where he could record huge sales and make more income.

Think where raw talents are got for promotion. What you cannot do with your own skill, others can be nurtured to do it for commercial benefits of both of you

Think of places that are fertile for certain business activities. Meditate deeply on places around you or outside that you discover. All places are good for different business activities that could pave the way employment creation. Transform the place as a viable business idea. In the course of this research, I saw a motor parts dealer who established his store at the entrance of a mechanic village where all the vehicles using the parts are largely concentrated. I knew of places very close to nature with dams, trees and natural aesthetics that could be right for resort, hotels and sports arenas for fun seekers but were idle.

Think of the primary products and services. By this, we mean arable and pastoral farming; sea and space exploration to discover the primary inputs. The products, as raw materials, feed the processing and manufacturing industries and create rooms for services from service providers.

In short, to create ideas, always and always **think** on everything new in different things to improve on what is in existence with people, associations, companies, institutions, governments, agencies, sectors, faiths, ideologies, products, services, places and objects. The **thirst** and **search** for more (greater) knowledge through exposure to greater courses and attending relevant seminars, no matter the costs, would serve as essential **aesthetics** or **inputs** (facilities) that could better the lives, spice up events, places and add values to institutions and property. By so doing, lucrative ideas of what the idle ones can do would be successfully created.

In addition to 'Thinking', ensure you read tomes of books and prints. I read inside newspapers about National Directorate of Employment and bank of Industries how they fund good projects from graduates with good business proposals. Move up to listen and cogitate over what are presented on electronic media including digital and social media to create employment opportunities. Today, youths are into blogging business and thereby earning legitimately from even vblogs too.

STEP TWO

With the above, numerous **ideas** have been created towards creation of lucrative employment **opportunities**. List the results, of your choice, by opportunities and the categories of users by their status and never do these:

a) Waste productive time or create idle time. Every time spent in a place creates opportunities to start a job. Task your senses. Wake up to your responsibilities. Never procrastinate. Plan on the viable use of your time.
b) Make minimum use of the peak periods to record huge sales or patronage
c) Wastes all assets available or at your beck and call gratis
d) Ignore the policies that are relevant to nurture the good business ideas
e) Never sell at the wrong markets. Display your products or services at the right places. Train with football clubs and not at ordinary pitch for coaches and the right scouts to discover you. Act with the popular thespians in their film locations. Locate at the open places and not at the obscure places for buyers to easily locate you.
f) Never produce inferior things. No compromise of quality to build business empires from an idea. Quality is your watchword.
g) Never fail to enter partnership agreement if there is great need to start up or transform a viable idea into products and services

STEP THREE

Place your choice in critical position of examining. Put them in order of popularity or market acceptability. It is right to produce what people buy in the market. What they buy is what they need to satisfy their thirst. Consider demography to sort out the segmented market that would form your customers. A product that is produced for a small population may not have adequate sales that would sustain its growth. Shine your eyes. Task your brains. Engage in small idea that would attract large buyers or clients (users).

STEP FOUR

Pair the product and services from the idea by the target users. Take a few samples. Pupils need educational materials like books, learning kits; teachers are in need of teaching aids in different courses of studies in different forms. Book library could be replaced by digital libraries probably for different specializations

STEP FIVE

Identify the essential factors that would aid nurturing the choice idea. Identify certain mitigating factors too. These are the Strength, Weak-points, Opportunities and Threats (SWOTs). Such inputs include all the available free existing facilities and those at the beck and calls. Engage in collaboration to end the capital-intensive jobs becoming zero-capital jobs. Read how to do this in the book 'Jobs with zero capital Volume Two.

SUMMARY OF THE CHAPTER

In the light of the sections so far, we have seen that STRENGTHS, WEAKNESSES and THREATS identified in all bodies (man, places, events and institutions) are **eye openers** to varieties of OPPORTUNITIES. In addition, all the components of SWOTs pave the way for opportunities to create lucrative jobs and wealth. Simply say, all create opportunities. The strengths, the weaknesses and the threats to businesses, institutions, persons, associations and ideologies are pathways to employment opportunities. We have done justice to them in the course since outset. Now, can we go into far depth reflecting on the word **'opportunity'** as defined by different minds?

We have, based on the read so far, defined several practical or operational definitions of the word **OPPORTUNITY** in view with employment generations. Search for **opportunities** as you have learnt in the course of reading this 'unputdownable' material and seize them to create something new from the old and existing jobs opportunities. Open the next chapter and learn a great deal about opportunities. It is proved that opportunities are limitless as they are continually created to create new jobs especially from the existing jobs in particular!!!

BRAINSTORM

a) Read each of the sub-chapters again and identify jobs that are identified in each of the sections. Enumerate them.
b) Prepare the new features that you can introduce to turn each of the jobs into new jobs for others
c) Identify the probable challenges facing the enumerated jobs. Create new jobs from the challenges as you have learnt from the chapter.
d) Use your nation as a case study, churn out jobs on the basis of what you have been exposed to in the writing to espouse such jobs. Domicile the jobs.

CHAPTER TWO

2.1 **WHAT IS AN OPPORTUNITY?**

All along, we have discussed tons of ways to identify **opportunities** to create new jobs and generate wealth for the nation. Several measures, as being emphasized, open several windows and doors to employment **opportunities** to become one's boss at least. Producing walks along with providing servicing vice versa. There is no production without discovery of what could add spices to life and lives. When a vehicle, for instance, is produced or manufactured, it has opened up transporting and haulage businesses opportunities with the value chains. Through transportation business, insurance firms have patronage. With the latter, banking sectors become good partners. The financial sector cannot exist without those who manufacture and supplies all the machines and apps needed for operation. And the cycle continues. All the serviced-and-manufactured-based institutions create opportunities to start lucrative jobs (Emphases mine). Let us ruminate over more instances for illustrations. The financial institutions, conventional and specialized, are established to finance viable business ideas. The bank of industry is instituted to support industries, small, medium and large scale. The Bank of Agriculture is established to support all who are interested in agribusiness especially those who meet the conditions to access the funds in forms of grants and low-interest loans. The students and products from agricultural institutions have banks who can support their viable business ideas related to agriculture. In all institutions, people should access right information from all institutions in order to be guided to new employment opportunities. If it is a school, there is a vacuum to be filled, a trained and competent teacher whose interest is in teaching should move to the management for job as full time or part time. Think about the objectives and mission of an institute to start a business of choice. What about the policies emanated from the government? The change of policies creates employment creation opportunities. I could recall that the change and somersaulting of policies and objectives of institutions are tasking to the senses towards creating opportunities. The establishments of ministries, departments and agencies is suffice to open the lids of lucrative employments.

Generally, to me, all business institutions, situational events, the places of worship, the service stations, charitable organizations and social clubs among others create avenues to start one jobs or the other. Abandon them as no-value is a waste of resources (Read comprehensive but concise details from the third volume- '**Wastes to wealth jobs**'). In fact, the poor economic situation in the nation is an eye opener to increase the sources of earning income. It teaches the persons, the firms, the institutions and the governments to open new doors to shore up the income. The loss of social values and degraded ethno-religion tenets is seen as the great opportunity to start new jobs. Go deep in meditation. Information in the prints like books, magazines, journals, newspapers in different languages open flood of opportunities to start lucrative jobs and wealth. Also, the releases on electronic media contains limitless of employment opportunities. Information in books are used for training of the minds. Information of places provide opportunities about the needs and vacuums. Information from the national bureau of statistics guide users to be their bosses. Information about the natural environments pave the way for jobs. How can a firm start a job that lacks adequate information? What about institutions and individuals? Several policies from rudderless government has prompted me into writing several books. I decided to write a thorough research on how to understand business environment when a critique of my first international book commented about the content. Several reports and films call for rejoinders. Many distorted histories need to be re-written for corrections. The research institutes provide periodical information useful to churn out jobs. What is the reason for the graduating students not converting their final theses and projects into use? Everywhere you look, there are free information that individuals and institutions can transform into secured jobs. The senses are subjected into integrity and quality tests if the information at our nose are left unused. What about the unused assets and quality manpower? Do listeners to electronic social media and readers of the prints ruminate over the contents and concepts to starting employments? Do people and institutions know that we are living and advancing with the use of information? **Information is key to employment opportunities**. Opportunities are products of information. Search for information. Do not keep idle information. Process and act the information at your fingertip into becoming physical products and visible services. Acting information, like a thespian acting a script, paves the way for wealth creation cum distribution and employment **opportunities**. There is the need to examine what the word 'opportunity' actually means to different scholars as revealed in their documented definitions.

Opportunity, according to Oxford Advanced Learner Dictionary, means 'a time when a particular situation makes it possible to do or achieve something. It is a period when the circumstances are right for doing something'.

With the above definition, our focus is the opportunity or opportunities before the unemployed roaming the streets searching for employment wasting precious time instead of establishing their own businesses. It is solution to stem the tide of the scourge of unemployment across the nations. **And the opportunities are the 'jobs'**. We can hence say that what would add values to lives starting from the source of earning comes from the use of opportunities. How can a breadwinner with several opportunities of converting assets available to him be so embittered for losing a paid job? I have read about a banker who converted one of his cars to hire-cab after registering with one of those rendering the car-hire service. And also engage in some other paying jobs with his spare time when he is not engaged. Losing a paid job is an opportunities to discover self-entrepreneurial ability and enliven the spirit with the available inputs. In fact, it is always a gain to most employers of labour today. Were they not sent packing, how would they be able to discover their strengths and potentials to start-up? When a room is exited, another room is entered. No man lives on the street permanently unless he is a destitute even the refugees are provided make-shift houses in camps.

In retrospect, to get the message clearer, let us examine some definitions from other sources. Google search engine defines opportunity as a set of circumstances that makes it possible to do something or a chance of employment or promotion. Its other synonyms are chance, occasion, opening, possibility and time. When a business lacks a department that would have driven the business and such is provided, employments have been created. When a football team is losing game after game for not having certain specialized role in the team; may be a sharp-shooting striker; it is an opportunity for those who are suitable to play the role. The long dry season in the arid area is an opportunity for those who have the resources to invest in water business. How would someone who supplies water for domestic use to the places where water is scarce? Imagine the gains from doing such business as a producer and a seller or supplier in such area. It is a relief on the part of the urban population for someone or people to import the foods from the rural population to their doorsteps. And this would serve as a production booster for the farmers. Likewise, all producers, in all forms, see the huge number of buyers as a catalyst (enabling input) to continually producing in a larger scale. The biting and long winter would also create opportunities for the mobile sellers of domestic needs. Starved people and nations has open doors to employments and wealth to the producers and suppliers from neighbouring nations where the business environment is enabling. When I decided to start producing cassava flour; I had listed the places where the buyers are densely populated. I equally enumerated the social connection that can help me secure big supplies. In short, there is always a lack that would open eyes into opportunities to start-up.

In Free Dictionary, it is defined as a favourable or advantageous circumstances or combination of circumstances; a favourable or suitable occasion or time or a chance of progress or advancement. When a nation is in economic recession with sliding national currency to the United States dollar. This has created wealth-revenue creating opportunities for the creative minds in the nation to export what they could locally-produced or fabricated products and services to earn big from the exchange rate of more national currency for a few dollar. Imagine how much an author selling his adequately protected and promoted e-books and audio-books online would be making if massive adverts and strategic selling promotions are done. A book that sold 100,000 at 5 dollar each would fetch the author and publisher 500,000 dollars. At the parallel market conversion rate, such has become a multimillionaire overnight with little efforts after taxes. Would such who have one or two things to sell online pray for appreciate national currency? Nay! Simply say, even though majority, especially of the manufacturers importing raw materials and machines spare parts, who need forex for payment of foreign technical expertise and for the importation of the inputs would see the sliding national currency as a bad forex policy but no the former. It pays the creative artisans that could package goods which meet international standards to be wealthy overnight with the use of the emerging technological innovations at their beck and call. I wrote some fellows that the best time for a nation is the time of economic recession. The economic downturn shows the reasons for diversify of economy or the discovery of new sources of earning legitimate income. Recession opens eyes and brains into work on new channels of earning income in addition to the present sources of earning. It takes people to visit the national export and import council site to unveil the products that are needed for export and earn forex. Such includes the intellectual property like books, films, songs, designer wears among others. A nation whose youth population are facing the bleak future from the rudderless leaders deserves charitable organizations that would volunteer to raise better orientated youths that would take their destiny by their hands. Before you know it, the youth population has become ambitious, industrious and creative. No matter the circumstances, the inconveniences and the situations on ground, opportunities are eternally created by each situation to get started. The brains only need to be tasked and the hearts are open.

Macmillian Dictionary defines opportunity as simply a 'job' that is available. We can infer that every situation, negative and positive, creates opportunities to start lucrative ventures. Several instances can be shared. The shortage of school in a nation with fast population growth rate creates avenues for proliferation of schools by private investors. Institutions like schools, hospitals... that lack adequate staff have created rooms for the employment of competent staff. Conversely, the over-supply of schools creates room for the proliferation of the providers of educational materials. A geographical business environment that lacks aesthetics has created room for the providers, private and public investors to create jobs. Business or investment that has low sales has created jobs opportunities for independent distributors and sales agents. Government lapses and problems always open doors for consultants. I could recall that the low income from crude oil has forced government into increasing taxes in order to generate revenue to run the institutions. Our office went into research and found out that there were several un-provided services and social utilities that would have created large sum of revenues in billions if implemented. The shortage and the scourge of unemployment triggered the personnel in the dynamic research department of our publishing firm into researching how to create lucrative jobs. This effort has created several best sellers.

With the used definitions of the word '**opportunity**', we can conclude that every report in print or on air, every executive and legislative bill passed into laws, every programme relay on the print and broadcast media, every contact and contract, every resolution made by boards or institutions, every final conclusion in a meeting, every endorsed final thesis and project, every objective guiding the corporate institutions, every event and situation, every adventure, trip and sojourn of man, every social connection and educational qualification, every need, desire, interest, hobby, talent, skill and want, every contest, seminar, symposium, training, every amendment into constitution, every institution in place for private and public use, every learnable skill, every garnered experience and service, boosted work experience, high profiles, credibility of authors, every exalted position and public status, every quality product (manpower) from institution, Every adventure of a man; every passed bills of the state and the national assemblies; every change in climatic and weather conditions; every news inside print or broadcast on all media; every establishment and institution opens doors to employment **opportunities**. Every content of a book; every product and service; every documentary; every social connect; every information and device at our fingertip; every interview and biography; every policy of government; every mission and vision of a business; every public opinion on issue, every divergent view and every ideology in existence open floods of revenue making and employment **opportunities**. Every existing business-profit-based or charity based, every self-infliction and natural disaster opens floods of opportunities to creating lucrative employment and spread the wealth. Exposure of children to places especially offices and institutions may be the foundation of interest to aspire to become certain personalities in life professionally. The visit to games and theatre villages had created interest in dramatists. Opportunities in academies are for many to grab. This reminds me of the popular Yoruba film artist, **Kafilat Kafidipe**, who accompanied her elder sister to a film village where she was given a script when the person assigned for the role failed to turn up. It is advisable for the effective use of opportunities that come one's way. Every vacation, every tour, every notice, every inspection always open rooms for opportunities. When people visit markets that lack comfortable comfort stations, when a motorists do not have parking spaces in the markets, then jobs have been created. State whose passed legislative and executive bills are not effectively implemented have shortchanged the people. We examined this in the third volume as part of 'wastes'. I could remember many youth corps members that develop interests in one form of vocation or the other during their participation in the employment workshop and skill acquisition programme for the members. Unless one often stays indoor; unless one is an introvert and not social; unless one has senseless senses or impaired senses that one would not find one employment opportunity or the other. In the recent in Nigeria, Ministry of information and culture unveil the digitalization in broadcasting business. With this, all television stations in the nation would go digital meaning more television stations with different contents and more employment **opportunities** for the practitioners and the value chains. It is expected that new media businesses would proliferate. Firms can decide to have their own stations to boost what they have in products and services. I partnered with a publishing firm abroad for having its own television to boost its sales and popularity for its products. We are expecting book media where books are read and reviewed for viewers who are interested or deals in books such as the libraries, bookstores, institutions among others. The proliferation of online and offline broadcasting station has paved the way for sellers and producers to have huge sales. I tried to partner with a radio station that is running online and offline twenty-four hours to publish and market my books on a mutual agreement. The platforms, just like the popular cinemas, the popular shopping malls and other business and educational institutions, are **opportunities** to explore for business deals. Let me give my readers a challenge on the broadcasting media digitalization. Create at least twenty stations that could be on air 24/7 for different viewers and espouse the details of the target audience. We could have arts and fashion television stations. Video adverts are the new thing in the social media handle where products and services are promoted to attract more buyers. Video adverts are acting the generic function of a product or demonstrating the effectiveness and efficiency of services. Works are limitless for the ICT professionals. And it is a way to boost the patronage for all entrepreneurs and artisans who embrace the vogue in electronic advertising. Invaluable readers, just tell me what does not create an opportunity in the world of ours in different forms and sizes. Everything at every place at all times paves the way for lucrative employments and revenue generation opportunity. Even in the buses, planes, ships during discussions within, listening to radio stations, viewing subscription-based and free-to-air cable television stations and reading (books, newspapers, magazines of local and foreign origins, opportunities to start-up are freely discussed for users who have interests. Free e-books and free libraries are enough to ignite entrepreneurial instincts in man with a right thinking cap. Do not just ignore any freebie. Such could open the doors to success in life. Seizing the opportunity at your fingertip could serve as catalyst to your success. It is onus on the travellers to another nation to study the **opportunities** from the vacuums or what could be added to the existing values and norms in the new nation. No society is perfect no matter the ranking and the hype as far as advancement in all spheres is concerned. To me, the advanced nations need new, unique and better software producers for their set objective of faster growing economy. They desire intellectuals that add voices to their status as a nation. I chose to answer a debate throwing to the contestants over taxation during the electioneering campaign in one of the nations. I tried to strike the balance from critique the two sides of the coins. And the better option then was that taxation policy should not send the investors away from the nation but to encourage more investment instead of keeping the money in bank fixed deposits. If the tax policy is not anti-investors, they would invest more for more jobs to be created vice versa. When an electronic breaks down, when the gadgets at home malfunctioned, when the roof is leaking, when insecurity pervades a place of residence and business, when the roads are full of potholes or lack road signs and street lights, when the warehouses are full to the brim and the patronage is at all-time low among several other inadequacies, then employments **opportunities** are created. I was admonishing a friend to key into the advancement in the ICT and the sliding national currency to dollar in the parallel market to make fame and money in forex. This is a friend that is a thoroughbred professional in the repair of electronic cars. I told him to create a blog in his own website. Use the blog to answer generated problems of the selected models of electronic cars; proffer simple practicable solutions from the 'first aid' to the owners or the drivers. If about 200 questions are generated and answered per month for readers to download for a price in the website, one can imagine the amount that would be earned as forex on regular basis aside the possibility of getting invitations to attend seminars to enlighten the public from the potential clients across the world.

In the light of this, many jobs can be created for different people from different discipline, in fact, all courses of study. Nutritionists could sell online meal recipes and methods to cook variants of meals of different continents; parenting could be discussed under questions and answers on issues like bedwetting, etiquettes, sexuality and sex education among others. Today, many sites have become popular as dating site; some others could proliferate and go further to create specialized relationship sites where discussions about marital life disputes are solved online. People who are tired of reading prose would be the right clients for the questions and answers blogs treating different issues. I used to educate people that they must have channels of making money and not one-job people and institution. Nigeria, as a nation, finds it hard to have enough forex to control the exchange rate simply because of its inability to meet the demands of users (manufacturers, service providers, basic traveling allowances, personal needs like the payment of school fees, medical charges et al). By this naira declines to hard currencies particularly the US dollar and British Pounds. This is as a result of dependence on the forex from oil sector alone for many decades. Had the nation possessed other sources of generating forex as in exporting of intellectual property, locally made goods and technical services, there would not be scarcity of forex for the users for their businesses and non-business use. The latter would suffer when the patronage of the job go south. And when a job does not fetch anticipated profits to foot the domestic bills, other jobs would supplement. What stops an engineer to keep diary and memoirs for publication periodically? What about other professionals? It is never surprising seen football stars that are into film making. It is not ridiculous for a popular singer to be a stakeholder in fashion shows and exhibitions. What I cherish most is a business that runs businesses that would add values and reduce the bills of other business in the conglomerate. An entrepreneur who is a manufacturers with his fleet of trucks needs its own auto-engineering workshops and fuel station in order to cut costs. This is a better option where outsourcing is unreliable and expensive. In the world of blogs, considering the geometric rise in the internet connections, cheaper data and interests of people to patronize online products and services, specialized blogs and sites are enough for the forex to be sufficiently made for personal and national use. And information travels in the speed of light.

Every business owner that is profit-based should employ offline and online methods. This is involving of reliable brands in the global market on the basis of positive market record tracks others with bigger facilities to sell the contents of the products and services. Someone was discussing how a business that had devoted time and invested money for the patronage of their service. Such should not give up advertising. If it can, there are other strategies that have not been explored. In this part of the world, attract customers or clients with freebies. Do you know how much the social media handles invest in dollars and hard currencies and yet provide free entries from people, businesses and institutions? They are not fools. They knew that the number of people on their sites would determine the potential customers or clients of products and services that advertise on their sites. This method is an opportunity to start good business. Start with freebies. Such business that does not have clients despite all adverts should give freebies just as honey attracts the bees into the artificial beehives. (Get other relevant materials from the books on business and economics on **www.amusa-abdulateef.com**)

In retrospect, it is easy to tap into the identified ones and start lucrative jobs. Also, to be one's boss, it is a must to identify with one of the above to start taking the right steps. Being one's own boss requires discovering the inner person in the person. Inner being must have confidence to excel before the physical being walk the talk. A discouraged man from within would never heed good counsel of out-spoken 100 wise men showing him the benefits and lights in doing a business. One must be able to discover his or her areas of strengths and weak-points to start with. In many cases, innate talents or inherent skills may be the foundation of building the entrepreneurial person in the person. The next step is to identify how to hone the skills. Is it to join an academy or a skill acquisition centre? Would the natural gift be nurtured into fruition in the four walls of classrooms? Does it need technical input to become a reality and practicable? Another step is to kill the procrastination trait. Never extend the day to start by a second. Get the relevant inputs by tools needed and work with set time. Never nurse or grow the spirit of 'I don't think I can'. Hold to the 'I can' and 'I will be successful pursuing the course'. I was initially discouraged by a close pal as regards writing and publishing. Today, I am by all measures available a credible author. When a need is lacked or insufficient, employment has been created for people and institutions. It is so simply because it takes synergy of several think tanks who own factories to provide the need. Take an instance of the food we eat. Shortage of food requires the works of farmers in the farms; farmers who are into large scale plantation require the services of farm workers especially farm machine operators; after harvesting, the transporters contribute their services. For the automobiles to be in good conditions to ply the farms, auto engineers and others feed on them. One can see the limitless value chain. When a vacuum is created, provision of the needs is a form of employment creation for those who can proffer the right and relevant solutions.

To this mind, everything in events and issues, places creates avenue to create jobs and new jobs. It does not catch me unaware when I saw a writer on 'Virginity' for the young daughters of Eve in particular on the virtues of remaining virgin till they are married legally. In the same popular and widely read newspaper is a columnist who used to write for adults and married on sex and sexuality in a straight manner. Another writer writes on fashion, art and leisure when a portion is reserved for the writer of moral etiquettes at homes, offices and public places. What can you say of the writers? Don't you see new employments opportunities from the wisdom and intellectual property of the writers or the columnists? Looking at another instance and the employment **opportunities** created, the need to safe a language from extinction through publishing of useful books on different issues, producing documentaries from interviews from the ancient speakers, the re-producing the compilation of the values in the language, producing films in the original languages, creating museums where artefacts are kept among others would create jobs for people and promotion in theatres across the world; another instance is the right business environment and otherwise creates way for employment **opportunities**; proliferation and closure of businesses pave the ways for creating new jobs; a proposed policy on education that sciences and Mathematics should be taught in the indigenous languages, if adopted and passed by the national assembly and duly assented to by the President, shall create jobs for writers, researchers, publishers and distributors of transliterated books. The teachers that are taking the subjects must undergo trainings from trainers. Proliferation of blogging jobs create rooms for the contributors of articles and videos for a good price. I could recall that a blogger friend told me about the huge sum earmarked for the correspondents or contributors in order to boost the traffics and the number of likes to the blog. A freelance writer of contents could generate hundreds of dollars in a month from the comforts of his home with no invested capital in cash but only intellectual capital and time. If a blog contribution is put at 100 dollar per month per blog and the writer has five blogs to write for. Such would be earning 500 dollars per month. Under-performing is an open room to start lucrative jobs; falling sick and natural disasters are windows to start good jobs; competitions of rival competitors are channels to create employments for the idle ones; dull and active atmosphere is an opportunity. Such could be in form of newly added values. Sometimes, it is a form of integration. In other sense, it is discovery new areas for jobs creation as in an estate management company that joins houses, malls and offices premises cleaning services and security to their jobs. A close pal was a staff in a popular private architectural firm. He endured till the owners retired at old ages. He was entrusted with the firm's assets including clients. Within some months, he became the estate manager of the buildings. He became the lessor at good prices. Through the connections and exposures to building jobs, he graduated to become building contractors working in a partner with professional builders. A trained disc jockey friend added selling of songs in compact discs and films. He grew the business to become independent producer of singers treading the path of wealthy and popular **Richard Branson** of Virgin records.

From the reading and studying of biographies, lessons are learnt. We have seen people in history that rose from ordinary secretary to become the chief executive officer. This serves as motivation to end depression of someone at the lower cadre in service. He who desires to be served must be ready to serve others. Big counts move to the right and the lower counts are to the left. The farther to the right in counts, the bigger the number vice versa. Decision, an opportunity, is with everyone to make. The former Head of Interim Government in Nigeria, **Earnest Shonekan**, came to mind. To improve the knowledge and skill values and this leads to increase pay; schools shall be the right destination. Many professional courses have different branches they can diversify to. Arts teachers could run visual arts workshops. The talented entertainers under paid employment at cultural agency could become independent producers of films, drama among others. This is like a specialized legal practitioner that is also into property management as an arm of his profession. Let us cite more illustrations. If the business environment has all what it takes, there is room for added value jobs in the distribution of products and services; if is the other way round, there is need for the contribution of both the public and the private sectors. For instance, if the new businesses have dearth of raw materials, it has given **opportunities** for suppliers and transporters and right logistic personnel. If the educational business lacks teaching and non-teaching staff, private tutors could apply to take up jobs. If a business folds up for financial loss, there is chance for new set of management that can transform the business into profit-making. This is true with the selling or taking over of the public institutions by the private owners under public private partnership. What about the build, operate and transfer in the support of the government to provide social infrastructures? And if there is proliferation of businesses, new vacancies are filled. And numerous indirect jobs would be created. As being emphasized, opportunities for employment could appear in any form. We only need to put our thinking caps to task to unearth convertible **opportunities** into lucrative and decent jobs.

Stroll the streets and list what is lacked in terms of public facilities; give the idle and wasting assets (human and non-human) in the nation; what about the list of tourist attraction places in your region? What do you make of the talents in the nation? enter varieties stores for a window shopping, there are brands they do not have and interested to have on stock, list them and make provision to become supplier; as an artist or painter, the popular shops or offices may add values with your aesthetic works, meet the owners. It is rare to meet bestselling authors, award-winning artistes, popular figures in all facets of life on the roads; you can only meet them at public functions; package what you have for them to be your own boss. Never ask for free money (stipend), ask for favour to be on your own by displaying your natural talents with proves. Meet the authors at the reading of his or her book. Meet the film producers at the film premiere. Meet the social clubs and the faith-based association at their headquarters or through the right contacts. I could recall a popular woman-journalist that got her job after meeting a popular publisher in a social function. For seekers of jobs interested to connect with the right public figure, move along with your photocopies of certificates before tracking the persons in mind. Let me use an author to represent producers, it is easy to sell millions of copies if I engage the bookshops and libraries including the retailers. What should I do? Sign an agreement with bookstores to produce entrepreneurship book section in popular bookshops that have branches all over the places including the services of the retailers and the libraries. Be mobile suppliers after studying and properly list their needs. Many who are into time-consuming white collar jobs like bankers, hoteliers, brokers and itinerant service providers are in dire need of private shoppers. They need mobile service providers. Mobile technicians are scarce. Mobile shoppers are not adequate. The same could be done to engage all in the production even some service sector. Do you know that many idle youths in the streets are naturally gifted in one talent or the other? Open talents hunt academies to catch them young and prepare them for scouts and agents that would expose them to right sports clubs. Turn the orphanage home into skill acquisition homes and turn out self-reliant people.

Service in service in the service stations is another open opportunity to start a job and becoming one's boss. Schools, formal and informal, need roaming or part-time teachers likewise other service institutions. Bankers in the banking rooms and departments, those in governments are not in control of their lives. They communicate with mobile gadgets to employ the services of people. But sometimes, it takes mobile service providers to make visits to establishments. Most institutional heads need those who fix things and installations for them. They need people who would do the domestic chores for them. Spare parts sellers could locate within the premises of the auto-repairers. This is what we referred to as creating **shop-in-shop**. All the outlets you see are not 100% stocked with all varieties. Make efforts to produce what will add values to the four wall business outlet or be a supplier to engage yourself and earn huge gains. In short, every office, workstation has opened limitless opportunities to start lucrative jobs. There is no way an institution, a street, a person, a place, an office.. would not lack several things. Hospitals may lack equipment and facilities. In fact, many states may lack primary, secondary and tertiary medical institutions. They may lack certain specialized staff. Think about **service in service** to start lucrative employments. Add spices to shows, seminars, workshops, institutions, sports venues, ceremonies among others. Let me give a few more instances. The proliferation or the licensing of media stations under traditional and digital ones in the establishment of private radio and television stations have created rooms for independent content producers, private presenters, independent OAPs, contents writers and mini-studios.

In addition, I could see limitless opportunities in the news about the exportable materials from the nation to the buyers. What do you make out of the pieces of news that you read in the print media or hear from the electronic media? Are you able to tap the **opportunities**? The list of importable items too is an eyes opener for those interested on importation. There are people who have the financial resources but do not have the idea of how to add values to the wealth, can you think and work to get engaged? There is no day news and productions in the media stations fail to create several employment opportunities. I started my resource office targeted at rendering assistance to projects of the final year students. Another arm of the centre is aimed at providing free tutorials in unique ways and free library service. I have seen guys that threw up non-governmental organizations for the nurturing of the youths into adult. Events in a nation could trigger the proliferation of several non-governmental organizations that are charity-based. Many are scouts' agents at the neighbourhood fields where excelling and talented youths are discovered at their prime. It is part of success story of our centre building teen-authors, teen-Mathematicians from contests in writing and mathematics clinics respectively. Let there be incubation centres to build teen-technicians and inventors. The need and lapse at a station, office, place, institution.. would always create endless **opportunities** for employments. Let us refresh.

By opportunities, we also mean doable and creatable jobs
The creatable lucrative business ideas
Not just for creating goods and services but for gainful employments
Starting from making use of chances at hand
Especially in the identifiable limitless needs
Identifiable from the use of innate faculties
In the criticisms of events and things around you
Get the needs provided and supplied
And self gets employed without delay
This is the path the successful have trod

Opportunities, by these we mean ideas
And this could come from problems and challenges
Never see a problem as one, but an opportunity
An opportunity showing the path to greatness
It takes a wise to proffer solutions to solve a problem
And the gains is in making success and good name from it

What comes to each one as opportunity differs
In individuals and businesses, offices and families
Ethnics and religion circle have fair shares of opportunities
Identify yours to stay awaken, as individual or business
Awaken and apply the faculties and act with the limbs

Opportunity may come like a lightning
Just like the rains in the rainy season
Failure to tie it down could be a major mistake
Tap everyone at your fingertips
And join the millions who are their own bosses

Opportunities are the creators of jobs
Every entrepreneur in history grabs them for use
Never stay idle, grab yours and get started to move up

Reading this eye-opener book is a great chance
Likewise reading tomes of books teaching you things
And many other things to learn in due course
Everything in life is an opportunity
And opportunity begets several opportunities
All firms you see used the opportunities to start operations
Opportunities are limitless and boundless
It exists at all places, time and with different creatures
And therefore jobs creation via seizing opportunities is limitless
Opportunities open eyes to wealth and jobs opportunities

Ask me what we called opportunities
Where you live and the aesthetics plus facilities are some
The type of business and geographic environment
The people, the business and others that make the environment
The unlimited needs and rights of the creatures create opportunities
The class, age, status, qualification, exposure, intelligence.. of those you move with
The associations or the affiliations you are co-habiting with
The occasion you attend or witness paves the way for opportunities
The utilities and facilities in the environment you are
How you feel, perceive things and think are paths to great opportunities
The stories and gossips that are convertible to books, films and documentaries
The scenes you witness freely everywhere and time are opportunities
You levels of application of the natural faculties
The people and creatures you meet through books, films and interviews
The internet services at your beck and calls to add values to your knowledge
The biographies at libraries and bookstores for you to surf
All the places of resorts that you have read about or visited
Numerous are opportunities that could pave the way for jobs creation
All the vacuums created in the nations by mismanagement and maladministration
Shortage of artisans or the professionals create chances
The availability of resources at commercial quantity of human and non-human
All these create limitless opportunities for those who could reflect or understand
Cudgels your brains to identify several ones
And pick out one of your interests to start a lucrative job"

N.B. wherever you see opportunities, think of generating lucrative ideas

Based on our socio-economic researches as written in a few lines above, we can conclude that there are limitless definitions for the term '<u>opportunity</u>' at different climes and different people that can be used <u>to create lucrative business ideas</u>. We conclude that **opportunities beget limitless business-inquisitive ideas** as God guides the senses. **Opportunities** embedded in all the past events, institutions... the present challenges, problems, situations, values, tests, crises and what could be produced for the future. Future opportunities could be identified from today. I see new phase of books in turning the contents of books into interview and reality show. And this is part of my next step in the course of publishing my works. Needs and wants are major path to discover potentials or opportunities. **Opportunities** could take any shape and appear in different fashion and sizes. Loss of jobs and sales has produced researchers and writers on employment creation and sales generation. Lack of comfort stations in poverty stricken nation is an opportunity to create thousands of such stations. One can imagine the lack of institutions in such nations and the number of employment **opportunities** that have been created. It depends on the level of the use of the senses to identify opportunities in opportunities. What we learn (from reading, listening, studying from observations), the level of natural intelligence, creativity, versatility and brilliance, where we reach (by all means of transportation), the height we attained in social status or position, the time we spent or being spent, the followers we enjoy, the customers for our products or services, the status or goodwill we possess, the number of branches we operate from, the quality of staff we work with, the affiliations we belong to, the past and present connections we make, the position we find ourselves, the talents we are naturally endowed with, the assets like the mineral resources beneath and above your soil, seas and air above you, the innate skills and the acquired, the inherited inheritance or the legally amassed wealth, the knowledge we have, meeting high personality or august visitors, the increasing number of products and services from existing and new institutions, the policies and the passed bills from the executives, the earmarked sum as intervention funds for specified sector, witnessing each passing day in good health and freedom, the affiliations we are in, the events we have witnessed and most importantly being alive aside all other positive actions of man... are all **opportunities**.

Those countless opportunities create the smooth path for employment creation and generation of wealth for distribution in the nation. A nation could create e-marketplace where collected products and services of the artisans are promoted online for the participants to increase their selling opportunities. It is a meaningless and purposeless mission for one not to fashion out opportunities after reading through a newspaper. It is a purely waste of time when a man is unable to create a solution to a problem in a day. Solving such problem is a path to become one's boss. Get me clear. A security threatening problem is soaring unemployment to nations. Searching for jobs people can do is a solution which we have published in books. Dull environment is a problem. Creating entertaining atmosphere is a solution. Shortage of certain fast moving good or popular product could be a problem to sellers at the markets. Getting them supplied has solved their problem. Wherever you find yourself, think about the problems therein. List them out for critical assessment towards finding lasting solutions. Proffer practicable solution and you have started a job! Keep this fact with you. No man, no creature, no structure, no institution, no corporate organization, no government or administration.. has everything needed. They outsource for resources in short supply or totally lacked. And you should brace up to be the missing link.

To deserve the above, always try to learn a new trade or the better strategies to promote your trade- learn the secrets of buying and selling; learn the art of repairing or maintenance; learn other people's languages, learn other special skills like typesetting, computing, driving, swimming; traverse the lands, explore the seas, read a book every day, task your brains, join a group, socialize with the right class of people, spare time to stroll about, go on vacation and holidays, stay away from negative habits, follow the right people, be a member of the progressives and thinkers, watch interviews with different professionals, enter or register into workshops and seminars, attend exhibitions, enroll at schools to improve your knowledge, engage a mentor or a role model, stay and chat with the elderly to gain wisdom, the access to books in the libraries, reading and ability to understand what is read and then identify a vacuum…are all **opportunities**. Learn a skill by chance and act the skill. Acting the skill improves the art. Failure to act it is losing the chance. You soccer talents, display the skills to get shirt. Show the acting skills on stage to secure the script, you thespians. Those are the real opportunities knocking at your doors! Many never have such golden chance in their lifetime. Those who had them died wretched as they lost them to their greediness, selfishness and gluttonous self. Reading this kind of motivational stuff that would open your eyes to several jobs that could open doors for you is a best use of time, an opportunity. At this point, we can finally define opportunity as the positive impact(s) of the resources, endowments, access, connections, the knowledge, the wisdom, the life experience, the talents, the skills, the educational attainment, ability to appropriately apply all the faculties (senses) and move the limbs, the attractive personality to build good human relationship among others on the doers (selves) and others (neighbours-within and outside) in this transitory life. Mother Teresa was reported to have defined '<u>life is an opportunity</u>'.

In fact, this is the opportunity that is said to so careful about in the common maxim that says '<u>an opportunity lost may never be regained</u>'. Failure to make the best use of time on earth to better the lives within in anticipation of heavenly rewards under the submissiveness to God's will is a wasted opportunity. A lost soul here would never exist again on earth but there. But for all livings, there is great chance for a wicked to become righteous; a miserly to become generous and so on. We can generalize the term opportunity in the light of **Macmillan** definition as '<u>proffering solutions to problems paving the way to gainful jobs</u>; acting at the right time before a situation gets out of hand is an opportunity; saving a business from imminent liquidation at the right time is a great opportunity put into good use, restoring normalcy when crises are at the corner using anticipated approach is a good use of opportunity. All these are wrapped up with the saying "*Make hay while the sun shines*".

It is established in the course that there are infinite opportunities to create lucrative new jobs at least from the existing ones by many idlers roaming the streets. This is a bit different from our publications on jobs creation. It is part of the identified 'wastes' in different forms that could propel creating employers of labour. At least many should be self-employed if the **opportunities** being spelt out here are considered. With the opportunities in the face of the people, the unemployed should be able to develop the art of entrepreneur. Not just developing it but start from picking interest in self-employment at first with the idle M's such as materials, manpower, market, machines of others close to them as those idle M's are opportunities for the users. A journey of one thousand kilometer starts with an ambitious step as quoted Confucius. Many have the ability or chance to download and upload opportunities to make money but fail. I once told a jobless guy. "Do you have parents of wide life experience?" 'Yes, I have' he answered. "Then, get close to them. Download ancient stories about warriors, herbalists, medicinal plants and their uses, the ancient proverbs and wise sayings with their meanings based on exegeses. All these would fetch you big perks if later sold to users in the cities". The wise parents with such life experience would have died with knowledge of plants, animals, birds and men of repute in their times. They would have dropped dead with tons of ancient proverbs and wise sayings in their brains. The moment they are downloaded, they are later uploaded for the commercial users. Download all that you understand from the attitudes of animals and birds to create sports activities. Engage your understanding of colour in peacocks and other birds and animals to paint your fabrics and artworks, you the skilled graphic artists. Create comics from the acts of birds and animals to start animation jobs for amusement. Many people neglect what they see, ear and inspired with and hence losing great opportunities to be their own bosses.

Imagine the opportunities slipping away from the guy until he was corrected. Listen to words of wisdom, listen to the sage; act or rehearse what you read in prints, always be in seminars- paid or free to add to your wealth of knowledge and skill, get a mentor, never play arrogance, learn from all classes of people, learn dialects of different men, different tricks you should learn to save the opportunity at your beck and call, stay among the learned to learn a new thing, and with all that you learn, you are on the right track to be your own boss! By the term '**opportunities**' we mean all assets, all resources at one's disposal to create jobs **opportunities** and spread the concentrated wealth among the citizens with the use of working ideas. It could be private or public assets, public or private resources in public or private places, businesses or social services, institutes or not, hidden or open. Convert the convertibles. Reflect on how to convert mistakes into products and services. Act the scripts. Convert what you hear or see (imagine) into products or services. Convert the idle land at the back of your home into a farm for plants or animals (pets). Transliterate the ancient stories and myths. Sell what you transcribe into product that would create opportunities for service providers.

Sincerely yours, selling, a skill and an art, is an opportunity to become renowned sales executive like the American Billionaire politician **Ross Perots** of this world. Learn the art. Imbibe the skill. Tread the tracks of the successful ones. Be more versatile by learning the marketplace language. Speak the marketplace terminologies to break barriers. Acting the script or of the popular published on stages, theatres and in films. Culinary skills that you possess are enough to turn you into becoming award winning chef. Break out of your cocoons, encourage your writing talent and skill. Improve it with reading different books of different authors, researchers, script writers, columnists, journalists among others. Enhanced writing skill is developed from improved knowledge as this is an opportunity to become famous and wealthy from what you put in black and white. All best-seller authors start from the first ambitious step. It is a convincing idea on the basis of ability. 'I can write block buster scripts' or 'I can author bestselling books' kicks it off. It is not the first book that makes many gain that status at outset. 'I have flair for reading tomes of books of different titles' or 'I am endowed with the charismatic voice and can read in the presence of large crowds without the fear of intimidation' is the spirit of public readers. Reading and understanding is enough to start creating fame and money from reading to big shots at gatherings and schools. You are on the right track to become successful compere and motivational speakers.

Make something out of the speaking skills that you have if you are a charismatic personality; it is an opportunity to be publicist. Channel all the identifiable opportunities to create several jobs **opportunities** for yourself and others. Work on your skills and talents to produce products and you have turned your nation into a producing nation. Remember the importance of selling to all the products. Without selling, products become glut in the market. And the producers are in the brink of collapse especially in a multicultural environment. The excess products and multi-service institutions have created **opportunities** (selling ideas) for independent sellers or retailers.

By multicultural environment, we mean different ethnic cultures, theological cultures and political cultures among others. Sellers, especially independent sellers, have opportunities or ideas to transform the products into money. Therefore, sellers are inevitable for all products. We sell what we discovered from the identified opportunities begging for exploitation for gains.

OPPORTUNITY PRIMARILY HAS TWO INEXHAUSTIBLE FACES BY OPPORTUNITIES

In the light of what we have written about, identified **opportunity** has two sides like a coin and each of the faces has potentials to create numerous value chains jobs. How do I mean? Each of the sides is capable to increase poverty or wealth, employments and unemployment, increase per capita income or otherwise, national socio-economic and technological growth or not. Let us reflect some cases. If there is mass failure of students in a public examination, all the stakeholders must have a meeting charting a new course to turn round the situation. Some of the resolutions could be massive recruitment of teachers or retraining of the teachers; the re-equip of the classrooms, laboratories, libraries and other facilities in the schools; re-writing of the curriculum by certain experts drawn from different educational disciplines among others. All these create jobs for different categories of people. Sometimes, failure to cut the cost of education as in the increase of tuition fees may force many students into learning a skill or trade where some earnings shall be made to pay the fees. Many drop out of school to face their natural skills squarely and this is the pillar and foundation of their success today. Harsh mistress forced popular football star, Cristiana Dos Santos Alfredo Ronaldo, out of school to hone his talent and interest in football. Today, he is super rich and influential from the proceeds of the round leather game. He is a face of Portugal. Shortage of housing estates for the nationals always lead to the participation of the private investors. With the involvement, thousands of jobs are created. Increasing tons of perishing food crops had pushed many into working on preservation and processing business and this adds to food sufficiency of the nation from food insecurity. Indigence of a nation, a family or the profit loss of a company is seen as a great opportunity for each to find lasting solutions. By so doing, new jobs are created and wealth is spread. When there is shortage of rainfall, nation think of the alternative which include dry season farming via irrigation. A nation whose natural resources are not fetching adequate forex looks inward to discover new resources. In fact, many easily diversify into new grounds. Poor dissemination of knowledge could spur new publishers just as the proliferation of electronic media houses especially with the emerging technology innovations. (Read more details in the third volume '**Wastes to wealth jobs**')

REFRESHING

"A wise in his wisdom says in his poetry
Three are the kinds of people on the land
Those who run away when a problem is seen
Those who only discuss away the problem without acting
The best ones are those who meditate and proffer solutions to them
The last people are the users of opportunities
For the benefits of mankind!"

2.2 THE FACTS ABOUT EMPLOYMENTS OPPORTUNITIES

Opportunities, as being emphasized, open rooms for countless **opportunities** particularly the chance to be one's boss by creating value chains from existing opportunities (jobs). As being emphasized, in different forms (shapes) and sizes (measures, degree) come lucrative new employments opportunities. It is easy to start a job from converting what others produce as a seller. Contents can be promoted via good platform as a way of earning legally. The establishment of the mobile telecommunication business has created limitless opportunities for the over-the-top (OTT) servicing firms not to talk of the value chains from sellers and promoters. Several reality show producers and entertainers are partnering with the telecoms owners to create jobs for their crew. Through internet service optimization, several internet jobs are created. Surf internet and discover limitless jobs in the sites. I told a guy that there are platforms on internet where his garnered experience as certified electric auto technician engineer could be sold for good prices as freelancer or as a forum to solve technical problems in his social media or personalized blog for the job. A highly revered writer and mentor introduced me into writing 'faction' stories. I demanded to know what he meant by 'faction'. I thought he wanted to say 'fiction'. Nay, he bared his mind saying "It is writing biography of a person in form of non-fiction". All the true names of persons and places are changed but the message is true about the person and places. Since then, I have ventured into writing several faction stories to teach the next generation about political and economic histories of nations and people. Writing about product or service for instance; critically look at the product (or service) and you would be able to develop another product (or service). Critically look at individuals, objects, needs, institutions, bodies, environments, events et al. What do they lack, what can add aesthetics to them? What such lacks is a vacuum to be filled. When I read a book as an author; I studied challenges and vacuum created waiting to be filled and I would invent those things to add in order to make it better. To the writers and producers of films, number of new books and films start from the end of those ones in the public view. I improved on my story writing from learning from the pens on paper of great writers within and abroad. Reading such published books is an opportunity to add pep to my writing style. A salesman who reads tomes of books on selling would learn better ways to develop selling strategies and create customers while retaining the old loyal ones.

By this, he or she could create avenues for employment of new people from business expansion from huge sales. Compare what it costs a woman to take care of her head with that of man. Think about the hair by natural colour, the texture of the hair, the head dandruff or scalp, the eyelashes, the ear rings, the neck bracelets, the beads, the hair cream and lotion, the hair washing or treatment soaps, relaxers, the scarf et al. The aesthetics for each of the head depend on the purse of the users determine the expenses. No particular aesthetic company can provide to satisfy all the needs to take good care of the head of both sexes, young and old of different status in the society. Compare what a man spends on his body parts with that of woman too. An existing product (or service) creates at least an opportunity for another firm to create better (if not similar) product (or service) of the same generic function in ever competitive open markets. New products and services can be created from the existing products and services with additional facilities, ingredient(s) or features likewise new services that could bridge the vacuum created by the existing services. It is very easy to create **opportunities** from an identified opportunity based on the creativity and versatility of the thinker or discoverer.

Opportunities could concentrate in a place or roam about. It is like a lost sheep, wherever it is found, tie it down and make the best use of it. Someone bought a washing machine for private use for his auto-car market. Before you say **Jack Robinson**, clients have become to increase to use the machine at a good price. The washing car shop become an arm of the auto business. Many have changed or diversified away from their original trade to another simply for the opportunity at their doors. I have reliable information of a popular bookseller, **Rasmed**, that has become a renowned publisher today. Many fast-rising publishing firms, in Ibadan, Nigeria, are owned by sales representatives for publishers who were their former employers. One can say they are closely related. What about a technician that becomes estate manager? It is not just a fate but grabbing a dangling opportunity that came his way without wasting time before it slips to the clouds. Here was a hardworking and trustworthy friend that was sociable whose customers with property scattered around used to confide in to link them with trusty estate managers. He took the opportunity up after a good counsel to become what he is today! This is how many recruitment agencies and suppliers of designers started (Ref: **Jobs with zero capital vol. one**). On the flip side, those who still nurse the fear of starting small with the items identified in the books- Jobs with zero capital Vol. One and Two, such could seize the opportunity of the established financial institutions to fund their business ideas through written of viable proposals. I counselled some with good business ideas that do not have interest in the interest-based banks to visit the non-interest financial institutions for sponsoring of their viable ideas. If you come across someone who seeks a favour, think about the gainful opportunities from your conversation. A request and favour could pave the ways to lifespan opportunities. The story of a rich tyre dealer, **Lamidi Ajadi**, in the ancient city of Ibadan showed that the man got direct distributorship of tyres from the producers who came all the way from Lagos. Others who were with him ran away when they saw that the visitors were whites. They might think they were sent from the seat of power to make arrest. Bravery and courage to meet high profile guest created the business partnership where all suppliers were done without depositing a penny. The tyres were on sales on return basis just as the publishers of today are doing to attract sellers and buyers. Do you know that those sellers can expand their businesses with new opportunities before them? Many of the sellers could become producers of the raw materials needed by the finished product-producing companies; many could add such business that would add values to the existing business. What stops the wealthy, influential and popular tyre dealers to add wheel balancing to their tyre stores across the nation? What stops such to invest in selling tyre-related parts including relevant lubricants in the vulcanizing industry? Imagine the sellers of tyres of all automobiles divest into rubber planting plantation? Imagine such invest in the recycling of used and expired tyres to black oil (at least). Number of jobs shall be created by the initiatives. Every think-tank on the three R's (reduce, reuse and resold) of converting wastes to wealth shall create several employment opportunities. Meditate over a waste around you. Go into research for more information on how to turn the recycling a commercial success. In a simple talk, all existing business opportunities would always create new employment opportunities to boost the wealth of institutions, individuals and the nations. Imagine the fabric designers moving up to have fashion stores, exhibitions, fashion reality shows or the establishment of fashion academies not to talk of backward integration of investing in textile factories. Imagine the livestock and poultry farmers add meat shops and eatery to their divisions of offices. Imagine schools running bookshops, commercial-based digital libraries, research service station among others in their ventures. Schools can produce quality professionals from the four walls of classrooms if subjects are converted into practice. Several employments have been created. Who would tell me that all the existing businesses do not have room to open new employment opportunities to effectively engage the idle ones roaming the streets as endangered species? No one dare have such stand!

In different dimensions, opportunity paves the way for self-employed (at least) or employer of employees at most. In the two cases, it is either transformed into a product or a service. A major challenge facing a new entrepreneur is the making of sales in order to run profitably. A business that does not make anticipated sales could run liquidated in a short of time. Customers determine the lifespan of businesses and business institutions in the market and the morale booster of the producer (entrepreneur). In most cases, what consumers buy determine what to be produced and what is placed to the market for sale. Outside the product concept, new entrepreneur must learn the secrets of selling to the target customers who are the very important personalities in the success of the business.

In retrospect, the next line is the selling of either to target consumers or clients. Before selling becomes a success in this global village called world where what affects a nation could spread to another within a few seconds, then, there is the need for the producer to be up-to-date in the technique of selling in order to create selling **opportunity**. The arts of producing and later selling must be learnt. The skills must be acquired. Both the arts and the skills have certain steps to tread. This is what we collated in the twenty six laws of selling. Recall that what is saleable is makeable by the producer.

Therefore, the producer must first see himself as the real seller. The identified laws of selling are therefore meant for the producers or the prospective entrepreneurs. They must be studied before the identified opportunity that could be transformed into either products or services becomes a success.

Emphasizing on the selling opportunities created by the increase in the products and services needed in the markets or the expansion of the industries to accommodate new sales executives, sellers take large percentage (about 70%) of the workforce in all industrial sectors. In fact, as proved in one of our publications on jobs creation, everything is an art. Selling, producing, buying, servicing and every action are products of arts-innate or developed (acquired).

In retrospect, for a seller to be successful, he/she must have developed interest, be passionate, lively, approachable, neat, polite, charismatic, mildly aggressive (if situation warrants), humane, capability to scan the buyers' environment for easy segmentations for penetration. They should be able to develop appropriate selling charts as regards the movements and how to sell (selling devises) depending on the products or services put up for sale or listed. In the book "What investors should know about the business environment before investments', we identified these movement charts and selling devises or codes such as business to business, business to market, market to offices and several derivable codes. Most businesses, existing and the prospective ones survive in the selling no matter the quality of the product or service satisfaction. A self-employed person that does not place significance to learning the art of selling his wares would fail in the marketplace. If those roaming the streets intended to grab the opportunities provided by those producing firms within and outside the shores, no one would be left searching for jobs. This has been the position of this book so far. It is an eye opener to such opportunities knocking at the doors of those who are ready to explore or exploit them for gainful benefits. Teaching prospective sellers of different products or services is an opportunity.

Truth be said, selling involves transaction of either product or service. We mean both products and services are saleable. They are what we sell. We sell what we can see, hold, ear or perceive and appreciate. We use different platforms and skills or talents to sell the products or services. Sometimes, we sell with our ability to speak different dialects. We sell with our ability to socialize with different people of different profiles or class. Sell your own product or service; your own skills or others, your own talents or others. With the intention or interest in selling, many dying business are raised from dead.

Therefore, everyone must learn the secrets of selling as an art. One of the greatest secrets is selling different products at all seasons. Never be a mono-product or mono-service seller. Create different products that sell at different seasons varying at different climes. Through several locations and employment of sales agents, volumes of sales are recorded. You make money all year round. And from the products or services, you identify the cash-cow. Never get satisfaction in being a stationary or rigid seller. Be a dynamic seller. Own your shops outlets and employ hawkers. Be mobile offline seller and add online if you can. Communicate with target buyers periodically with the communication instruments in vogue. Invite them to online shops at discounted prices and gifts. Create chance for online buyers and window shoppers. Sell credits and cash to gain many. Many training grounds could not contain all the selling tricks. In books, many are found. Sharing one of such with the readers, we therefore culled the following information verbatim from the aforementioned book from the same author. Two options are there for people with no jobs. <u>If they cannot create or manufacture a product or provide a service, then they should brace up to sell the commodities</u>. It takes a lot to be successful seller. We shall treat what make the **art of selling** in later paragraphs.

Sellers, they are like the certified pharmacists that recommend drugs for patients. The buyers are the patients and the pharmacists are the sellers while the products and the care represent the drugs and the services respectively. There are secrets of selling to make your mark; indelible marks in the sands of time. **Take selling a corporate job**. It is an <u>inevitable art</u> in a successful company. Since selling is for those who could not produce (manufacture), then the opportunity to sell manufactured products and quality services is open. We have illustrated what to sell between pages **34** and **37** of the book '<u>Creating New Jobs From The Existing Jobs</u>'. <u>Learn to understand the a-z secrets of selling and this is an opportunity to be successful in selling</u>. Failure to learn it could be a **<u>misuse opportunity</u>** when there is chance to do so.

In all nations, two employment **opportunities** come side by side. It is the making (producing and manufacturing) and selling. Not all can be endowed to become producers or service providers but a very big fraction in millions have the ability to horn their selling skills to become successful sellers of those products produced by the entrepreneurs. A good instance is the conversion of millions at a swap to become digital seller for the goods and services in a national marketplace. In short, a fraction of the populace would have to go into **production** and bigger fraction would be into **selling** aside those employ in between as administrators.

The proliferation of manufacturing industries including the service providers is an eyes opener to start selling, distribution and marketing jobs for those who desire. Without doubt, a major problem facing the manufacturers and service providers is dearth or dwindling of sales that could be classified under low or no sale. There is room for independent sellers, marketers and distributors. Having seen making huge **selling** as great opportunity to generate employments since not all can be producers and providers of services; and all existing businesses find it inevitable to expand and diversify, teaching the potential sellers how to sell is a path to employ people in their hundreds directly and indirectly, we need to treat secrets of selling as an art in production process and going-concern of a business, then all salesmen should strictly follow the following 'a' to 'z' secrets of selling (extracted from another title- Understanding Business Environment, right or wrong') to target buyers (of different buying attitudes) at different places. This is an **opportunity** to learn more on how to strategically increase sales and indirectly creating rooms for employment for others.

A-Z SECRETS OF SELLING

a) He/she should be aware that some buyers are seasonal and selective purchaser: Parents buy books, kits and instructional materials during the holidays. Umbrella, boots and rain coats aside different consumables, electronic gadgets (heaters, burners) have their peak sales during the rainy season. Sports business sells at certain periods of the year. Tourism business is sold to target tourists at the right time by the sellers especially the travel agencies. A seller whose sales movement chart considers the peak periods is out to make huge sales. Choose to sell the right product that adds values to customer' needs (**Law One**).

b) He/she should be aware that tastes differ as environment is dynamic: It is different tales with different folks. He should study the environment where his target customers are largely found. The environment should be known with its psychology of buyers, similar sellers who are rivals to compete with in order to strategize for creation of anticipated market shares. He should therefore have 100% knowledge about the product or service and the buyers' environment before the commodity is being put up for sale to the target customers. A seller that does not understand much about the advertised product or service and the environment would simply fail in the market. <u>Understand the environment and the content of the product and much about the buyers</u>. It gives the seller the ability to sell the message within a few seconds or minutes. It is just like an interview session where the applicant is given a few minutes to identify his skills. With this, the buyer's psychology is bought, and mind and body are attracted. <u>This is the selling point to him/her</u> (**Law Two**)

c) The seller could also create social sites especially blogs, in this digital selling craze, to adverts the products being sold as the representative of the producer. With constant upgrading in blogs sharing the benefits and generic functions of a product on his list, new customers may be created. Persistent persuasive promotion would attract the 'deaf' and 'blind' customers. Since it is not sacrosanct that potential customers should buy a product or enjoy a service no matter the quality and the low prices but constant promotion and convincing illustrations from the social media handle, the dedicated specialized blog and the site of the sellers. Advertisement, a consistent one, is itself half-selling of the product. Awareness about the products should be created for the target buyers before they are formally released to the market by the duo of producer and the sellers in their respective <u>business and social sites</u>. Advertisements activities should not be done by the producers alone. In the modern selling environment, products and services are known from social selling or digital selling. Spare sum of money or gifts to enhance quality public relation in order to get anticipated patronage. This mode of selling sells the products or services beyond the boundaries (of class, status, gender, affiliation, nation, races, religion). Target all. Do not limit your sales target. You can grow it every day. As you tenaciously hold on to the old customers, try to create new customers through selling baits periodically. Sometimes, the minority could be the buyers that enable your product sold out. Therefore, the number does not matter for all products or services being sold by the sellers. Those who are not targeted but are able to come by the adverts would recommend the products or services to others. Some products and services have to be consistently advertised online and offline to the target buyers in trickles. Some could attract instant patronage if massive advertisements and promotions have been done before release. Live streaming and social media videos have added values to promotion of products and services. This is done by producers and sellers to gain presale popularity and probably booking in advance, before they are officially released. Many publishers and film makers are in the fun of doing this. Imagine the potential of sales a seller would record if with the permission of the producers he places such item in his sites for all the existing customers and prospective ones in the market. He is the mouth-piece and the representative of the manufacturers. He should be social-media friendly commanding many followers and even create rooms to get more followers on a daily basis.

By so doing, he would be able to create a social brand for self and the products and services being sold to the target consumers. Beside this, relevant advertising methods or channels should be adopted by the sellers to win the target market. In open market, sellers could use megaphone to speak to people simply because market is always noisy. He could use electronic media to get clients in offices. Short Message Services that are flavored with aesthetics, Blackberry Messenger, instagram, whatsapp and bulk SMS including all social media handles could also be effectively and efficiently used to reach out people with the appropriate or universal language in all the business environments or nations with a click of buttons. He should be able to afford all the electronic gadgets that would enhance his social status and reach out to large number of people who are the potential customers. Reach out to target customers with effective means of communication and baits. (**Law Three**)

d) He should set up criteria to rate each product or service being sold to ease the shoppers' intention to diagonize or analyze the products put up for sale. This is doable with the feedbacks from the customers. A product could be rated based on volumes of sales per hour or per day; sales volume is a function of prompt delivery and supplying the right product at right or attractive price to the buyer at the appropriate place. It could also be done via the quality as commented by the users or buyers. <u>Make self-assessment as per prompt delivery and feedback of the buyers.</u> (**Law Four**)

e) He should be polite, neat, enthusiastic, business environment –friendly customers-friendly, approachable, sociable (with public servants, civil society and law enforcement agents) and trustworthy to retain old customers and gain new customers. As the representative of the manufacturer, he should exhibit quality moral values such as being passionate, patience, prudency and prayerful. He should also be dutiful, diligence, determine to set and meet target sales volume, self-discipline, dynamic and dedication to duty. A seller should be the first patron of the product being sold. Imagine a seller eating one of the edible products being sold in the presence of the potential buyers. His office should also wear quality and inviting aesthetics to attract clients. Making more customers in addition to the old customers is a great priority to him. He is aware that losing a customer through dissatisfaction could lead to the loss of one hundred. Gaining one customer is a potential to gain at least ten more customers as a publicist. <u>Looking gay, neat and tidy are inevitable when meeting new people target as buyers.</u> (**Law Five**)

f) Sellers should learn to speak several dialects of his target customers to effectively sell the product. An independent seller that could not speak the dialects of the target consumers should employ a multilingual person as partner in progress. Sometimes, a part-time grass root man could do this for a stipend. Some could even do this gratis provided some of the products are given to him/her gratis. Some versatile and humane seller would start from the top to reach the grass-root. This is by selling the intended product or service through the political leaders or tribal chiefs. <u>Someone who understands the language of the others has been free from their tricks. Learn the target buyers' dialects. (**Law Six**)

g) He should be able to create seller-sellers and seller-customers business relationship to enhance 100% patronage. By so doing, the feedbacks, comments, enquiries, suggestions to improve the product or service would be received at a very low cost to the producer from both his own recruited sellers and the buyers from the sellers. Each product has different approach to its selling. The seller must prepare different approach at different point in time for categorized class of target buyers. <u>Social impression sells products and services; sellers must create good impression about self and products or services being sold.</u> (**Law Seven**)

h) He should never compromise selling inferior goods for quality products. Also, all legitimate product or service must be done. Therefore, his producers must be genuine establishment producing genuine legitimate products or services. He must do that to protect his own goodwill (image) and that of the producer(s). <u>Seller must strictly observe the law of apple. An inferior product among tens of quality products could turn the buyers off. Avoid it like plague.</u> (**Law Eight**)

i) He should be dynamic with changing business environment with up to date knowledge about micro and macro economy. A seller could get a foreigner intending to patronize his product or service, his knowledge of foreign exchange should be proven without hesitation. <u>Knowledge of dynamics through seeking for more knowledge sustains all business survival.</u> (**Law Nine**)

j) Arithmetic skills are inevitable for any successful sellers. He has two bosses- manufacturers and the buyers. He treats the customers with respect and dignity. Condition may warrant he sells on credit therefore he must be able to keep all business transaction records against the date/hour of transaction. <u>Inevitable to sustain the going-concern of a business is the arithmetical skills, a must to develop.</u> (**Law Ten**)

k) He is always time-conscious as what he sells is time-based. He is aware of a particular product or service that could be sold in a very large quantity to attract large profits. His market success is the producer's success vice versa.

Being time-conscious is working with time, being dynamic and technologically-conscious of the trends in the market. <u>Time is a priceless asset for the survival of a business, attach high premium to it</u>. (**Law Eleven**)

l) He should be wary of legal restrictions in the societies he operates. There are society watchers in the shoes of the human right activists. Any product or service that could harm the ignorant buyers must never be sold or else legal wars could start between the seller and the activists. <u>What is illegal to be produced is illegal to be displayed and sold</u>. (**Law Twelve**)

m) Just as the manufacturers, he must be able to define the right environment for each product being sold based other factors like the traditional socio-cultural values or value-system of the people. It is possible for a seller of beef in the Muslim-dominant nation to sell pork in another nation outside the Muslims nation to make huge sales and profits. Ensure you sell at places where there are large crowds who are prospective buyers. Such places of events are convention grounds, trade fair pavilions, festival and carnival grounds, cinemas, tourist places, sports arenas among others. The places are enough to create what jobs to do and the feasible business ideas. Think. <u>Patronage is got at the right environment vice versa; locating it first is a must</u>. (**Law Thirteen**)

n) He should be able to analyse each product or service being sold to the public based on the SWOTs analyses. Failure to do so, he may not make much sales among the educated or elitist buyers who may be the biggest customers in term of purchases. <u>A novice at selling can never record a gain</u>. (**Law Fourteen**)

o) As a promoter who is out to sell skills and services, he must be a type that mixes with rank and file of the society as a social class. Sellers in the personnel department should be creative to sell in volumes anticipated by the producer. Multi-Level Marketing is a creative selling strategy. Main sellers like the franchise dealers should employ more sales agents with good remuneration. The recruited sellers must be given a sense of belonging in the type of uniforms and kits to enhance their sales potentials and they must be located at strategic locations to make huge target sales. I was surprised when a publisher of one of my publication intended to develop my book in YouTube, a social 'film' media. I wondered how a personal guide book would be acted into a film on YouTube; yet, it shows creativity on the part of the sellers. Imagine converting the road hawkers into corporate uniformed or customized hawkers with better commission. What about trailer sales? There are one thousand and one ways to make huge sales. It only depends on creativity, versatility and dynamism of those assigned the authority or responsible for selling. In the modern world, electronic adverts to make sales and payment are the trend for renowned seller to adopt. <u>Failure of a seller to be a brand is a path to financial loss from low or no patronage</u>. (**Law Fifteen**)

p) His social status demands for acquiring certain brand of car, certain attires or customized uniform and kits and communication devices (phone, laptop with internet facility always) to facilitate his movements (transportation) and networking (communication) and endear him to the target buyers who are mostly migrants. He is out to sell what could make brands out of others who patronize him. Purchasers (brands-in-the-making) buy from sellers with a quality brand in personality. He is a social brand that is inevitable to sell a novice but quality material to the users in the public, near and far. Many music stars are brought into limelight by the sellers (promoters) that have the social status and golden touch. <u>As a social brand himself, Sellers' products or services must have the ability to make different brands in others</u>. (**Law Sixteen**)

q) He must not have a preference for buyers on the basis of their ethnics, beliefs, values, affiliations, associations, personal aspirations, ideas, school of thoughts or ideology (politics, socio-economic) or locations. If the category of the target buyers falls in any of the stated classes, his mission is to sell to them without being selective. <u>Target all without discrimination to make high sales above target</u>. (**Law Seventeen**)

r) Aside being selling environment-friendly and customer-friendly, he must be humane, enthusiastic and kind (mild) at all times to the buyers, old or prospective. He must be able to win the hearts of the target clients, old and new to have effective demands for the product(s) or service(s). He should be aware that the volumes of sales would determine his own commission and elevation to bigger responsibility in the business and rating among co-sellers by the public. It is not amazing to learn that the sales volume of amazon, barnes and noble and some traditional and national bookstores are considered as part of what the New York best sellers use to rate a book a bestseller (Wikipedia: 2012)! <u>If you are not cheerful, do not open the shop</u>. (**Law Eighteen**)

s) Record keeping and rating of product based on sales and feedbacks from the buyers are some of his business responsibilities. Sellers use different style to keep records of stock. Some adopt first in, first out. Some are into last in, first out. These methods depend on the perish-ability or fragility of the product. <u>Keep the records to be aware of the stores in stock</u>. (**Law Nineteen**)

t) He should properly list his products and services under the right categories or based on alphabets, makers or brands, relevance, most popular, time of production after categorization into different classes like books, toys, electronics, foot wears, fabrics, among others. <u>Proper listing in different sections is the right bait to buyers</u>. (**Law Twenty**)

u) He should be able to create new markets by his recommendations and suggestions for the target buyers. Creating new market share goes beyond the nation but outside. There are buyers scattered all over the world. Digital selling and personal selling could be feasible to achieve this objective. Personal selling should be done with the use of <u>selling movement charts</u> below. There should not be limited target buyers. He should be able to reach out to all regardless of sex, status, cultural affiliations, social affiliations, religion association among others. This helps the seller to have anticipated number of buyers. Assuming a seller sets to sell one thousand buyers and he is able to 'sell the idea' (advertise) to hundred thousand, it would be easy to achieve the set sales volume. He should have eyes and contribution in the creation of bigger market with the producers. The larger the market, the larger the sales volume potentials and the more the commissions for his business. Wise sellers sell at the most appropriate market place. Market place could be organized launching venue, public presentations, road shows, seminars, symposium, restaurants, community services, fuel stations, religion places among other places. The first two are done with the permission and supports of the producers. Books are sold at campuses by supplying the schools bookstores. <u>The larger the market, the larger the clients. Create more networks</u>. (**Law Twenty-One**)

v) He should be able to communicate with his customers everywhere no matter the distance informing them about new stocks in stock for them with the price and the benefits (reasons of purchase). Communicate by uniform that you wear. Communicate by the speech you make in the public. Communicate with your good virtues and social interactions. He should be morally upright and have the ability to deliver the booked item(s) at the doorstep(s) of the customer(s) at the appropriate time of need. <u>Never create a gap between you and the buyers. Fill in the gap before they know it</u>. (**Law Twenty-Two**)

w) Privacy of the customers should be kept hence he become a trusted brand to the customers. A customer that trusts his seller would trust the brands of products or services being sold. Every buyer is an invaluable asset to the seller just as the seller to the manufacturers. Indirectly, the customer that trusts the seller trusts the producers. Book your appointment before you show up. <u>Treat the buyers like kings. Respect his or her privacy. Never betray the trust. Keep his dignity intact</u>. (**Law Twenty- Three**)

x) Anticipate more purchases by the buyer. Attractive goods catch more attention. List the relevant and complementary products with those ones or the one picked for purchase by the buyer on schedule. Online booksellers used to encourage buyer with such write-ups like: "Customers who bought this item also purchased these…..(the books)". Move along with your best products especially in the listings as these could allow more sales not earlier booked by the buyer. <u>Never hesitate to create attractive marketing slogan to update the buyers</u>. (**Law Twenty-Four**)

y) Sell by the rule. Never step on toes in the course of selling to your target buyers. Nations are guided by the socio-cultural values and religions dictates; therefore selling what is illegitimate is feeding the people with poison. This would be resisted at all cost. <u>Observe the laws of the buyers' land to gain acceptability and make your target sales</u>. (**Law Twenty-Five**)

z) Waive your price to sell more in volumes. A seller that is not ready to provide discounts to buyers may not be a market success. There are customers at different places that would demand for price reductions. In fact, segment your target buyers into three categories namely- primary users or buyers, secondary buyers and the choice buyers. Ensure the listing of the products is done under different usage categories. A product could appear in multiple categories if the use is so universal. It makes shopping very easy for the buyers and selection of products for effective purchase. Try to offer them to gain the market especially if the population is very high. <u>Price strategy is flexible; observe it when and where necessary</u>. (**Law Twenty-Six**)

These are the **twenty-six laws of selling**. A seller who observes them would make a market success in his selling business. In this case, the producers too should adopt the selling secrets in order to effectively sell their wares. Add relevant aesthetics to attract crowds of patrons. The impact has direct positive influence in the proliferation of business ideas by the entrepreneurs-existing and prospective. (Expand the scope about selling in a separate book from our stable titled <u>'Winning huge sales and increasing clients' base..</u>')

In the course of compiling this work, I met a seller with a company. His case is worth sharing. Their company gave them new sales target within a specified time to meet or face the consequence. The consequence is the opposite of hiring. Here was a company that failed to embark on promotional activities to regularly updating the target buyers about their products in the market. The friend told me about how all their efforts to encourage the management to invest in advertising of the products to the prospective buyers were to no avail. Unfortunately, the business was in an environment where the per capita income was very low, political instability, inconsistent economic and political policies, high level of corruption and the unemployment rate was rising every day. Does this kind of seller need to advertise what the company is producing from his own salary to meet the set target through attracting adequate buyers? His intuitive is being challenged or tested in this case. He must use all the social resources in his capacity to meet the set target. He must design right selling decision to enhance sales anticipated. He has to because if he fails to meet up, he may never meet the target and is facing sack which is a passage to over saturated labour market! To meet the target, he has to re-design his selling movements to gain more customers from the numerous potential clients.

Let him follow the selling movement charts below to make his headway. Besides that, the seller must develop a more acceptable character to advertise and sell the products to all people without any restrictions. He should never be restricted by his own personal values such as religion, ethnic, political ideology or affiliations, associations or groups he belongs. He should see all as target buyers wherever they are found-public places, private offices, worship centres, seminars, filling stations, recreation clubs, institutions and regardless of status-single or married, or gender-male or female, or age-young or old.

Having known the identities (features) of the manufacturers, the products and the target business environment; the seller must endeavour to create a broad and clear channel to reach the target buyers therefore, he must design a movement chart to make a prompt delivery and for the effective application of the laws.

Towards designing selling points and devising selling movement charts, the charts are the followings:

a) Business to business sales points or through selling under a global trade name
b) Business to home sales points
c) Home to office sales points
d) Office to office sales points
e) Institutes to institutes points
f) Organizations to organizations points
g) Open markets to open markets points
h) Town to town

i) City to city
j) Nation to nation

2.3 NATURE OF EMPLOYMENT-WEALTH CREATION OPPORTUNITIES

All along, we have done justice to different opportunities towards creating new jobs from the existing opportunities. There is need to give a summary of how opportunities look like. In short, opportunities to start a business idea could come in different forms especially **negative or positive** at different places and time or situations such as in:

a) Information or data in prints, electronic media
b) Tangible assets as in natural faculties and abilities aside the inherited or acquired assets
c) Spiritual assets as abstracts based on talent or inspirational
d) Links, status and personality
e) Grants or aids, loans

f) Sharing of knowledge or exchanging of pleasantries using any medium
g) Social connections, interactions or relationships
h) Boost or motivations in different forms-moral, materials and financial
i) Numerical strength and ability to discover new things, innovations, new designs, new features, additional compositions or ingredients
j) Events and individual perceptions or needs, group and association including institutional essentials, luxurious and esteem needs
k) Change in policy and the somersaulting of policy and objectives
l) Change in weather conditions and climate; change in situation and timing; failure and success of an event
m) The existing institutions, agencies, ministries, departments, the social clubs, the professional bodies, ethno-religion values, ideological changes or alterations, amendments to constitutions among related others.
n) The abandon materials that people and institutions referred to as 'wastes'
o) The improving information and communication technology and their products and services
p) All intellectual property of individuals, institutions and others.

Therefore, **opportunity**, either social or economic services, is meant to be discovered and convertible into commercial use as **viable idea**. Every wealthy person on earth has been a good user of opportunity that came his way. Every great nation has been a good user of opportunities like good and bad climatic conditions, fertile and unfertile soil, mass lands or not, vast and long seas or not, thick or scattered forests among other endowments within and around it. Both sides of the coins have inscription and messages. Every successful entrepreneur is someone who has made the optimal use of the opportunity, whatever form and size, in the past. One thing about opportunity is that it is never static. Opportunity is ever dynamic and challenging creating room for new set of opportunities. The application of the senses play major roles to discover and identify opportunities to start-up jobs and create wealth. They (opportunities) are treated in different ways and degrees. Some opportunities may require very urgent attention like the supplies of foods and medicals to the displaced people in camps. Rehabilitation and reconstruction of damaged linked bridges after a storm or any natural disaster. Restore of water and electricity supplies to power homes and industries. All these create instant employments for different tradesmen and artisans. Browse the biographies of the successful people in a choice facets of life to learn about their pasts. Many a star musician walks along with his recorder to record new songs as inspiration comes from creatures around him or those he suddenly comes across. A film maker also does the same. Creative architects must study different houses and structures at every place they find themselves. I know many who learnt the traditional pharmacology skills from the natives they sojourn with at a time of their lives. Artists could hone their skills or improve their creativity from the serene environment they find themselves. The operating environment is the opportunity being talked about. It is an opportunity (idea) that creates other opportunities (ideas) in the valuable artistry works from the artists. To discover the needs saleable, research into the minds of the buyers. Study where they live and their desires to enjoy good living. Consider the platform in existence that could aid your work.

And by so doing, the opportunity is bright to be a success. It is transformational into relevant ideas and hence products and services. Apply all the faculties. In the light of above list, it is true that opportunity is at everywhere to create ideas especially in:

a) In the internets and sites through the search engines
b) Inside the publications like the newspapers, magazines, bulletins and tabloids
c) Along the streets, in the trains, buses, aeroplane (while strolling or travelling) and inside homes
d) In the electronic media like radio, television, mobile phones…
e) In the sermons from the divine scriptures
f) In the cased publications like books of different professional disciplines from institutes, associations, affiliations and research stations
g) Surfing or recalling events of the past or cogitating (meditation) about all creatures around or beyond

h) In all situations and events like market situation, political events, history, religion and sporting activities, entertainment and leisure, tourism and festivals among others
i) In all dark spots or places like the slums, the ghettos and all kinds of environment man is found among others. A rural dweller has great opportunity to become farmer, hunter, herbalist, warrior and related jobs. The riverside dwellers are potential fishermen, sea explorers and relevant professionals.

REFRESHING TEASER

Opportunity begets limitless opportunities, I repeat
Just as man begets mankind and procreation goes
Limitless is the number of opportunities just as procreation never ceases
Since needs are limitless likewise the creatable opportunities

Learning a skill is an opportunity
Paving the way to sell the skills
And creating a niche for the owner

Sell the skill at the right places
An opportunity to reap in full, it is
Meeting VIPs is an opportunity
As it makes to create a brand
Speaking among the dignitaries an opportunity
Feasible to endear speaker to many big shots
And enhance developing greater public speaking skills
Representing the people is a rare opportunity
Make the best use of it to get followers
Invitation to big events is a worthy opportunity
You've got the chance to socialize with socialites
Opportunity is learning at schools and teaching by acts
As that catapults you into the elite clubs

Quality learning environment is for rich future
As quality graduates are human assets
An excellent way to build the nation in the future
Creating jobs opportunities from them all, how?!

Acquiring knowledge is an opportunity
It gives the path to lead the packs
Elected or selected to high position is another
As it paves the way for good representation"

BRAINSTORM

Let us look into **opportunities** to create jobs and wealth from sports with the use of **football as a case study**. As a football analyst and follower, you can create jobs opportunities beyond analyzing or be a fan in the name of watching your darling team. What steps can you take to start a lucrative job? Assuming you are a fan of Real Madrid and your best player is the Portuguese Cristiana Ronaldo. Follow these steps to get yourself engaged by packaging such in websites, dedicated blogs or recording compact discs (video) for customers worldwide:

a) Record his dribbling skills during training and on the field of play
b) Measure his firing shots at goals
c) Record all the free kicks taken per match
d) Record the number of goals he scored
e) Record the number of assists per match
f) Research for his personality in the training ground, on the field and outside the field of play
g) Determine his commitment based on what others say about him especially his coaches, personal trainers, team mates, fans, domestic servants and sports writers
h) His endorsements and awards

i) His likes and dislikes (turn-ons and turn-offs)
  j) His life philosophy
  k) His football philosophy

Each of the records breaking achievements of the star players could become source of creating jobs and money for several thousands of people across the world. This does not include the revenues from advertisers and endorsements. In today's world, several talents are in different sports with large followers. Creating such for them is an opener to creating employment opportunities and wealth. Think of working for Lionel Andrea Messi (the magical Messi), Pep Guardiola in football and coaching respectively, Muhammad Ali in boxing, Michael Phelps in swimming, Usain Bolts in athletics... or of international renowned singers, thespians, great administrators...

Imagine if the soccer talent sells himself. Imagine the publication or the production of the title "**Ronaldo, his exploits**" endorsed and managed by **Ronaldo** himself. Think about the number of jobs Ronaldo's museum would provide and the income from tourists to such museum. This motivates him the more in the field of play. And it is enough to change the personality. His skills improve as he is aware of selling self to fans. For the fans of different skills, let the artists among sell visual impression of the player or the star players in each of the entry points, imagine the sales per venue. Every nation has such popular figures in different fields. Working on them would create numerous employments **opportunities** from chains of sectors. Let the communicators among fans start promoting the celebrated player, coach or team and raise their incomes. For the writers, with the data per match, you can start publication of this guy per match!

Imagine what you would be making if transliterated in different dialects. Imagine what you can sell to English fans of his, imagine the saleable to the Catalan fans and foes; imagine the sales to the Spanish fans of this great and talented footballer per week... you should know that the guy has fans worldwide just like others. Do not just be a fan paying to watch him play, make efforts to make your own legal perks. Imagine comparing two Ronaldos in the history of football-the **Portuguese** and the **Brazilian Ronaldos**. Your artistic impressions of the star players could sell you to big employers for the skills or you could become employers of sales agents in all the venues. Sell souvenirs at the premises and be creative in the products put for sale. If you cannot be scout or agent for such, write through consortium of sportswriters (if you are not a writer by profession but as the initiator of the saleable idea and one who could finance the project).

EXERCISES

a) Use the sample above for other great players in football and other different sports like athletics, basketballs, gymnastics, judo, rugby, golf, lawn Tennis, Table Tennis, Swimming, Boxing among other crowd pulling sports. Package stories on the exploits of the legends and the reigning stars in each. Aesthetically packaged products attract the largest buyers. Therefore, this matters. Celebrate the likes of David Beckams, the great coaches lie the Alex Fergusons, the Jose Felix Mourinhos, the Pep Guardiolas, Arsene Wengers of this football world. Work on the legends on tracks like Carl Lewis, Usain Bolts, the boxers like Rocky Machianos, Muhammad Alis, Marvin Haglers, Mike Tysons, to the Klitscho brothers of today; Ivan Lendl, Steff Grafs, Serena Williams, Boris Beckers, Nadals, Murrays, Pete Sampras in lawn tennis among others in other sports. Celebrate the in different packages for commercial gains. Translate the products into different dialects to ensure wide distribution. Go into book publication. Let some go into online publishing or broadcasting. In short, by so doing, millions of jobs –direct and indirect, would be created across the nations!
b) Think about the successful coaches of the present teams in those sports. Do the same for them and see the result.
c) Recall the past. Recollect all the juicy stories. Reflect on the good, the bad and the ugly. Put them into stories in series just like the above. You have turned yourself into employers of labour.
d) Work on the team of your choice. Take the similar steps like the above and lucrative jobs are guaranteed!

e) Be a fan of all the teams in the choice league and create something different. Do the same for other sports. Be wary of rivals and this is the reason your package must give you the edge to create your own market share.
f) Be followers of all leagues of different sports in Europe, Asia and other continents, for instance, and start working in line with what we have spelt out above.
g) Let the social brands and 'trademarks' in different fields or specialization as they are big personalities worthy of being sold. Let each of the public brands sell themselves in different ways outside books written by them or the ghost writers start making money from writing and publishing them after authorization. 'Sell' the successful business gurus like the Briton Richard Bransons of this world, American Warren Buffets, 'sell' the Bill Gates of the world, 'sell' Steve Jobs of Apples… sell their exploits in prints and videos and you could imagine the patronage. Sell their events in the history for students to learn. Sell their products and philosophies. And by so doing jobs opportunities are easily created!
h) Create new style of organization of soccer events like a five-a-side tournament or all players team with no goalie. Let me give some other instances. Let each of the players display their skills or soccer artistry. Therefore, each player should play for a limited number of playing time on the pitch. Or separate team should play each half. This gives opportunities to the twenty-two players on the bench! Create something new. The ball is now in your court!
i) Critically look at the stadium, does it lack some things? Can you provide them? Study the spectators; do they crave for a thing? Can you create utility that can satisfy the need? Think for the bench, what do you think they lack or in dire need of? Can you bridge the vacuum? Think of the soccer managers; what do you add to create more values for the competition like side attractions, mid-half attractions…? Create unique soccer academy for different ages. Create soccer science library; create soccer artistry digital library. Create robot coaches, self-training kits and trainers instructing players on skills at the comfort of their homes. Create

flags for the teams. Create mock cups for contests. Create special shirts of the players in different designs. Create songs, anthems and poetry for the darling team. Create periodical journals selling the team the more. Create maps and attractive souvenirs for the team. Publish the past, the present and project the future of the team and legendary players. Dedicate special parks for patronage of the fans. All these are mouth-watering <u>opportunities</u> in the sight of tech-entrepreneurs! Do the same for other sports and you hit it big!

j) Imagine the celebrated footballers like Zinedine Zidane, Diego Amando Maradona, Ronaldo De Lima...come out from retirement to venture into reporting or selling video-exploits of their careers in their hey days on the fields. Imagine writing columns for papers and authoring books on football. Imagine they become mentors if they cannot go for coaching jobs. Imagine the Mike Tysons, Larry Holmes...from retirement becoming promoter of their past exploits in the rings just like the footballers. Imagine the money they would be making and the number of jobs opportunities they would have been created by the attempts.

<u>**N.B.**</u> Those fans outside Europe could make their money from publishing and production of their own materials in their mother tongues! Imagine the millions of jobs that have been created worldwide from just one <u>opportunity</u> created by sports for the die-hard fans! The population of sports lovers, especially football addicts, in the above case would transformed into several jobs opportunities. The fans should be aware that their tickets make the sports industry to thrive and the players to be so wealthy. They could make their own money from them too by go into the identified businesses. Let this in everybody's mind, we are all consumers and potential producers. We consume what the others produce and we should also produce what those people also consume. The sports stars would patronize the souvenirs made for them. They would purchase the shirts and designers in their names. They would patronize your boutiques and designer shops.

EXTRA CHALLENGE

Place other structures (business organizations, association, sports business) before you. Take the steps of the above. Create jobs opportunities.

CHALLENGES AHEAD

In the next chapter are several other social and economic opportunities (ideas) that can be transformed into jobs **opportunities**. Take your pen. Read to understand the jobs in each paragraph. Scribble down the jobs opportunities from each of the paragraphs. Start work plan for your choice job. Strategize on how to build the chosen business idea in each paragraph. Open the next page and brace up for the challenges for more **opportunities** towards creating jobs and wealth for the nationals and the nation respectively. Keep on reading and learning!!!

CHAPTER THREE

3.1   **OPPORTUNITIES KNOCKING AT THE DOORS 2**

Now, let us gradually rounding off on a grand scale with more windows to opportunities to create new jobs and becoming one's boss at one's set pace. Apply grey matter in all cases. At this stage, we focus on individuals, government Ministries, departments and agencies and the private investors, local and foreign, to seek, identify and create opportunities to generate lucrative employments. In the previous chapters, we have concisely discussed how individuals can identify opportunities to be their own bosses. We have done justice on the paths to identify revenues-employments opportunities by the government and private investors too. It should come to mind that government through its socio-economic think tanks can further identify the lapses and ineffective state of social services to create new jobs. The aim of providing aesthetic and filths-free environment could generate thousands of jobs for evacuators, sweepers, sorters and recyclers not to talk of the administrative staff. The opening of national e-marketplace wherein all goods and services within are registered (uploaded) at a price and then promoted could earn forex and generate digital selling jobs for millions. The think tanks for private sectors stakeholders could identify the missing points to create new jobs. Is this a hard task? Nay! Do you also know what? <u>Do you know that the employment and wealth creating strategies revolve round producing and selling</u>? By the word 'producer', we mean promoter of goods and services and manufacturers or processors, fabricators, publishers, consultants, provider of services, developers, innovators, inventors, composers, think tanks, proprietors that are universally referred to as the trail blazer or the entrepreneurs. And the word 'seller' stands for all wholesalers, distributors, marketers, promoters, advertisers, retailers, hawkers of goods and services. Producers are not limited to ages. They are not ethno-religion limited also. Everyone, regardless of age, gender, religion, ethnic group, professional affiliation, association and what have you is a potential producer. A child of below teenage may come with unique practicable business idea that would become the family business. An experience, good or bad, may be the starting point of a viable business idea. Many have become school representatives for the searching of right schools for his children. Many who are into travelling agents came into the business by mere use of connections they have with people outside the shores. Many a friend is selling imported cars that are exported by their pals living abroad. There are fashion shops in Europe and America whose stylists and designers are in Nigeria. Many software developers prefer to produce in India and sell across the world. I cannot count the numbers of those who have reinvested what they earn from auto sales into estate developing business.

In view of the above, all what we have discussed so far are on **what to produce** (in products or services) or **what to sell** (either as a tangible, visible goods or services). For both, there is inevitable need to identify the right track to be successful. Based on what we have passed in the messages, production of producer is simply focused on the identified need to bridge a vacuum and hence meeting a defined or discovered desire of consumers. It is either one is a producer (as illustrated earlier) of commodity (tangible goods and visible services). By the word 'one', we mean an individual, a government, an association, an alma matter, a professional body, a regulatory body, a faith, a culture, a ministry, a department, an agency, an institution, an event, a ceremony, a process, a time in history, a race and an object. Each of these can identify what to produce for target customers or clients for others to sell. For instance, under food security project, Ministry of Agriculture could identify modern ways to boost production with the introduction of quarantined seeds and modern farm inputs especially incentives for farmers. And by so doing, engage more hands than before. Production demands inputs from different specialized manpower. A producer is incomplete without the sellers. Just as the producers are inseparable without sellers, within and private, sellers also have line of staff as their strength to attain set objective. Truly, there is wisdom in the creation of things in pairs as the incorruptible scriptures reveal. In summary, all who desire to set up a business must either be a producer or a seller. You either produce for the sellers or you produce and sell the item yourself with your team or staff on paid employment. Sometimes, one may go solo by being the producer and seller as got in mobile technicians. These have technical knowledge and decide to hawk the service without a staff. And what is produced or sold is meant to fill a vacuum created. Without doubt, there is always a vacuum for think tanks to unveil. There are great and hidden **opportunities** to create new jobs as we have been able to do since the first dot on the paper. They need explorers positively. Yes, positive-minded explorers are needed to create peaceful worlds. They need those who can exploit them. They are at your beck and call. Ask me what? They are without doubt lucrative jobs **opportunities**-hidden and visible. They are hidden to those without the sixth sense and third eye. Those with the third eyes see them. Some bypass them every day. Yet, all of them are still searching for gainful jobs. These

opportunities keep knocking on your door at every second are opportunities. Some are migrating away without notice. If those far away seize the **opportunities**, they would re-package them and sell them to you. Those are the best people evolved for mankind. It is high time the brains (wisdom, natural thinking faculty) were put to task. Open your minds. Let your mindset be aware that limitless are these opportunities. No object, land, person, institution… is created idle. 'Waste' is man-designed word of the philologists. The word only appears in man-written dictionary. No thing is created or labeled a waste by the Creator from the revelations of the scriptures. Subject your thinking and other faculties into long and critical meditation. Natural ideas that would open paths to **opportunities** would come your way. And you find meaning and purpose for all the creation around you. I was about to defend one of my new projects at a place when I got another business to work on. This was an **opportunity**. And the previously listed projects are **opportunities** worthy of exploring. The newly discovered business was establishing sugarcane juice spots at tertiary institutions. This is fruit cannery business on mobile at small scale at relevant market. It is a new business as no such business existed in any of the schools before from previous studies. People like sugar cane just like varieties of fruits, but they do not know that there are latest machines to squeeze the water content from the sugarcane. Source for blenders and movable equipment to squeeze all other fruits to prepare fresh drink for the target consumers. Wherever you are, listen to people; study the need of the people and mood of places and several employment **opportunities** could knock the doors to your hearts and brains! If you ask me of the business proposal taken to the place, it was the first online library in the nation! Many schools, particularly tertiary institutions, believe in the establishing of the e-libraries which could only serve the community alone. When I was asked about my project; I told the interviewer that it touches the larger community and one of the opportunities created from e-commerce that would attract forex to the national treasury. Let all artisanal products and services be promoted on the national e-market platform and new jobs under logistics shall be created.

Again, listen to me. Ideas at your doorstep are looking for you- individuals, governments, MDAs, organizations, institutions, professional bodies, alma mater, tribes, associations, parties, businesses... Turn them into lucrative jobs. China is called the workshop of the world simply because of certain provision in the environment that are lacked in others. This is an opportunity for business to thrive there. Why did they see Dubai as shopper's world? What is in France that is so referred to as fashion world centre? Every appellation to a person, a nation, a company open rooms for employment opportunities, seize them. Heed my counsel. Except government is given idea on how to create new jobs and the private owners of businesses, both are thinking how to cut their costs on salaries and other social welfare on workers. Every opportunity is in two faces as illustrated in an earlier sub-chapter. Every failure or inadequacy creates definite and infinite **opportunities** to start good and viable businesses. Every success paves way for a number of opportunities to start jobs. Therefore, it is high time you stopped wasting you irreversible priceless ever-fleeting time on the streets in search of what is not lost. Asking or wondering of what is not lost! Yes, what is not lost! Not just that, what is available everywhere like the air is never scarce to find. Along the streets, they are found. In the newspapers, they are daily published. On all electronic media, they are in thousands. In the social status, they are in abundance. In the residential and industrial areas are different **opportunities**. On the shops, they are found. On the vans, they are advertised. Everywhere you look, you find them. Fortunately, they are created every day by different events and people-knowingly or unknowingly. Too numerous where you make your choice, they are. What is this again, you may ask? Listen to me, it is something that turns the idlers into active and viable. It is what adds values to them socially and economically. It is something that can make you wine and dine with big guns. It is what is giving names and goodwill to the doers. When someone has his name written in gold or in the sands of time, he might have specialized in one. It is the **opportunity** at your doorstep. Even though raw at first instance, brush it, wash it, grease it and it gives you a stand. Eh wait, apply your wits. What do the students intend to do with their certificates after years of burning candles and researches to present papers, projects and theses? That is the answer to all the parables.

Jobs are at the doorsteps of yours. Never again waste your time looking what is very near to you! Follow me paragraph by paragraph and start developing one or two.

Starting from social status; by this, we believe in the words from the incorruptible scriptures that men are created in ranks and files. The poor are in different class just as the rich too. Money, wealth of natural resources, skills, talents, personality based on qualifications, position of authority, marital status, affiliations and sex determine different social status of people. The need of a nuclear family is different from those of the extended family. The needs of the orphans are different from those with parents. The needs of the widows and widowers are different from those who are single parents. The needs of bachelor and spinsters are different from those of the married. What the mentally and physically strong need is different from those of the disables. The components in all environments like the geographical location, the climatic condition, the religion environment, the cultural environment, the socio-political environment among others are the eyes openers to jobs **opportunities**. What the segmented people that fall in different categories need are the openers into jobs creation opportunities. These open the doors to different jobs opportunities for socio-economic thinkers among the entrepreneurs and sellers.

In retrospect, all environments are inhabited by different classes of people. Segment the people by status to create endless **opportunities**. These are in need of different convenience things. Think for the disables, they need convenience of life. Create virtual schools and staff for the blind. A broadcast media station collaborate with a virtual school to start e-learning class towards prepare ordinary level students where such final year students who watch the tutorial classes on the station could have the episode downloaded with an app at a cheap price affordable to the pupils. What comes to your mind? Can you design your business, talent, skill along this pattern? Create virtual library with audio books or relevant materials for your target market. And this is an **opportunity** to create jobs for thousands directly and indirectly. Makers and sellers are in big money if the **opportunities** are seized positively. Wealthy and popular <u>Steve Wonders</u>,

<u>Dan Marayas</u> (of the blessed memory) of this world need thinkers among the manufacturers and sellers. Create better reading facility for the blind. Think for the deaf. Think for the sick. The successful motivational speakers like the wealthy <u>John Foppe</u> need thinkers among the business owners. Think for them and get your bucks. Driverless cars, voice-cars, fast trains are made for certain people. The nature of their jobs and schedules not excluding their incomes create the **opportunities** for the makers and suppliers. The rich deserve to enjoy their wealth. Create comfortable materials and facilities that would suite their status. If it is possible, the children of the rich would love to ride on computer-based bicycle pointing compass, appreciate distinct electronic toys, wearing costly and designer dress, eating class of foods and studying in special schools. The rich man lives distinctive life full of luxury. Create internet-compliant cars at any price, recordable pens, recording eye glass, mobile gym, detachable homes for tourists, video-pen, talking car, flying boats, and the minority buyers would patronize them from auto-makers. The class of the rich lives in clusters. Visit the residential areas they occupy and think for their needs. What they need create **opportunity** to get employed. Many could afford mobile homes, mobile gardens for relaxation, all these could be a lucrative job for the mobile events planners and managers. The poor men living on the land needs are plenty. Their families have different tastes as the income determines. They cut the coat according to the piece of cloths. Among them are the handicapped and the sick just we have those who are physically strong and healthy. Some are living in slums when some are living average lives. The needs of those people create **opportunity** for makers of different products and services including the suppliers or sellers. Those people living on the seas need floating schools, floating hospitals, floating post offices and floating relaxation spots among others; these are jobs **opportunities**.

In retrospect, create them and make your mark in the sands of time. Provide for the needs as a producer or supply them as a seller. Great opportunities to make it big are at your doorstep as your august visitors. Think for the classes of people therein too. Internet libraries in certain schools are possible based on the target users like the corporate bodies for video-conferencing, e-researching, e-learning among other uses. Not for the poor are the luxurious goods and services, create for the poor what they need at the place of needs. The above explains it all. Visit the orphanage; visit the rehab centres, visit the hospitals, visit the prisons and discover the needs of inmates. The place they occupy determines the need of each class of people. Get the needs listed and limitless opportunities have been created to make your bucks!

Are you a good observer? Do you read all prints between the lines? Do you ever think of what is the foundation of all inventions you see around? Then, you have to apply your faculties even the sixth sense. Let me take you to a journey around you. I am ready you to ignite creativity in you in a good way to develop jobs opportunities from what people do always. Do you know that the social sites are created from building electronic form of entertaining guests at home? You asked how? Yes, you entertain your guests with your albums and chat with them, do you? Do you create issues to talk about to keep the atmosphere warm? Do you give room for the guests to contribute their minds? Do you entertain them with films and other spices of life? Those are some of the views ingredients use to build most of the social sites. Remember that an auditorium or stadium that is filled up with spectators attract sellers of products? Yes, the producers and sellers who have the interests to popularize their products do so where there are large convergence of people like stadium. The more the attraction to the social sites the more the products are known. And this is where the sites owners are making their legal money! Add this to that. Do you know that people needs social connections to sell their skills and products? Do you aware that these people are like a bird of a feather in psychological and physiological attitudes? Connecting people of similar profession or skills in forum, or the applicants together lead to the creation of such site like **linkedin** where professionals meet the interested candidates for posts. **Goodreads** is a site created by those who think of helping the bookworms shopping for books. Do you see the opportunity of creating such site shopping for specialized book for scholars, institutions and libraries? A chance to display a product online has created another chance to have online selling and distribution sites. Can some people create book reviews sites for the potential buyers online and offline?

Now, think of different behaviours of people and even other living creatures; study their mode of life-economic, social and political even the technological and spiritual lives. All these could lead you into creation of sites that are relevant to them and you will see the rush into the sites for advertisers to place adverts on. Break the population into segments based on age group, sex, ethnic, qualification, affiliations, values be it religion, ideology, cultural to commence the operation of thinking for them. Take the path of the social sites earlier illustrated. And you would end up creating jobs from sites building. Study the existing sites, look for some vacuums, create a bridge and introduce something unique and by so doing you have created new products and services from the existing products and services.

Browse biographies. Make business out of biographies in electronic production and sites celebrating the celebrities in different areas of life endeavours. And huge adverts such activities would attract. Study business organizations. Do they need your technical skills or additional training forum? What could be done to enhance achieving the corporate goals? Turn the opportunities into electronic format to make money. Build relevant sites for similar organizations to enjoy internal and external economies of scale. The simple arithmetic to build a site is: People, business organizations, institutions, others (as segmented) **plus** their peculiar interests (listed after identification and analyses) **plus** technology (Information and Communication Technology skills). Think and work in changing the chalkboard or tempo boards into different types (by sizes, aesthetics, contents, colours, shapes) of electronic boards for the use of classrooms pupils. This is a tablet of knowledge that would contain all the subjects, practices, activities for pupils and teachers, tests with different forms of graphical illustrations. Turn the magic magnetic boards in different sizes and shapes into bigger ones for classrooms for schools from the elementary to the tertiary institutions.

In short, conventional publishers are advancing every day moving with fast developing technology; turning global physical books into digital books in the tablets especially related books under your label under one cover for all the levels of education. Many can run online libraries for specialized courses. They could partner with tertiary institutions to run bookless libraries in the schools. The same could be done at institutions like medical, engineering, technology among others. Through the running of e-marketplace to sell their books, they could employ several thousand of sellers online and boost the logistic environment of the nation. This is limitless jobs creating opportunities as creativity is infinite and never an ethnic-bound. What do you think?

Recently, university admission board (in Nigeria) introduced Computer-Based Tests for millions of students getting admissions into the tertiary institutions. This has attracted the attention of schools creating e-libraries where the facilities could be converted for a price by the prospective university candidates. The facility could also be used for e-conference centres for firms, box-office for film makers. Let the event halls step up their places to attract new businesses to partner in the use of the facilities. This efforts would make the facility all-year round use. At a time when the subventions to the tertiary institutions in the nation was dwindling, I sent proposals to them on how they can be financially independent from selling their intellectual property online. With this, all stakeholders would be earning directly and indirectly.

In the implementation of education restructuring, new books from authors alongside with instructional materials must be provided showing the new jobs for different classes of people and business institutions. In addition, nations shall create new jobs from ensuring that all specialized tertiary institutions only admit students and run courses that are related. If the colleges and universities of agriculture run courses that are agricultural-based, and supports are given the graduates, several thousands of jobs shall be created not to talk of added value chains of jobs. If the agriculture research institutes feed the agricultural-based colleges with the research findings, self-sufficiency in food production and raw materials for the agro-allied industries become a guaranty. Let the same applies to technological and humanity colleges and the result in employment creation and revenue generation are enhanced. Let us assume the other sectors are also restructured. New jobs shall be created.

Statisticians, update your knowledge. Be your own boss. Add information and communication skills to your knowledge to create relevant sites many desire to launch into. The collected data can attract viewers in large number among the researchers and students of different background. The huge followers would get you the commercial traffics from advertisers. Create sites for the unemployed and the vacancies in your sites with relevant data and enjoy the traffic to sell the site to firms here and there. Create site for schools celebrating education. Slots for admission processes and what the students would enjoy including the information that helps the followers should be included. And the huge crowds would create your business partners. Do not think with your eyes. Think with your brains. Do not be selfish with your collections. Transform them into commercial use in websites. Throw up competitive sites and grab your own market share. Give the booksellers a fight for their money. Create book serialization site to review the popular books for students and public readers. The attractive the sites, the large the followers in number and the advertisers are coming to place their products and services. Do special ones for films and make your trademark known to users online. Endless are the sites that could be created. Apply your grey matter. 'Competition challenges the intellect' as **Eddie Iroh** rightly quoted. 'It is good for the soul, for the intellect. Monopoly does not' he concluded. This is a job for as many ambitious related professionals as possible as competition creates room for quality and varieties of choices for consumers.

Where are you the freelance writers and broadcasters? Jobs opportunities are there to be created for people. Use the existing platforms of the print and electronic media to sell you intelligence. Let the celebrated freelance broadcaster buy some hours to sell his own television. This is television in television or cable in cable. Let the popular freelance writers or columnists buy some slots inside the newspapers and sell his skills of investigative impressions and adverts are coming their ways.

Are you a person who ignores what you heard on radio or other media outlets? Stop this act. You have lost golden opportunities to create lucrative jobs and make legitimate money. Over the media you would have such adverts on life changing business seminars and workshops, attend to the choice one to start developing viable skills. Many are products that are in abundance but are scarce in some other nations. Those who have the information would knock all doors spreading the message. It is done through the media. Ignorant person throws raw gold with his catapult for his lack of knowledge. Many a company need independent sellers and re-sellers of their products through the media they advertise themselves. Follow the media and be friendly with the crew within.

Imagine those living in the diaspora. I mean the migrants in other people's lands outside the shores of their own nations. It is a fact that you are living thousands of miles away from the homes of your ancestors. You don't need to add your number to those of the nationals roaming the streets in search of gainful jobs. For allowing you into the nations under any asylum is a grace. Never become a social burden to the hosts. Do not be either a parasite or a saprophyte. Live a symbiotic life. You are permitted in to contribute positive quota into the host economy and social lives. Work to add values to their economic development and the nationals. Engage in reminiscence jobs. Revive the food culture of your race in diaspora to make good money from their patronage. Revive the entertainment sector of your race to have places to relax their nerves after hours of hectic jobs in offices. Create indigenous relaxation spots for them in the host nation. Create viable businesses to employ your own people too. The population of the community of the speakers of similar dialect is enough to tap opportunities. Take a cue from the Jewish community in Europe and America. Many profitable businesses are created by them. The businesses employ their own race and the hosts. Emulate the Pakistanis in America and United Kingdom. Many a business that is legitimate you can import from your nation to add values to the host nation. Create indigenous newspaper for them to read to revitalize your dying dialects. Run indigenous programs on the electronic media under collaboration efforts with existing media outlets. In short, media-enhanced jobs are opportunities for the few to explore. Entertain them with the folktales in the media and your language never becomes extinct as you make your bucks! Run eateries selling indigenous foods to your own people. Create home away from home instead of chasing scarce jobs in offices meant for the home populace! A friend of mine, Adam, told me about his former place of work at Dubai. The company, owned by Indians, employed over 90% Indians as its employees. He could only identify two who are from Africa. Imagine the number of jobs created for its own indigenes. I read, in the course of the research about alibaba.com based in China. In a year, it claimed to have provided jobs for three million Chinese. Just as online businesses are employing thousands and millions, with the right platform in the environment you are, create jobs for at least your own people. Trace the employee list in any company; it will be clear as day that indigenous people take the largest share even if the local content law is not in place. Nepotism is in the veins of all even though the natural religion tries to unite us in brotherhood. If it were you, would you employ people that do not understand your language? Let the gifted among create lucrative businesses that would employ your own people there. This is an invaluable economic relief to the host nation!

Move up from there to enter other businesses. Establish your mark in the sands of time. Many young aspiring undergraduates are never aware that there are new courses of study that are in hot demand in the market. Many software applications are in need of designers. Many companies are in need of certain specialists that are in short supply in the market. It takes visits and counsels of career counselors in schools to educate the folks before applying for the oversupplied skills. It took a friend the second thought to decide to go for Fire Safety Engineering in his school for his second degree. A browse into the course in all the institutions in the nation, the course is never found. Being a new course showed to him as a course worth of study. Schools introduce new courses or re-package a course to suit the need of the labour market. And employments are created for staff and publishers of educational and informational knowledge-based materials. Imagine the teaching of how to create drones for different purpose of vigilance. Such experts in the creation of different types of drones would be a commercial success in the market later. Heed this golden piece of advice. As a student, whenever you are introduced into a new course, think over the success and inevitability in the market in the future and now; grab the opportunity if it is worth it! Sincerely, the making of drones would prove to be one of the latest sought-out for job at your fingertip. When companies are in dire need of a particular professional, they pay such heavy remuneration. Mark my word!

A guy, fresh from school, got some vital information inside the bus while coming down to his place. The discussion was on the viability of snails in hotels in a state. Fortunately, he knew a town where eating of snails was a taboo. In the town, snails bred in thousands. He was a fast learner of languages. He had the opportunity to have learnt the language of his previous host while in the service. By this, he was loved by the villagers. The young eavesdropper inside the bus, what did he do? He sourced for more information about the hotels at the place where buyers were concentrated. He collated the selling price of the snails with sizes. Off he went back to the town of snails where he was a beloved for understanding their dialect. With peanuts to encourage young scavengers in the village, he started loading the snails and sold at the hotels where his clients were waiting for the supplies. This was how he got the opportunity and made optimal use of it! He discovered what was saleable and at where. He made use of his educational attainments (intelligence and brilliance) to locate the buyers, got some of them, used those ones as business links to secure more clients, within and beyond, bargained the price, mapped out his movement and cost, and relocate the source where the products needed could be got in large quantity.

In a chat, a woman that came from a town of about 1000km was told that the jewelry she put on was just fifty cent (in dollar value). This was a chain she bought at over ten dollar. She was taken to the place where the precious gold bracelets were sold. She bought all she could with all the thousands of national currency with her. Within two days, she had sold out the materials and made over three thousand percent profits from the sales! This is the secret that many traders never share with others. She got the opportunity from chatting. Do you see the reason why the buyers must learn the secrets of buying? Eavesdrop to get opportunity. Throw challenges at people to learn from their wisdom and intelligence. Chat in the social chat rooms in the sites visited. Throw open debates to learn of opportunity. Listen and analyse people's comments, suggestions, enquiries and recommendations to discover opportunities. Apply grey matter when necessary to make optimal use of the identifiable opportunities.

I learnt in the course of research that children learnt more from songs and poetry. I took it up to produce poetry-like rhymes for difficult subjects like Mathematics. Some of the juicy children stories are re-written in verse. Many who are technical-based could develop technical games for the children teaching such difficulty subjects to tease their brains.

The complaint of customers of the post-paid metres has developed interest for pre-paid metres. Electrical contractors take it up as good opportunity to reap their gains through supplying the customers. Do you study the clients of different products or services? What do they need urgently? Make provision for them and get your perks!

A new resident found out that there was no green field in the residential area. What did he do? He created and developed some plots of land for commercial use of the residents for use at a price. This is how private car parks and car wash proliferate in the business districts and open markets. The need has created the opportunity to starting making a good business. Many residential areas with beautiful greenery lack greens keepers just like many golf clubs. Imagine the opportunity that has been created after the jobs of the florists and horticulturists! Cudgel your brains over the dump sites within, think about disposal of the dumps, think about sorting out the dump materials, think about recycling of the materials in the dumps. Think of other inevitable needs of different public and private places, provide for the need and get your bucks as desired! What does this teach you? Every provision creates another or several other opportunities for creative users of opportunities.

It is ridiculous to meet graduates of tertiary and technical institutions looking for jobs. It is high time they are stopped from being partakers in all forms of underemployment and casualisation through vacancies for contract staff in industries. Many of them are prospective entrepreneurs that can effectively employ those with the skills from other lower institutions and vocational schools.

Most of them, if not all, might have come across what could pay their bills in the course of study, but they neglect the opportunities. Most of the contents of the courses of study contain what could develop entrepreneurial spirit in them. For those who cannot develop one, the ability to sell other's products or services would have been taught. This writer was challenged in Entrepreneurial Development Course (EDC) class while dealing with Small Business Management (a course of study). The lecturer told us to prepare against the next class the feasibility studies of ten different jobs that are never in existence in our residential places. The content simply means that we should create new jobs from the existing jobs. The inference has produced the research-based book of the same title by yours sincerely currently on sale throughout the world. The challenge of the lecturer created the book. That is a form opportunity usually takes. Whenever you are challenged, dive within you, think deeply and grab the opportunity to produce a tangible product or service!

I am reluctant to tell you this. The certificates and garnered experience you have got have created enough opportunity to become a top echelon in the scheme of things. If you never know how to search for relevant jobs with them, learn the art. I mean the art of searching for jobs. Never wait inside your room searching for your astray pet. Do not sit back, I say. Up from that reclining and relaxing position! Wake up for something. Pursue the dream jobs where they rightly belong. Jobs are advertised in different medium. In different institutes are periodical bulletin where you find yours if you search for them. In the internet sites are different jobs that you are the most suitable person for. How many hours have you earmarked for the search on internet, prints and electronic? Create valuable time to surf internet. It won't cost you more than nest egg. Do you contact the recognized recruitment agencies? Do you know that you can also run outsourcing jobs especially recruitment of suitable workers for companies as a professional personnel management graduate? But, I believe you can rise to become celebrated outsourcing firm later in life among the renowned international recruitment companies. After all, those in the job started somewhere at sometimes. They never started as a big firm but the business grew gradually to be so recognized. This is the main theme of this work-job sourcing. It is a business to ease the burdens of searching for jobs called outsourcing in the modern business language. Many firms intend to transfer the procurement responsibility on to other private bodies' neck. Can you bear the burden for the gains attached? You would end up recruiting for banks, oil and gas industry, aviation and much more. Get started from the little. Get connected to the human resources departments of different industries. Good rapports with the head would do the jobs. Get the lists of the vacant posts within different sectors. List out what they want; what the person(s) for the job(s) possess as per requirements-age, status, qualifications, skills, proficiency, fluency, experiences and other details. Demand for the remuneration for each post. And with an interview recorded in the midget, you could get out to place the jobs on your notice boards. Let applicants pay for employment forms. File the photocopies of the documents with the recent picture. Keep two different files. Keep one with you and the other to the firm in need of employees. Interview and keep their files. Send the original with their pictures to the company. And by so doing, you are doing a fantastic Public Relation job!

The same way you outsource for manufacturers. Get the information about the raw materials they are in dire need. Search for information of where they are largely and cheaply found. Meet the producers or their agents (company representatives) and set for supplying business.

A guy started his cable television product selling business from selection of free stations. He only needs to have specialized theme. There could be faith-based cable products. He could go into sports only. In short, the facilities in existence are adequate to create new business ideas.

I know of talented comedians who are good in packaging their talents to attract crowds from all walks of lives and therefore become attractive to advertisers and businesses. They smile to banks and move with the big guns in the society. Several ideas could be created from the talented comedian. Create league for the comedians like in football. Create tournaments or tours for their shows. They add flavours to fashion shows, sports and entertainment industry. The corporate firms need them for their annual general meetings. The government circles need their services. Promote them with your social resources or connections. Never stay idle. Do not waste the resources and connection. Sell the talents to sports, entertainers for a good price. Sell them into the sports kits makers and corporate firms as their ambassadors. Think of what is saleable at their shows. Be agents to show case them and get your share. This is what makes the sportsmen what they are. The sports create jobs for scouts, coaches, trainers, psychologists, physicians among others.

Visit the classes or categories of markets and institutes (schools, public places, offices) of different classes of people to discover what they lack. The need they lack is an opener to get your perks. Be aware that every environment must lack a need. What they lack provide the chance (opportunity). Many a market lacks aesthetics. Many of them are in dire need of comfort stations. Many need relaxation spots within. Complementary products are what others need. Supply them and receive your perks. Many shops owners need different services-mobile or immobile. And the need is limitless just as the wants. Limitless opportunities are created to create gainful jobs. Jobs, in form of services like helping services or supplying some products to shops. This is possible by distribution for a fee. In the places are always some vacuum. Fill them and get your due perks!

The classes of their affiliations based on society or theology could lead you to banks. Provide or supply what they need at your segmented places and reap your gains for all the efforts.

Many immigrants need your services just as tourists need tourist guides. Do any of these for a wage. Those who started small end up big in size. A journey of one thousand kicks off with a step. 'Becoming a man is never a day job besides Rome was not built in a day' as the saying teaches!

Engage in the cultural jobs enhanced by the environment you are. Turn the forest into a large scale farm of cash crops. Turn the riverside into fishing grounds. How can a child of herdsmen be searching for scarce jobs outside the cultural jobs? Modernize and create ranches to avoid health crises at old age. Nations that are facing the challenges of the fights between the farmers and the herdsmen could create ranches with all facilities for the herdsmen at a small charge for maintenance. This is an avenue to create job for the guards. Develop the jobs into commercial levels and those in the cities would extol your courage! If you cannot engage in farming or fishing, be the sellers of the products as a profitable service. Sell to the cities what you buy at good price at the villages. Being a link is a valuable job, I insist. Invest your gains on the producers in the farms and seas; before you know it, you have become employers of labour setting the target produce and quantity!

Tap the opportunities at your doorstep or roaming the streets. Never turn blind eyes or deaf ears. Don't just read, listen or view for the fun of it. Get the message right. It must not slip away. What is it? It is a package from an author or celebrated writers, renowned poets and entertainers. Author of a bestselling book is giving you this mouthwatering offer. Charismatic and eloquent speakers have challenged your senses to start something new. They desire you to hit it big. Hit the ground running with the public launching and presentation. Get the work acted or repackaged in audio for commercial target. Become a virtual tutor with the content. Engage in seminars and workshop with the content. Re-compose the work into acting scripts. And in the process of doing any of this, you have engaged yourself positively with lucrative jobs! What you only need to do, get the consent of the author. Break the leg!

Turn around your skill of writing and ability to read and digest. You could become abridged version writer of bestselling books. What about becoming films and documentaries reviewers in abridged formats? Get the authorization knocking at your door, and be gainfully employed!

Start investing the perks and grow your investments. Get started and opt out of the association of idlers. Get your buck and start moving it up and down buying blue chip investments. You have started moving up the ladder where all would see you on top. Your eyes has been opened to the opportunities knocking at your door! Open the door for it or them. Grab the opportunity!

What do you make out of the materials on your domestic pets? Do you aware of the hairy goats and sheep of yours are needed by the textile operators to produce cash mere sweaters? Do you aware that the amount of milk being got from your cattle could turn into a commercial value? Do you ever aware that the tough pet of yours are being searched for purchase by security outfits? Turn them into jobs opportunity. It is sad for a student of a tertiary institution that was into breeding albino rats for laboratories abandoning the lucrative jobs for certificates that are not guarantee lucrative jobs many years after their attainment. Can you pick up such abandon job? Or can you go further breeding rabbits for laboratory usage? Those are opportunities staring at you, grab them. Do not just breed pets as pastime or for the fun of it, make perks from them!

A retiree came for business counsel. His interest was into commercial production of broilers. 'Why the broilers when there are many operating the same business? Don't you know that those with bigger investments could send you packing with price war?' I enquired. "What else can I go into that is related to breeding broilers?" He asked. Many things I answered. Stay unique. Learn the art of breeding turkey. And home bred turkey could be more patronized than the imported. What do you think? Many are into broilers neglecting breeding of turkey in commercial quantity for consumers. And the market share of turkey is very big if not bigger than the broilers. This he picked up as a great opportunity. He changed his interest to be one of the pacesetters in the commercial production of turkey. 'The early bird, they say, catches the fattest worm'

The soil and the climate around you make the right environment for medicinal and ornamental plants. How much of the space do you use for this? Turn the premises into a right usage. Visit the soil scientists and get the message right. Validate it and become engaged positively!

Visit libraries to read tomes of books. New books are stocked virtually every day. In the books are secrets revealed to the writer. You should know that the writers are inspirational. What you do not know, you find in prints. Get yourself updated. Keep learning and learning from reading. Browse books as you browse internet.

Whatever you find on internet is first of all reduced to print. Read into the past. Read into the present. Project for the future based on the content to make hay while the sun shines. The **opportunities** are ahead. Asking about the **opportunities** in visiting libraries? You could script the writs. Thinking about users? Film makers, publicists, advertisers, consultants, public commentators, researchers, strategists and many professionals of course! What are you in the libraries for? You are there as a solution maker for all burning issues! Do this and engage your time. Engage the idle time to improve your knowledge and earn the pay!

From the gains in reading and researching, develop children-centred films in different dialects. Create bilingual films teaching technology combined with social values. There is enough production of adult films. Create films teaching moral or religion-inclined values and projecting the future to the youths. As their books sell so also will be their films. Treat the children like the adult buyers. They are very important personalities who deserve some privacy and respect. Create sections for the children to shop themselves. This is a good **opportunity** for you the film producers!

I counseled a man recently on the creatable jobs from running spacious bookstores without having a rented shop. I introduced online bookstores and how to partner with the existing sellers across the continents. Many publishers in the advanced economy are engaging in Print On Demand self-publishing. All the operations are done online. It is high time bookstores owner established library within the four walls. And the guests are got through subscriptions. A few schools are enough to make his bucks. What about running mobile bookshops with trolleys and vehicles in major markets and streets? What about running online retail or even wholesale in the increasing the sales volumes of the stores? Imagine numerous **opportunities** at the door step of the owners!

Endeavour to create brain teasers for the children. In form of games, they could be created. In form of instructional materials, they could be formed. Produce them for commercial purpose and make your mark.

Speaking toys working with engine could attract children of the average income earners and especially the rich. Friendly pets should however be the most saleable. A good opportunity is it for the technology firms. Enter into this and create a niche. What about those ones as instructional materials for school pupils? Engage in mass production and get your bucks in droves!

At the entrance of public places, particularly the market environments, are challenges facing the dwellers. The producers and the sellers most especially are having weak sales problem. Proffer solutions and get your dues. One of the problems of the prospective buyers is solved in opening their eyes to gainful jobs. This is already solved in books on jobs creation especially this!

Go global and research on issues for sale. Many institutions are into search for practicable solutions to key issues. Work on them and share the abstracts online. Sell the abstracts to them online and you are called to the rostrum to deliver your paper. Sell abstracts backed with relevant video clips. This is a good package for all international organizations and institutions for a good price. All these are done for the deserved perks in your accounts!

What you read and learn from media outlets are enough to provide you an office and pay your dues. Wasting the knowledge and the exposure would do you no good. In the papers are several news headlines that create scripts for film makers. In the adverts are vacancies to fill.

Several opportunities are on your table, you the tech-entrepreneurs. Wherever you look, they are there in thousands. Create virtual tutors and tutorials for different professional disciplines. Become a technical virtual tutor if you have garnered so much practical experience. Specialise in autos especially electronic cars. Turn your solutions into online and offline jobs. Update your software as the virus makers update theirs. Become a virtual service provider and get your account credited with cash. Sell your capability and technical ability through the blogs. Be unique in the package of yours. This is a good opportunity you must not afford to lose!

Re-write your collections in different dialects especially the popular ones. Publishers and producers are in dire need of the collections. Make efforts to write dialect-based dictionaries, collect the proverbs, folks and tales of the ancients from the elders and on the path of honour you are treading!

Shop for all types of libraries (book and bookless e libraries) and you have started a good job. Many owners have less time to do the shopping. Become a mobile librarian if you can afford the task. Do the same for the bookstores. An arrangement with the owners could give you the chance. Endeavour to hawk best sellers for the immobile bookstores owners and you start making your money. Sell to the executives and immobile managers of big companies. Create clients among the top schools within and outside. As you shop for booksellers, shop for the libraries of firms especially consultants of different profession. Stock the libraries for them with latest books in different formats and earn it big. Mobile libraries are some handsets devices, iphones and ipads. Create special tablets containing the technical or electronic vocabularies and idioms. In different sizes, shapes and designs for different classes of target buyers and users. Think how you can help uploading books for the technically ignorant users for a price. Many libraries need upgrading. Turn convectional library into virtual section. Locate areas where there are none, establish libraries as a commercial business. Encourage reading contests within the room. And you have engaged yourself rightly and positively.

Visit social sites. Not for fun but for facts and reliable information. Get the facts to develop the scripts. Ensure you test the facts and all information as studies show that some information are simply adulterated and misleading. Do not just develop scripts, you could develop but distinct blogs if you have software programming and engineering background. The contents of which would proffer solutions to burning issues. Imagine collating the right jobs for specialized professionals. Imagine collating solutions for climate change from sites. Imagine gathering marketing solutions for firms facing weak sales. Take problems to the sites and get the ways out. Do this and get the buck from users. Get to sites and connect yourself to businesses. Do not join a business for the fun of it. Like a business because of mutual benefits. And your resources and quality could endear you to them for lucrative jobs. Can you sell other people's products or services of firms outside your shores? Jobs are there for grab. You are an inch to becoming a seller of the product! Many online book retailers are in dire need of private but interested sellers like you. Visit their sites and work things out! That's an **opportunity** at your door step, it is up for grab.

Are you still on internet? Are you really internet-savvy? How do you handle the limitless information from different quarters on internet? Do you make commercial use of them? What about the service providers like the social media? What do you make from using their platforms? Or do you think that they are online for fun? Nay, they are eyes openers to business **opportunities**! Are you versatile and creative in the technological devices? What stops you from picking up several **opportunities** knocking at your doors all days and nights? As you used to do for vacancies and advertisements inside prints, do you apply the same for the classified and unclassified adverts from the online media to identify jobs opportunities? Several online jobs are there waiting for exact person like you! You are meant for the jobs that are really designed and meant for you, apply and supply your resume online! If you have no contribution in production to internet, attach yourself to producers or promoters to become their affiliate sellers at a commission in forex. Boost your profile on the social media with right responses to issues and by this, you have huge crowd followers. With increasing followers, you are a stone's throw to be earning from shared advertisements. Most bloggers start from releasing captivating contents! Check their blogs!

The internet-savvy idlers, do you intend to make best use of the limitless contents within the search engines? Many foreign transactions you can enter into except you ignore them or intend to engage with evil intention. Never go there, you scammers. The long hand of the law would soon catch up on you. Talking to genuine users, many good business you can transact on internet, engage yourself and make the legitimate perks! Investors itch for business links. Work things out, do the job for an agreed fee. Invest in mobile and immobile assets needed by prospective investors. The return on investment is huge. And the jobs **opportunity** creatable is huge. With your own money you start the search and take along the embassy on the agreement and the job. Get it done and get your shares!

What do you do with idle funds at banks? Invest the buck and get greater bucks. Add values to the idle stagnant money in savings and deposits into better lucrative venture. Become franchise producers of products with good brand and start making more money and fame as industrialist. Buy technologies in internet. Finance the technologies with your stagnant deposits. Take the path of the gurus in the information and communication technology business. Enter into partnership with collaboration with export-import banks to buy raw materials for sale or selling finished products as an independent body. Create more houses and movable or detachable settlements for the homeless for good return on investments. Invest in mobile comfort stations for users in the public functions. Grab the golden opportunities to become realtor in collaboration with the mortgage banks. Do these and engage many-direct and indirect workers from those roaming the streets in search of gainful jobs.

For you that have no penny at banks but naturally talented and skillful. Many a deposits are in the banks as intervention funds for your use. Visit the central banks to be aware of where the cash or grant is domiciled. Explore the chance and bail yourself out of joblessness. In banks, within and outside are such funds accessible for climate change, researches, sports development, entertainment industry, mining sector and many other capital-intensive businesses. A letter of credit from many banks could turn your practicable business ideas, raw skill into products for jobs creation to millions on the streets. Imagine the number of jobs **opportunities** that could be created from the provision for miners of liquid and solid minerals in a nation with vast deposits of the natural resources. Discover the source where they are deposited in commercial quantity, get the proofs, prepare the right proposals and the letter of credit would facilitate the funding aspect. With the development in the sector, many industries start springing up absorbing millions directly and indirectly.

A friend created opportunities for creative sellers or agents. Not just a friend, many investors are in the same shoes. They need intelligent people that can create market share for their investments. Get this done and you have made effective use of the **opportunities** for money making. Yes, you own no system, neither printing machine nor spiral binding machine you possess, fortunately, someone very close has all. Many are services on his list. Become an agent based on agreement on the service fees for each of them and get the customers from outside. Tell no more, this is an opportunity at your door step, grab it and work on it to fruition!

Make something big from that idle complaining webmasters around you. Get them seated. Discuss the charges and face the task squarely. Facing the task is getting the clients. Source for clients and make your gains. For every website you did, maybe a certain percentage you share. Create attractive side effects in the sites for prospective advertisers. For every updating of each of the site, certain percentage of the service charge you take. What an opportunity at your doorstep. Use your social resources to get the connections and the more you get, the high the income and keep investing your own!

Turn all the past time activities into lucrative business. Do not just record with your smart-phone, digital camera and systems for fun. Be objective and re-define your focus on the reasons for being a fan. Turn watching your darling teams into commercial gains. Video recording of events are lucrative business that can butter your bread back to back. Videos, in different brands, sell than papers. Take the path of YouTube inventors. Over four billions are watching online productions daily across the world. Imagine the traffics. Imagine the target adverts. Imagine the gains for the efforts. Limitless things (products and services, events even natural disasters) could go viral on air using the internet facilities at your fingertips. Two things I advise you to do to make a breakthrough. Always work to create a practicable content. And strive to produce believable package for commercial success. But, to make huge patronage, aesthetics matter. Create relevant and sensible side effects with your skills in electronic or software engineering. Take a few instances, at football matches, lawn tennis courts, golf greens, swimming pools, athletics fields and other sporting arenas; picking out a football match among the lots, record the thrilling events like the dribbling, the shots, the free kicks, the savings and the hard tackling. All these can be edited by your mobile production studio to sell to football fans after the matches. You could decide several titles for each of the package even from a match. Several titles for the videos from a few matches could fetch you big bucks within a short space of time. Creative side effects from sounds, colours, quotable quotes and some other features could attract crowds of lovers. This is done based on your analyses and others viewpoints as an added values to the video shots.

Teach football science and techniques through your videos. Teach skills through others. Teach teamwork as it ensures success (winning) in some. Teach how matches are won in some cases. There are several aspects videos can show and teach the watchers at their leisure at home. You could wipe out corruption from video recording business. Map out your business plan. If you intend to wipe it out from the streets, start recording your own focus and edit them at the right time for sale to relevant organizations and foundations against such societal vice. If it is corrupt officers taking bribe, shot them at the 'spot of action' and package them for public viewing. If you desire bigger publicity and more earnings, try to go into sports-based blogging. Work with legal practitioners or social activists and you shall reap the gains. Video of the past events in economic and political activities would sell just as the re-publishing of the past news in prints. Develop historical jobs in your clime. Follow the landmark cases in courts. Commercialize them in prints and videos. Publish research findings that are publishable with several inputs through your own revisions. Producing them verbatim is plagiarism. A research is always an eye opener to further research, suggestions, recommendations and comments. Package them into a global standard for money-making.

Start a franchise business with your business skills and interest. Represent foreign brands in the nation and other nations as their sales representatives. Your own company can re-produce the products if you pass through the tests of the original owners. Shop for products that a target population used to look for, enter business agreement with the producer and sell as a dealer to the built customer base in your nation.

Design your own or create your own special designs for makers to sell to target customers. You can design all existing products that would suit the tastes of your clients. Put your graphic art works and creativity into work for companies to produce specialized patented products for you only. Doing so, you are miles apart of the other sellers. Patent rights await you if the designs of the products are yours. Just like the author, the design of fabrics to the textiles is produced to your shop only. Popularize your own brand of products created by your natural intelligence.

Many developed business ideas in the advanced nation could be replicated in the poor nation. Many nations overseas are creating millions of jobs through online and offline business. What stops the poor nation to develop the sector with the available and accessibility to internet facilities by the developing information and communication technology knowledge? Imagine the number of jobs that could be created from online retail business, online media, digitalized business and practices among others.

Schools in Europe and America are creating jobs opportunities for their students. Can the other continents take a cue from this attitude to engage the young ones? Not just this alone, all potential graduates should be nurtured to take practical courses from their chosen courses of studies to be their own bosses. After graduations, they are adequately mentored and empowered by relevant authorities. And by so doing, no graduate would roam the streets in search of scarce jobs. Let me quickly chip this in. you must be aware that many courses that are very costly always have the lowest number of applicants to fill the vacancies. Search for them through adverts and interviews and go after them. Let me ask you a few questions. How many pilots are rendered jobless after trainings? If they are not employed by the commercial airliners, nation's defence would employ them. How many marine engineers are roaming the streets, the same thing that applies to the pilots applies to them. Think for more!

Explore the open door economic policies of the administration to have adequate knowledge of the opportunities of jobs creation from the part of government. Through several bodies jobs opportunities are created indirectly by the government of the day. Move to all the ministries, departments and agencies of governments at all levels; browse their gazettes. Ask for information of what they lack and the budgets of each of the MDAs. In the budgets are the needs for the good of the nation. Do you see anything that can add values? Put up efforts to interview those in vantage position to furnish you with right information. For instance, export and import promotional council always compile the lists of those importable and exportable goods. Make plans on such jobs that can be exhumed from prevalent government policy. Grab the opportunities and start something very gainful!

Create blogs for book and films reviewing, arts, science, festivals, religion teachings, corporate shows, political events and all these would attract very huge traffics. Take permission from the author and publishers of this kind of publication. Design different side effects with the machine to gain followers. Beat the imagination of other sites owners. Become reviewer of texts, graphics and video clips. I mean, review all the best sellers in books, the block busters in films and rest in the specialized blogs and just imagine the traffics. The bigger the likes across the sites, the higher the number of commercial activities and the pay into the business accounts!

Create software for different sectors of the economy. Create management software with a difference. Stop creating virus to attack software. Apply the ICT knowledge positively. Just like books, there is no limit to the number of software for all users. There is opportunity in upgrading and updating of software just as revised edition of books and re-mix of songs and poetry.

Many nations are in short supply of forensic laboratories. Establishing them would have helped stem the tide of crime waves in the nations and speed the judicial system. It is not just forensic labs but of forensic experts for all professional leanings. If a criminality is committed, forensic experts are called upon; if a fraud is perpetuated and all evidences are almost destroyed, forensic software unravels the mystery. This is a challenge to all professional association to imbibe the courses on forensic to solve crises. By adopting this, several employment opportunities are created with their value chains.

What do you make out of reading the Divine scriptures to mankind? Oh! You should have hit it big, had you made the best use of the directives and guides in them. Turn the stories of the prophets into poetry, act the poetry and get the buck for a job well done. Read to audience to make your bucks. Solo acting could attract you to many. Many are solutions to all issues of life. Get them scripted and locate the film makers. Introduce blogs to educate and inspire the growing population of online visitors and users. Get them extracted and solve the crises. Remember many people in the world follow the scripts. Imagine the work and the gains for you. Surfing the scriptures is a great opportunity knocking your door begging for ambitious and religion-inclined like you!

Never hesitate to develop your skill at the right time just like the Bill Gates of this world. Failure to do so, other people might take them up before. Early bird, they say, eats the fattest worm'. If dropping out of schools could help the super musicians and tech-entrepreneurs to be outstanding today, kindly say bye to the four walls in order to develop the discovered skills and nurture the talents of yours at the right time. Instead of becoming the trail blazer; do not be afraid of being labelled a copycat. All inventions are copied by the human discoverers who might surfed the scriptures and studied the natural environment and the creatures within. Ask yourself, what is the paper qualification of the sportsmen in history? I mean the likes of Cristiana Ronaldos, Lionel Messi, Rafael Nadals, Roger Federers, Andy Murrays, Djokovics, of this world! Of course, most of them are not traced to the four walls of classrooms in tertiary institutions but to the relevant sports academies where their skills are discovered. Simply say, the stars are products of academies. Diversify, create entrepreneurial academies for the breeding of entrepreneurs.

Limitless opportunities await you the friends of vendors. Infinite opportunities are on the tables of addict readers of printed materials in offices and joints. Many read but not between the lines. For alphabet, dot, word and paragraph in columns, every news headline, every cartoon (on paper or animation) and graphic illustrations, every advert placed in the prints, many opportunities are begging for use. Read between the lines. Cudgel your brains and get the business ideas crying for you to choose from. Many classified adverts are placed to source for sales agents. Many are placed to source for other services. Every problem written about is cry for solutions, proffer them and contact the right users. The issue of unemployment across the world pushed the writer into all the jobs on jobs creation. A piece of news is enough to create research topics for the creative researchers. Read through the contents. Cogitate and meditate and you would get something out of the news. Study the events being reported and something would come out as business idea. You can start writing biographies of political elites in the good books of people as you take every note of the bad ones for posterity would want pieces of writing about them later. Many old stories called dead stories are good for refreshment and learning from the past. What can you collate about the celebrated thespians on the pages of newspapers? What can you make out of the interviews and editorial reports? They are worthy materials for references in works. Gather them and starting working to exhume ideas for your take-off. Start compiling your facts for publication. Can you get something out of what you read? Doing this, the opportunity has been given the right treatment. If not done, it may slip away and you are left searching for scarce readily made jobs! Create new markets based on different segments and sell the wares. What the selling departments fail to do, your exposure should help you to do and make your mark. Take the path as it could open doors for you!

What comes out of your brains after listening to news, interviews and issues of discuss on the electronic media? All the contents will suffice to develop your scripts. Enough you have heard to design your business idea. Enough you have garnered to become something out of nothing. They are catalysts to get things done! Spice your business with the experiences of the successful gurus you have learnt about in biographies and interviews. Develop new business ideas from these and you have made the best use of the opportunity of using the electronic devices!

Along the roads and highways are billboards. Advertising of services and products cannot be rightly done without the boards. Can you make something out of this? Yes, of course. The opportunity of becoming one is there for you to pick. Gifted in writing captivating piece of adverts? A gifted engineer could design speaking billboards for good price from the business owners. Many a billboard that is electronic-based should be in different designs and content for the public as additional aesthetics to the nation. Embrace the great job. You have landed yourself a big job in the selling product and service! Start collating different better jingles. Work with those with knowledge of graphics in animation. And develop animating adverts for the firms. A lucrative job you have started, grab the chance, it must not allow to swim away like fish in the sea!

One thing is factual. Not all graduates or products from any school would be employers of employees. The employees are produced at the same school to serve the interests of the employers. This makes the synergy work and a confirmation that we are created in ranks and files by the Creator. This is the purpose of creation. Endowment differs from nation to nation and man to man. If you are interested in becoming an employer, you must be ready to pay the price. If you are self-defeatist who is contented to be employee, so be it. Mind you too, be ready to pay the price in order to rise to highest office in your place of work. In the nation, your source, never try dreaming becoming guest worker, your innate entrepreneurial skill is enough to get you on the right track. If you have the intelligent and versatile, you can turn many dying businesses round, you the employers-to-be. You should develop the magic wand. Create business lively environment around you as any in the shoes. As aforementioned under the internet-savvy but idlers still searching for jobs, many jobs are begging to be picked. Sell products of companies especially manufacturing companies, of bakery or catering business, sell services of many service-rendering businesses such as insurance policies, banking services, security services among others. Empty the warehouses of the processing, bottling and other manufacturing-based to engage yourself and make your bucks. You can only do this by thinking for the firms.

Think, strategise on getting the right users at the right places. Work on the strategies before your intention is made known to the management in form of persuasive proposals. You could it big if you are multi-lingual. You could it bigger if that is added with all your social connections. What you have around and within you is enough to turn you employed. And extra efforts could turn you into producer yourself a la amazon.com of this world. Start from selling others products and save to start your own. Start selling others' services with the products a la Ross Perots of this world and you get on the track of becoming a billionaire like him. Sell research findings. Develop additional values to a finding or some findings to get yourself registered in the history book of successful researchers. A wise used to say "To be at the position or step into the status of the most successful, then you must tread their paths to the revered height".

Watch the lips of the public officers and head of departments. Never mind the usual propagandas. When the societal or national ills are mentioned, the truth is said at last. What they say are the path to start a business for you creative solution-oriented mind. Imagine a statement '20million enjoy electricity out of 160million'. Jobs opportunities are for you, the producers and sellers of renewable energy, energy saving bulbs and electricity generation plants. Form a consortium and engage the right ministry for contracts with government or the institutions in need of suppliers. Public Private Partnership (PPP) is adequate to create jobs for thousands. Imagine the ban on importation of a staple food. Jobs are knocking your doors if you start production locally. Listen to news and interviews of those public figures; read into the challenges facing institutions and your efforts to proffer solutions would engage you meaningfully.

Many poor nations lack aesthetics. Road, streets, residential, commercial houses aesthetics are in short supply. Create different aesthetics to turn them inviting. And by so doing, the path to start lucrative job is started. Create comfort stations at miles apart and many you would employ as your staff. Create commissioned hawkers of your souvenirs at gatherings. Imagine the income that would be banked for you! Create private public parks close to open markets and imagine the perks that come your way. The lapses of government are an open **opportunity** begging to be explored. Villagers that lack electricity need to enjoy cold products. Establish cold room within to sell products to them. Create health centres at villages and start making your money. Diagnostic and scanning centres are lacking in the country-side, provide them and get employed! Create your gardens and parks for tourists to relax. Certain fees for users would land you among the satisfied employers.

What are you doing with your natural talents? Many read the theory before they develop one. Never waste the talent that can feed your generation and even outlive your generations. Many research institutes need your services for their publications, productions and public relations. International organizations are looking for you as their independent publicist. Turn the popular books of publishers, as a freelance, into major languages for them to make higher profits. Re-write the names of popular poets. Re-produce their works into major languages you understand. Help the factories empty their stores. Lead the vans to distance to sell to the natives for a good remuneration. Selling the products through advertisement in major languages you understand is worth millions in value to the producers. Move up to reach mutual agreement with them and make your mark by becoming a brand for the firms. A new face of the product or service or the awaiting ambassador!

Many an interview is a good source of jobs creation opportunity. Many business ideas are being churned out for viewers of television and cable. I never watch the lips of the interviewee without making something out of his or her lips. We have highlighted this under the reading of newspapers in search of jobs. Take what you learn in the section to have a rethink of what we meant by interview on television channels. From documentaries a friend developed snailery, poultry and many other agricultural-based businesses. He never watched the tubes for the fun of it. In watching television documentaries and features, he created several jobs!

Many factories are facing similar problems. It is dwindling fortunes. This is a result of weak sales. Can you create clients to empty the saleable products? Apply your social connections to minority that could be biggest buyers. This is sales agency work that could turn you into billionaire like the Warren Buffet and Ross Perots of this world. Selling other people's products and services when you do not have yours is a great opportunity to hit it big and create your own brand as reputable seller. Many publishers I know started from selling other's books. Many technicians today started from working for others. Develop your interest from working for others, on the job you learn the skill and develop the arts to become your own boss. Target marketplaces of the average income earners too! Make the effective use of your multilingual talent. Before you know it, profits start to amass. That is the starting point to reach the height. Sky is your benchmark in the selling business! Sell other people's products with authorized permission as in transliteration and translation of bestselling books into different dialects. Re-package block buster films into different languages or becoming subtitles in bilingual and many others.

Many an asset is turning rot. Look into the streets to make discoveries. Check out the residential and business districts. Visit parks and markets. Stroll to industrial layouts. Find the vacuums or the missing points. Critically studies the materials for schools. Interview people to unearth what is urgently needed. Visit institutions and unveil what they are lacking. Go back to your inner room and dish out what could be provided or produced to bridge the vacuums. What are you doing to turn them into commercial values, you idlers? Sell the education outfits to potential students for a good charge on agreement. What can you sell to the teaching staff to boost their performance? What mobile service can you render to add values?

Do you know that 'messengership' has become a big job for people through modernization? I am talking about the DHL, EMS, IMNL and other courier service providers of this world. Do you see where you can make a difference? How do you run errand for different business institutions? What about doing the same for the staff of those institutions? Employ yourself. Task yourself in the publicity business. Turn yourself into public relation officer to reputable institutions. Get their permission after showing your stuff in persuasive proposals; one or two would give you the job!

Imagine the number of jobs that could be created from the idle and underutilized assets in each nation. It is ridiculous for advanced nations having scourge of unemployment when the assets could create the jobs in excess of needs. In United Kingdom are over 4,000 libraries. Each library has thousands of readers in a quarter. Can the library organize employment seminars for the authors of entrepreneurship books on its shelves under 'meet the authors'? The practical presentations and demonstrations of the authors in the seminars shall ignite the passion of becoming one's boss by the readers in the library. Is this a propaganda? Can the library employ jobs consultants to create jobs for the readers in their libraries? Imagine if a library is able to create 100 new employers per month through counseling and chats on books on career building, not less than 400,000 employers have been created per quarter. Imagine the effective reading and analyses of such books like 'Creating new jobs from the existing jobs' or 'jobs with zero-capital' or all other works in the catalogue on jobs creation. The sharing of the content online with many online readers and the periodical bringing them under s roof for proper business discussion under career guide would do the magic. The job is finished with the gathering after the interest has been created. The multiplier effect on the labour market would be great! Failure to use the opportunities of the books in the libraries by carrying along the readers through discussions by the librarians and the consultants working within could end up being a great lifetime opportunity lost.

In the same library, many books could have solved the problems of many institutions and businesses if the contents are well explored by internal and external readers. Failure to use the books and materials within appropriately, the effects on the business environment viability remains a mystery. Research begets researches. Products beget product as in complementary or composite products. Service gives birth to services such as complementary services as creation is eternal. This shows that jobs beget jobs- direct or indirect, full time or past time. There is no ending in the creation of jobs!

Conversely, as illustrated earlier in the work, in a nation that is so poor and backward, the measurable lapses are opportunities to create gainful employments. If your nation lacks libraries at strategic places, take it up as profit-making business. Attract readers to libraries through freebies, side attractions, contests with mouthwatering prices. Create readers' club with affordable subscription periodically for the attracted visitors. Aesthetics and working facilities and business ethics could attract many the more especially if you work on the right users. Imagine another nation without social infrastructures, public private partnership would do the job and the lapse has created jobs for thousands!

Population, sparsely or densely distributed, literates or illiterates, cultured or not, religious or not, social or not, of left wing or the right wing, is a great asset that has with it limitless opportunity to start gainful jobs. What they need is what you create for them to buy. Segment the market to nature of needs. Segment them by their age group. Do the segmentation by qualifications and status. Never hesitate to do same by their values, religion or cultural habits. If you cannot create one, be a seller for the producers of such needs and make your perks. The financial status determines the market price.

Research institutes are enough to create jobs opportunities. The findings (final analyses) are there in the archives for years meant for public consumption. Dust off the dirt enveloping the materials. Study them and get engage your mindset. If you are never aware, the findings are there for you and I to become our own bosses. A working and enhancement legislation could do the final job. In a nutshell, the institutes are opportunities that are creating opportunities for idlers!

Conversely, in the nations where they are lacked, create institutes through affiliations and you are on the track to produce opportunities for nationals.

Each school has the potential. I repeat, each institute has the wherewithal. They have the facilities and manpower resources to produce employers in thousands. In every course of study are numerous practicable jobs. Task your brains, the graduates. Cudgel your brains, oh you the products of the schools! It is high time you stopped your fruitless search for readily-made jobs. Think self-employment instead of the scarce white collar jobs. Start as a sole proprietor. Start yours and continue to rise. All your role models had witnessed these several times. 'Winners never quit as quitters never win' so goes the saying. Be wary of the twin words of employers- hiring and firing. With him are the cards. He flashed at you whichever he wishes at any time he wishes. This is the reason of grabbing the opportunity knocking incessantly at our doors. Not just knocking the doors, about to open the doors for you. It is staring at you. Welcome it and draw it near for exploration! On the job you learn a lot. Off the job, you learn from others. Experience never comes naturally. It is learnt from role models and personal involvement. 'It happens to me' is an experience. 'This is how I solved the challenge' is another experience. All these are opportunities. Business is like a seed. Plant a seed, nurture the seed and reap in multiples of the seed. Invest your nest egg, nurture it, and you reap in hundreds or thousands. Every business has a beginning. Ask the multi-business owners today, they start small with a business idea! Explore the real opportunities to start small and rise; the rise and the fall and the rise again! Your exposure would give you the experience to model others in the nearest future.

What about the figures of the registered industries under the company allied commissions? Revive the dead business enterprises for new owners to continue managing. This opportunity is calling for user to make optimum use of it. Never delist the firms for new as 'old wine, they say, tastes better than the new. Change the management and support the new for business resumption!

Sell the renowned clinics and specialized hospitals to probable users or clients abroad. With this stuff, you have added values to your time. Hit the ground running and you have sought the chance.

How many illiterate drivers are on the wheel? Many, many of course! What do they know about comprehensive insurance policies? They need to know as the itch to know. What the employees within could not do, you could with your socialization with the men on the wheels. Get things right! Take the right steps and you are given the job based on agreeable commission.

All businesses, small, medium and large need the banks. They need the banks and the banks need them too. Make efforts to discover fertile businesses. Owners (discoverers) of many could fund the business with letter of credit. Connect the duo and get your perk. Banking services just the underwriters are huge and dynamic with time. Learning the more would expose you to many or all. Sort them out and recommend what for what user business. As the middleman, you get your returns for the efforts you made! At your fingertips are the dying businesses, make your choices and pick interests. With this, you have broken out of your shell!

Many things around are left to waste. Many a zero-demand could turn to wealth. Think about these and start your own. Many wastes are wealth in disguise. 'In trash are treasures' the English says. Expand your knowledge by reading the tomes of books. The right books are the works on environment. Explore them and catch the interest. It is not a big task when you select your area of interest. Converting the rubbers into pellet would take some steps. Conversion of waste papers into toilet rolls would take some steps. Conversion the old stories reported inside the daily, weekend or periodical prints create numerous jobs for many- direct and indirect. Make efforts to set up one or two, and you have created lucrative jobs for self and many outside there. Simple indeed!

Much has been taught in conversion of other people's materials and minds. Many starters need other people's money. What you sell to them attracts other people's money. What you place before a mentor for mentoring would give you piece of other people's minds. By minds, we mean their intellects, wisdom, practical life experience and the brilliance. Some few hours out of the whole twenty four at your service is what you spare. Get this done and start growing your own.

He has idle system and other typesetting facilities at his beck and call. Not to mention the typesetting capability and his prowess in all the desktop jobs. Alas, this is the same person looking for jobs. Let him make efforts to reach at schools. Let him make s business intention stroll to the offices. Get the works and type within for a fee. Secure jobs from target clients. Supply appropriately. Be time conscious. Do perfect jobs for next turn to come in patronage. Do this often to get the name (goodwill). What follows the name is the gains (rich) attached.

What is the commercial value of the bus or car in the garage? Of what use is the driving skill of the idle guy? Turn the engine on and turn the idle bus into money making asset from commercial driving. Before they get to know, you have got enough to register the bus as commercial.

Register the bus with proprietors and proprietress at schools. Periodical fares would bring in the perks. A good path you have started to get up there leaving the union of idlers. Be wary of idlers, devils find evil jobs for them.

Start nursery business from within. It is less costly with the compost from the backyard dump. Nurse medicinal plants for pharmacists; nurse flowers for florists and landscapers. Nurse scenting and bright colouring flowers for developers, hotels, hostels, hospitals and schools. Never allow the opportunity to slip away from your fingertip. An opportunity lost may never be regained the wise counsels. What you have others lack. Grab it!

Turn the vast premises into recycling plant. Sort the wastes out into categories. Sell some and channel your efforts into the recycling for reselling for users. The lifespan of most dumps is eternal. Recycle business is lifelong business. This is knocking opportunity before you, grab it; exploit it. Exploit it and get the best in commercial value out of it!

It is not a huge task publishing your works. It is just a matter of planning. Some steps you need to take and kick start the business. Many a publishing is done with zero-capital. Start with small number of page-book to end in the large volume of pages. This writer started from self-publishing from the nest egg and some seed capital. It is not sinful thinking big. Every tall building starts from a foundation. The foundation of all the big business is from the small business. Just as the old man was once a baby, get started with the small in size. The size is not the key issue in a business but the quality of the stuff.

Socialize with people and get right business idea from them. In their mix, listen first and speak less. Speaking more may stop you from allow many to contribute. What each contributes might show you the path. Wherever you are, listen to chats. In many a chat, scripts are written by wise thespians. On the streets is the scarce most wanted infinite wealth. A dump by one is an asset to you. I have read about a wise that made his first million from selling the chicken. He sold the chickens to the war displacing people. Another listened to gossips inside the cab. He was coming from the land of snails. This was a land where eating snail was a taboo. This is proving the saying that 'one man's food is another man's poison'. From what he heard, his business started. Having overheard a city where snail was scarce and costly. Not just cost, but in a very high demand. He dropped his bags and did the research. Researching to validate what he heard. He got to know and got the buyers. In thousands they booked in advance. Within a week, the first supply reached the buyers. And from that moment on, the man hit it big!

Hearsays and eavesdropping pay sometimes as most pen professionals used to do. In many cases, never are they eyewitness. It is what they gather from eye witnesses that they wrote. This is so man is limited with resources. And he has no invisible mysterious eyes to know the hidden and all events at all time. Simply to put, they earn their living from what they ear and sometimes see. With your mobile set, the work is done. Record the voice, record the pictures. All these are source of perks. Work things together and get something done. Events are happening every second, and man is never tired listening to breaking news and acts. This is showing the rare opportunities of getting something done positively.

Do you need a certificate to get started? To me, I believe, you don't! Your packaging, intelligence, politeness, creativity and cleverness would land you in deals with the right quarters.

Resuscitate the periodical printed comics for children; use the natural graphic arts within your veins. It is high time you created unique comics for different classes of readers. Discuss prevalent issues in arts. Arts in comics are enough to bring you fortunes and fame. Start telling amusing stories in pictures or art works. This fetches you money than easting time searching for the scarce commodity called jobs. Fantasy and adventure books for children and tourists among adults would change your status from receivers of checks to the issuer of checks. Make them bilingual or multilingual and get the market. Coloured one attracts many potential buyers as aesthetics.

Start updating of the business environment where you are. Help the industries with the efforts in the print. Research and supply the information to the producers. Expose the right markets to sell different wares in your prints. And the target buyers would surely patronize the prints. If you never aware, you have helped them in researching for what they need. Imagine your sales figure if the update in the stock exchange in all capitals are reported by you. Imagine doing the shopping for buyers in form of periodical publication. All these would butter your bread back to back. They did not employ you but you have employed yourself to serve them. And the money is being received from their account willingly. Think for the big guns. Think for the firms. And your deserved perk after work is assured!

Satisfy the thirsts of tourists. They need relax spots. They need fun fair. Create the directions in prints. And sell the prints in hotels and where they are in stadiums. Features of sports events in a session attract huge patronage. Imagine what you make from producing the features of soccer matches and selling at venues of matches. Imagine what you get from reading and digest what is read in print. Ability to read and write is enough to get you lucrative job!

Mathematics is never the friends of lazy students. Can you make the students Mathematics-friendly? Asking me how? Get seated. Get some others who are Mathematicians. Solve the problems of relevant period of past questions. And your product would sell like cakes! Investing your income matters after each sales record; think on investing and grow your investments. What you do to create Mathematics-friendly pupils could be done in all other subjects. The market is always there for you to be market success. Tap the chance and become big time income earner behind the class.

Solve the managerial crises in the institutions. Zero-tolerance to internal and external crises could prompt you into good work. Research into the problems and proffer solutions as independent bodies. Create aptitude tests for the training of employees. The products of these services are worth invaluable document to the target users. And many or the specialized firms or institutions would pick you up as consultant. Create for educational institutions and get rewarded from huge patronage. Map out practicable strategies that recognize the modernity or strategise for firms, institutions to be challenges-free and you could hit it big! When two of my research-based books reached the palms of a gubernatorial aspirant, at the moment he bared his mind. Imagine the position awaiting me if he eventually gets into the exalted office!

Make efforts to catch them young. Who are these targets of mine? I mean, the pupils learning at schools. Trees are nurtured from shoots or seeds. It is good to catch them young. Create 'I can do it' spirit in the young ones from schools. Develop brain teasing quiz on different subjects for them at schools encouraged with mouth-watering prizes. For some fees they register for them. With support of some firms, foundations, NGOs and wealthy interested individuals you hit the ground running. Start working producing young mathematicians, young artists, young architects, young farmers and young professionals from specialized academies. Create teen-authors, potential entrepreneurs from the four walls of schools. Turn the freelance writers in different departments in schools into money-earning undergraduates. Engage the thespians in the art and theatre department into poets and artistes. Let them earn as they read. And this could be their professions to be upgraded after schooling. Make efforts to creating teen-technicians and engineers. In each subjects, you can break the ground. Supportive efforts though to schools, but the latter cannot do without the efforts. Under the 'catch them young', opportunities are limitless to explore, you employable graduates of different disciplines!

At the idle period of mine, meditation is my job. Everything you see around comes from the ideas of many thinkers. Ideas, bedrock of all innovations, come before invention. I decided to engage myself. Teen-mathematicians became an option. Producing one-day teen-author became another. Tourism-on-the-spot became the third. Starting with the first, mathematics clinic became a starting point. From familiarization came the mathematics contests. Positively, I engaged myself and others of course! Imagine creating aptitude tests for pupils on the dreadful subjects. And one could imagine what the gains one could make!

Move a bit away from the focus on pupils. Work on different tests for the employees. This is enough to win training on the job business. As it has depicted you as one that cares for the business!

Plant trees in nursery bags to sell for users. Greenery environment is attractive to all. Generate income from nursery of medicinal and ornamental plants. Imagine keeping of flying fish. This is enough attraction to the tourist among pupils and saleable to the zoological management.

Turn block buster films into animation-packed. This is another dimension of selling to others in the public. With authorization of the owner or maker, you could get started from this.

Turn bestselling prose into poetry. Write them in verses after summarizing the contents. All these are done with the permission of the copyright owners. Serialize the prose into films. And the publishers could enter into agreement with you. Turn reputable poetry into plays. Act the lines to the admiration of the spectators. Here are jobs that are slipping away. An opportunity you must not ignore.

Conversion of juicy stories into animation could attract new market shares. Engage in one to employ yourself. This remains an opportunity calling for you! What about the jingles of many successful firms on television or electronic billboards? Convert them into animation format to save their cost for thespians. Do this and get your pay!

Start developing inspirational scripts from cartoons and quotes; do the same from news and events; do this targeting all and not just the kids. Make efforts to write voluminous prose in verses with authorization. Doing this is creating new market for the owner and publishers! Turn many popular prose into gripping drama and start making your perks. An agreement with the owner would kick start the job! Make abridged version of several publications with permission of copyright owners. Doing this would popularize the books for more.

Create educational jokes teaching the pupils and general readers. With constructive and technical jokes, you sell many products. Many technical products are hard to sell. Create relevant and the right jokes to empty the stores. This is rare opportunity knocking your door. Grab it before it slips. Spare time to engage your time and earn from their purses.

Learn different attitudes from behaviours of all creatures to get things started. Close observation and periodical meditation on them could trigger thriving idea.

With the mobile set, you could engage your brains and limbs. Events are up for records at every moment of life. Upload events for sale to users. Attract the buyers by searching online. Log on to users and you get many of them. Many print and electronic make their names from reporting breaking news. The event you witnessed is very hot to them. Reach agreement and work as a freelancer. In 'thinkstock' the publishers would buy and keep. For background information, the film makers are in need. Sincerely yours, the uploaded events could spark off block buster films from creative makers!

What do you learn from the booksellers in the preface? They turn their selling skills into becoming publishers. Have you ever come across the online retailers advertisements online looking for interested sellers for the products placed online? Those are opportunities at your fingertips. Grab them!

What do you make out of your quality technical skills that you possess? Create software- solution-based software for different challenges facing technical firms. Turn yourself into software installers for agreed fees. Turn into mobile trainers on software solutions. Becoming mobile engineers never belittled your skills. Many social sites you see around started from blogging. Sincerely yours, blog job is a one-man business that attracts zero-capital but the ICT skills and the available devices. Create social sites that are specialized by profession. Imagine creating such for sports lovers. Imagine you create blogs for entertainers only. And you flavor the sites with genuine information. As you attract crowds, you attract businesses advertisements. That is a different direction from the immobile service provider. A new job from the existing job, we call it! Live ahead you time.

As a fan to a particular team, make your perks instead of laughing, yelling and clapping at stadiums. Prepare the saleable souvenirs, graphic artworks, image impressions of great players, for the retired famous players and the team managers and set to claim big bucks. Loyalists and supporters would buy the gifts showing appreciation to your worth. Follow your team to a greater length. Scout for them in wherever position it is dire need. By so doing, you become independent or unofficial scout. Packaging towards making your mark matters in all cases. Be a fan and as well as a scout. Repeat the same for all teams if you have interest in all. This is a path to generate more income to your purse. Make yourself and the products available at the right venues and you are the right track to hit it big!

Do you follow film makers? Do you follow certain thespians? Then, big business has knocked your door, grab it! Do the same as in the above and a viable business is commenced. Visit film locations if you have the innate talents or skills to act.

Train at stadiums with star footballers to get notice. Train at boxing gyms to get discovered. Sell your saleable wares at the locations of choice. In locations, it is either you sell your skill or person or you celebrate (sell) others. Employ some others for other sites. Commissioned hawkers would attract higher sales in volumes as you cannot be in two venues at a time.

Site your 'selling depots' at the entrances of a fair. Let the writer sell his skill in the writers' associations within and beyond. Every writer has the right to belong to several associations. Pick interest in the internet and join international writers. In the union, you make a breakthrough through right links. Display your sketches of graphics arts at appropriate exhibitions and someone there would lift you up! Not just lifting you but show you to the world to appreciate. Seller of instructional materials locates very close to schools. Toys' sellers site close to daycare, Montessori or crèches.

Let the full time housewives turn the facilities at home into factory. Expose and turn the culinary skills into great business. Many renowned chefs started their skills from homes. Study at the leisure in home library to add to your knowledge. Valuable is the time spent to read and write. Many issues worthy of publishing are there to write about. Turn the idle room into a crèche. Multi-lingual day care could turn to nursery school. Running convenience stores is a good business. Think for brides and get their jobs. Bride party, bride costumier, bride suite, beads making among others are good jobs for them. Become online sellers of your skills for good price.

Numerous migrants from Africa get to their choice destination through students visas, foreign scholarships, visa lotteries or several forms of asylums. If the chance is not created by those host nations, would the successful ones able to search for green pasture beyond the shores?

I have research based materials on jobs creation to make good my intention of zero tolerance to the scourge of unemployment across the nations. I had the option of either publishing it here or abroad. I considered the publishing where the product would attract global standard and got more popularity by the facilities in place by the publishers. I opted for the publishers abroad. I got the opportunity of working with them from browsing of internet! Just as many establish lifespan relationship online through the internet, likewise several business relationships can be created. This is good opportunity knocking at your doors, grab it!

Many a nation through bilateral relations has created avenue for transactions. The farmers in farms, the producers in the cities that are ignorant of the signed documents could still be suffering from weak sales. The opportunity to create new market or new customers has been created but they fail to use them at their business peril. Many business owners fail to use the services of import-export banks and facilities to improve their business statuses. Import cheaper but quality raw materials to feed the local industries to increase the jobs opportunities. License individuals who are interested or the relevant agencies are put to task. Exhibition of products are on-going in different venues but many entrepreneurs are never aware. Whose blame if the opportunities slip away? Had they seize the created opportunity, their businesses would have grown as this is sure fire!

In the course of my research, I got aware of some parents who are the managers of their children who are blessed with natural skills. Ask Lionel Messi about his manager. Ask Steffi Graf about her manager, ask Ronaldinho of his manager. Many a parent never promotes their talented children at their own peril. Those who do so are making money and fame from the talents! They started from encouraging the lads; took them to relevant academies to develop the natural skills more. Sometimes, they take them to mentors for proper mentoring. Some are kept under the roof and watchful eyes of a talented coach. In the academies or under the tutelage of coaches, they are fine-tuned to become the accepted stuff; a global product in their field of specialization!

You do not need to speak a world most recognized language before you sell you talent or skill. For a few years of playing in England, Tevez could never speak English. His football talent is paying his bills. He finds his opportunity to create wealth and fame outside his own native home! Where would the natural talents or the skills be more accepted? Locate the right place and off you go to the destination.

Government can create jobs instead of creating higher levels of poverty. The increase in the low income of people through the empowerment of people with cars, bikes and tricycles for commercial transportation is a great **opportunity** to increase small scale industries from the increase in the number of artisans. Let the artisans be encouraged by several relevant inducements. Some implemented policies can create jobs for all the sectors of the economy such as housing and engineering. If 1000 building artisans are employed four times in a year to rehabilitate structures-residential, industrial, hospitality in a year, not less than 1000 structures would be in their charge from a one-million structure in a nation.

BROWSING SAMPLED NEWSPAPER FOR JOBS OPPORTUNITIES

Name: Sunday Punch

Country of publication: Nigeria

Volume: 19

Number: 19,750

Publishing date: July 21, 2013

Publisher: Punch Nigeria Limited

JOBS OPPORTUNITIES

1) Under the title 'we are ready to receive Amaechi-presidency'. Readers who are following the truce between the governor and the presidency could start compiling all the materials, use relevant quotes from the horse's mouths to sell in print or online in special online sites. It is noted that all frontline stories of any newspaper is the hot news that the editorial voted for as the selling point. Jobs for communicators, freelance journalists and columnists for associations, institutes and schools.

2) In the same page (one), the theme-'Jonathan, Obasanjo in secret 2015 talks..'. The two are Presidents; one is a former and the other an incumbent (as at 2015). Many questions come to the minds as regards 2015. Investigative journalism is at work especially the freelance. The buyers of the story are the public and political researchers.
3) Another selling point in the front page is the caption: 'crashed marriage: I have learnt from my mistakes'-Funke Akindele. What is the opportunity here? It is researching and writing about the causes and the effects of crashed marriages especially of the public figures. Proffer solutions as a creative behavioural researcher and marriage counselor.
4) Another catching story is the story through pictures showing the protesters against senate resolution on girl-child marriage. The issue calls for social researchers to start working on the right of girl child after definition of the girl child from different schools of thought. Remember that dearth of unemployment catalysed this effort to create jobs for many. We are surfing the papers to expose the readers to certain jobs they can do from the pieces of content in the paper.
5) Another caption in the inside page is under 'women employment'. Under the theme, the donor donated 20,000 naira to empower the women. How best can women be empowered in this system of political and economic failure? Would cash or the provision of both cash and equipment pay? Start researching on how best to empower women of different categories like for the full time housewives, part time housewives, literate but single women, illiterate and single among other categories. Yours truly has written a book titled 'Housewives are prospective entrepreneurs'. Use your own style and produce something more unique such as women finances, parenting and women in business, entrepreneur women among other titles.
6) An advert showed this: 'Win VIP tickets to the African Fashion shows in London'. What comes to your mind as readers? Do you need to be a designer before you are selected for the show? Do you need to operate a fashion house in Nigeria before you participate? Do you need to have acquired certain qualification outside fashion skills? No. you could be an agent for creative fashion designers displaying the wears especially if you

are a creative person. Create the designs and make some designer fabrics presentation and you are qualified for the shows and exhibitions.

7) In an interview with EU ambassador, it is quoted "…there are not enough activities taking place to provide jobs…There is a lot of importation of things like fruits in a country that has plentiful land'. The interviewee has opened the eyes of the readers to opportunities. What the nation lacks has been stated. There is opportunity for fruits farmers in the nation. There is also chance of making it big as an investor supporting the farmers in the course. In agriculture generally, opportunities are there for the purposeful and creative readers.

8) In another interview with a librarian who was quoted to have said "We lack good libraries". The content shows that public libraries are not adequately stocked wherever they are available. They are too few for the readers and users. The opportunities have been created for private investors in library business-in schools, communities or national. Such specialized libraries for researchers, theological libraries, Mathematics and scientific-based libraries, children-based libraries, corporate and public policy libraries, in either convectional or digital form or even the combination of both are calling for opportunists. With this investment, imagine the number of volunteers and library workers that would be positively engaged.

9) Under another interview, there is a quote of the interviewer to the interviewee who is a professional building engineer that says "There has been shortage of houses in Nigeria…". The answer is best imagined. This is a good opportunity for the real estate developer and mortgage banks to invest and make their legitimate dues. A nation where construction is carried out often employs more people directly and indirectly. Imagine the number of manufacturers of the building materials, the suppliers of the materials, the professional servicemen that would work on the building, the direct workers and the financial institutions.

10) Under young entrepreneur page, the interviewee plays a role model and mentor for the readers. It is a story of a plant science and forestry cum environmental science graduate that becomes an event planner and manager based on the skills she learnt from her mum.

11) Under a classified advert are different goods or items for sale. Can someone create business opportunities from this? Yes there are many. Study the items for sale. Identify with those you could get buyers for. Make enquiries from the advertisers through the phone contacts. Strike an agreement on the price as a sales agent or you agree on trade discount and freebies to attract sales. Then, make efforts to market the items first to your target market newly created by you or those in existence.

12) "Kogi offers Dangote land for refinery". This caption is an opportunity for professional proposal writers. They must work with consortium of relevant professional bodies to give their proposal to be external consultant for the proposed refinery. Are you capable professionally or technically? That is a good opportunity knocking at your door!

13) In the newspaper is a full page advert of a cable television. Can you make something good out of this as freelance graphic artists, journalists, writers, promoters, advertisers, producers, artistes, talented motivational or charismatic speakers, orators and planners? The best bet is to package yourself for the jobs opportunities!

TESTS

a) **P**ick a newspaper or magazine. Read between the lines. Choose your favourite column- Sport, entertainment, commerce, features, interviews and other sections of your choice. Create jobs opportunities as we have demonstrated above. Develop feasibility studies for each of the work with different people of different profile in mind. Mind you, each of the feasibility studies could fetch you a million if you sell them to the right buyers. Good luck!

b) **D**o the same for electronic media. Visit the major roads, study the vehicular movements, study the passengers or motorists, a market, mall, fuel station, school and any other public institutions around you or outside your jurisdiction. Chat with friends, neighbours and colleagues at work. Browse internets and conduct interviews. Administer questionnaires to determine their urgent needs. From what you observed, think about their needs that could create room for jobs opportunities that are crying for discoverers (socio-economic thinkers) like you. Remember that needs are limitless and likewise the jobs opportunities. Recall that needs change with time and tide of life at different climes under different situations. Work on them or chosen interest among the listed needs of target users to create new jobs as a creative seller or as a producer.

PREVIEW TO THE NEXT CHAPTER

We have identified the two extremes in production. It is either one is a producer or one is a seller of the products and services of the identified opportunities. It is an additional gain for the ability to interpret the terms and the use of body language. There is a good chance for s/he who can critically study contents in all institutions and places to be producers of goods and better plus unique services in order to be new employers of labour. Open the next chapter to learn a great deal on how one can become producers and sellers of tangible goods and visible services. Imbibe the steps as guides to become successful one.

3.3 STEPS TO BECOME PRODUCERS AND SELLERS

In the light of our discussions so far, definite and infinite **opportunities** for one to either be a producer or a seller has been set. At outset, we have identified opportunities to be **producing** and **selling** as the bedrock of identifying employment and wealth creating opportunities. Having dealt with the selling and how huge sales could be made and more secure and lucrative jobs are created, we shall critically looked into the inputs towards becoming successful producers and sellers.

TOWARDS BECOMING A PRODUCER

On the basis of our findings, it is an easy task for a nation to create millions of jobs from the promotion of small and medium scale industrialists from the list of opportunities from different ways in all facets of life and sectors that we have illustrated in this book from the first talk '**author speaks**'. By calculation, in recognition of the definition of a small scale business as a business that employs 100 persons, directly and indirectly, a nation that is targeting providing jobs for fifty million only needs adequately motivated 500,000 small scale business owners. This feat is achievable within a year if the opportunities we have exposed the readers (individuals, institutions, government) to are unambiguously enumerated, critically examined to identify the sub-jobs from the value chains of each and then fully supported with right incentives at the instance of those who can collaborate in the creation of jobs as illustrated in the book '**Creating new jobs from the existing jobs**' by the same author. These are the governments at all levels, the philanthropic institutions, the research institutions, the voluntary organizations-profit and charity based, the professional associations or institutes, the alma mater or alumnus, the faith and ethnic-based organization, the foundations and all other stakeholders in the nation to lift the interested entrepreneurs. Meanwhile, the small scale can be developed into becoming medium and large scale as the incentives keep pouring in from the right institutions.

Nevertheless, in the course of becoming a producer in any scale, there are major steps to take by the government via creating enabling environment through incentivize the would-be entrepreneurs. On the part of the individuals, especially those who have developed interests in starting a job from selected opportunities and have discovered the gains accruable to the endless **opportunities, such must also follow certain steps to nurture the jobs into limelight.** Doing this could pave the way for creation of new lucrative jobs as a part of added value chains. **Firstly**, both the government and the would-be-entrepreneurs should never stop learning about how to grow the business by identifying the probable challenges within and outside the jobs under the regular SWOT analyzes. Government through its MDAs should learn how to maintain stable micro and macro-economic environment with right and reviewable policies and how to boost and promote the local content, products and services particularly the indigenous industrialists from external competitors and unhealthy competitions. **Secondly**, ensure you enumerate the ingredients (features, compositions) needed as an interested maker-in-the-making (manufacturer, processor) time to time to meet global competition of your desired tangible goods or visible services. **Thirdly**, learn how to organize your resources (human and non-human) as demand requires. Bear it in your mind that becoming the technical director of any business institutions requires dynamism to ensure the vision is achieved within set time.

Just as we did for boosting arts of selling opportunities, this is also created by lack of certain needs and wants of people, places events and institutions. Bear it in mind that you are becoming a brand by becoming an entrepreneur. Quality product or service must be your watchword. Give a critical look at the existing products and services, make additional contribution to create something new. The existing products have created **opportunities** for the emergence of new products and services. This comes first before goodwill and money-making. For the inevitable steps as an entrepreneur, the prior-steps are inevitable:

a) Develop enthusiasm for the **opportunity** or ever emerging opportunities at your beck and call. Never be a quack producer or provider of service. Learn more from the most experienced to become a professional whose impact is felt by the clients. Your product or service must add values to the lives of the consumers or clients. Expose your team to periodical seminars that would bring the best inputs out of them for 'ever-best' products and services. Be passionate in getting it or the topmost choice among done.
b) Make a good move to learn from mentors and humble enough to listen and learn from your subordinates. Subordinates like boss who recognizes their contribution (physical and mental inputs) and always ready to learn from their natural intelligence and wisdom. Identify appropriate mentor who must have been a successful person in the trade. His wealth of experience would assist in your establishment.
c) Keep diaries of all the day to day running as you are still under the guide of the mentor. The diaries would be a reference material on the job when it is needed. Leader is a title to have control entrust on a person over others by virtues of criteria. Everyone is a leader at his own right. Generally, we are all pupils who learn always and must never tire of learning from cradle to grave.
d) Be a learner under all the workers in the mentor's business to gain more from their practical experience. Scribble down what you learn and never hesitate to enquire about what you do not understand.
e) Meditate over what you learn daily to discover new paths to meet global standard, tackle the internal and external environment and outwit competitors
f) Never start from your own level of knowledge. Take the path of the chosen successful mentor. If you desire to be like Brian Tracy, write in his style to enjoy patronage of Brian Tracy.
g) Always act what you learn to develop more skills
h) Promote the products and the sellers with their locations using the right languages and right graphics that are not offensive
i) Set target for the sales department and provide the facilities require to enhance effectiveness and efficiency

j) Create aesthetics where necessary to attract the crowds of genuine buyers. Work in aesthetic business environment. Produce aesthetics and quality products for buyers. The aesthetics attract them before the quality is tested.

In addition, a successful entrepreneur or producer must have selling skill possess by the professional sellers too. With the right and dynamic selling strategies, such would not be in the dark over the profit-making of the business. With this in mind, producer must see self as the first certified seller of his product or service. Dynamic selling skills must be a top priority hence the independent sellers and the engaged ones in staff would meet the set objectives of the producers at minimum cost.

There are different skills and art of selling that must be continually designed by the producer to educate and guide the sellers to commercial success. Selling, as aforementioned, itself, is a good job for many people as products and services keep increasing. Such increasing output has paved the way for jobs opportunities, direct and indirect. You have read this under the 26 secrets of selling listed at earlier sub-theme. Apply them. He who fails to learn the art of buying and selling would fail in business. Successful salesmen employ different tactics to enjoy patronage of customers as time and tide change. Nevertheless, a seller must not have preferential treatment for buyers. To him/her, all buyers are potential customers regardless of their social profile. To ensure good sales and generating target profit margins, these steps must be taken by the producers:

a) Learn the art of consumers' intention towards buying your products. Customers must be convinced about the quality of your product or service before you anticipate patronage. Keep learning from reading books of researches on selling. Enroll in workshops and for a where the art especially modern strategies of selling are rolled out by different speakers from different sectors, backgrounds and climes. Let it be at the back of your mind that a strategy that works in a city may never work in a close city in the same state and nation. And the quality and the cheapest in price do not propel huge sale. There are more to the duo for a seller and maker to record anticipated sales. Products are bought from different makers at wholesale prices with trade discounts and some other freebies. If you fail to buy at the rate, then your own product will be too costly in the market. A costly product is a turn-off to the buyers. See yourself as one of the competitors making efforts in the sharing of the market share.

b) Learn to understand what makes a product or service a quality and of global standard. Study the compositions, the content, the benefits and other features that make it worthy of placement among the products in stores. Failure to know this would result in stocking your shop with fake and inferior products. Stocking your stores with such products would lead into the losing of your brand name, goodwill and facing the wrath of the law. Ensure that you can be proud of your product or service at anywhere and at all times. But, never close eyes to be better. No end to creativity for the better product and service.

c) Learn how to test product acceptability in the market before you stock them. Never hesitate to sort consumers' opinions about the generic functions of your product or the extent of satisfaction clients derive from using your service. Task your customer care service unit to get right feedbacks from the clients and consumers.

d) Like the independent sellers and general distributors, do proper listing based on our assessment of each product as they are beneficial to satisfy certain needs of customers. Take for instances, in a bookstore, you can categorise a book into different category such as under motivational, reference material, employment generation, income generation among others. The more the category, the more the chance of selling in volume.

e) Ensure you are into selling of varieties especially complementary products. Let a seller of children cloths be selling their shoes, slippers, strolling or bathroom wears for all sexes of different age, colours, sizes and shapes (designs). A seasonal product seller and even a mono-product seller would be at financial loss during the other seasons of the year. Always be dynamic and creative. Employ new think tanks, if there is need, to boost your production quality in order to retain your old customers and gaining new ones from all corners under different market segmentations.

f) Create more sales outlets at the appropriate places where people bypass or very close to business districts if not within the districts. Never use only one outlet as the volume of sales would be minimal.
g) Employ mobile service for certain categories of your buyers. Employ sales agents or hawkers if you can provide the facilities.
h) Inform your target buyers in your list about your new stocks as soon as they are delivered. In short, keep the records of the bio-data and contact addresses of your customers especially the phone directory and email. Update your buyers regularly. Share their dates and felicitate with them at the right time.
i) Sell with gifts and some other forms of discounts for all categories of buyers in retail and bulk purchase.
j) Attract them with ever-changing aesthetics in the outlets.
k) Speak to them in the language they understand. Learn to speak their mother-tongue especially in the placement of adverts of the products on the listing.
l) Join the producers in promoting the goods in your outlets and the locations closer to the target buyers.
m) Learn how to retain the old customers and gaining the new customers.
n) Create aesthetics when and where necessary. Be hygienic and sell in highly aesthetic shops.

N.B Highly recommended is our research-based book on selling titled "Winning huge sales and increasing clients' base"

CHAPTER FOUR

Having discussed widely how opportunities come in different shades and sizes for employment and wealth creation, we shall introduce how new jobs are created from the existing ones by virtue some of the identified opportunities. All the jobs are also eyes opener to creating new ones. The level of creativity and versatility is very important.

4.1   NEW JOBS OPPORTUNITIES FROM THE EXISTING JOBS OPPORTUNITIES

This section is specially focused on churning out some of the limitless new jobs that are creatable from the existing and non-existing opportunities as part of the gains from the reading. Each of the listed jobs has tendency to create jobs for over one hundred. They could be grown and developed into medium and large scale businesses for greater number of jobs from the value chains.

1. Reading billboards: In order to boost the reading culture and producing bright, competent and highly educative students. Digital boards for advertisements can be converted into reading tablet for free readers at business districts, campuses, hostels, hotels, relaxation joints et al. A portion would be for advertisements and the two third of the board would be reading page. Such reading tablet at campuses, hostels, business districts... could be speechless (mute) billboards or the speaking ones where the pages are being read out as programmed by the software engineers.

2. Entertaining electronic board: We see this as a chance of increasing the sales and popularity of the thespians and the title. Entertainment billboard is a free medium where films and songs are freely transmitted to the public. It is an avenue to showcase the artists and their products and a path to make money from downloading and selling of compact discs or e-formats of the intellectual property.

3. Book, films, songs…reviews on media institutions: These intellectual property can be created from all sources. Reflection on the prints and broadcasting contents could trigger writing, books publishing and productions of combination of media with the materials as in education radio. This is another form of selling many idle ones can pick up. If the works of intellectual property owners are reviewed in the media by the people, they become sellers like those who sell at stores.

BUSINESS IN BUSINESS

1) **Blog in blog:** In today's business world, firms pay for attractive tweets to crowd-pulling bloggers. A blogger rides on other popular bloggers to sell his brand to create followers. Individuals can produce blogs for different themes. They could move up to engage in vblogs. And the combination of the two is feasible for those who have the tools and brilliance. I admonished a guy to choose a blog that needs to be updated on weekly basis than the ones that require daily update. A good example is specialized book review blog. There is no limit to number of blogs that can be created as versatility and creativity abound every surface of the earth. Congestion on satellites may serve as major obstacle as the traffics of blogs slow down the services.
2) **Social media in social media:** The internet facility has created room for several specialized or professional digital media to be created. Many have started operation of specialized online radio and television stations through the existing social media. Nations desire competition in order to downsize the costs of advertisements for the industries and institutions. The platform and the template is not as technical to discourage interested investors of money and technical skills.

3) **Television in television:** Media-entrepreneurs could package reality shows, files, events reporting businesses, sports analyses, fashion, films promotion, service publicity among others on the convectional traditional media stations. The traditional stations are in need of such bumper package from external presenters to add values to their brands and attract advertisements. The inception of digitalization of the broadcasting media would create more employments for the people from different professional leanings.
4) **Radio in radio:** Like the above, independent and creative entertainers, seasoned broadcasters especially the freelancers... should package interesting stories consumable by the listeners. Most wasting or idle air time should be repackaged by the director of programme to unveil new freelancers with right packages to turn the time into commercial use. Those who have contents and do not have the funds to establish radio stations could partner with the existing radio stations to air their projects.
5) **Print in print:** Journalists can practice their jobs by going specialized. Imagine printing reviews about products and services and get them as part of the prints in popular newspapers. Such can take this step- Pay for four centre pages to produce your materials in the daily, weekend and periodical productions at a negotiable fee. Sports journalist, a freelancer, can partner with the existing newspaper firm to produce his or her own sports package. What about music writers, fashion designers, photo-journalists, institutions to advertise what they stand for like the estates managers slots being printed to promote what they have to sell or lease out to the clients among others?. Many columnists today use the platforms to popularize themselves. They achieve their present status from the use of the print media. In fact, many direct readers to their blogs and sites from the regular featuring in the papers.
6) **Event in event business:** In social functions, independent sellers of souvenirs and those who would add spices to energize the events are highly appreciated and rewarded. Public figures cherish paparazzi and side attractions that can add values to their personality. Such include v

ideography, photography, visual artists. It takes the creative minds to identify what events that could be added to spice an event.
7) **Bookshops in bookstores, malls, fuel stations….:** If you are reputable writer and author, partner with reputable bookshops that have locations at right places with huge records of sales by history; create your own section where your works are displayed on the basis of agreement. By this, you have your own 'bookstore' within the bookshop. You can do this with the broadcast station. By this, you are making customers from their customers and earning goodwill from their goodwill.
8) **Faction stories from biographies:** We are in a world where stories of people could be scribble down to produce books. But unlike the biography and autobiographies, you are only privileged to a short story and you build new stories to tell the life story of the person. Such could be turned into films and documentaries in form of animation or for the advertisement agency including building reality shows.

GENERAL TESTS

On the basis of what has been taught in the work, churn out and develop new employment from the following list:

1) Motivational and sports media stations
2) Mobile schools, clinics, malls,
3) Stock exchange broker on mobile phones
4) Specialized educational and vocational activities
5) Recycling of old 'intellectual property'
6) Scouting and nurturing of talents, skills…
7) Franchising as a business
8) Eradicating piracy and substandard goods for a price
9) Mobile entertainers (poets, artworks…)
10 E-journalism and i-reporting; e-school and i-learning
11 Unique Reality shows

4.2 THE GAINS

The opportunities exposed people, institutions and associations (of different values) to in the research-based work would make a nation prosperous. There would be adequate employment opportunities from numerous opportunities from different points of views. In addition, the level of productivity is enhanced and the vicious acts go south as more people are engaged positively. A benefit to the individuals would have positive multiplier effects on the overall especially in the quality of living.

In addition to the benefits to the nation, there is improved aesthetics as the land is free from all forms of social nuisance. The human liabilities would have become human assets as more capable manpower resources have been created. There is proliferation of businesses. The wealth of the nation is no more concentrated among a few citizens but rather evenly distributed. The nation's Gross Domestic Products (GDP) and Gross National Income (GNI) continue to swell. In the comity of nations, it becomes a highly respected advanced economy that would be a business model for others.

TO THE NATIONS

a) From the limitless opportunities and how to discover them based on the contents, the nations are free from human liabilities as gainful employment is generated in thousands for millions directly and indirectly to benefit from
b) The national environment is free from nuisance and filths hence it wears new and inviting aesthetics
c) The anticipated increase in the gross domestic product leads to the corresponding increase in the national income; and as a result, the per capita income increases. These are the result of the proliferation of several sub-industries from different sectors and sub-sectors as a product of using all the opportunities in all disguise.

d) There is increase in the number of independent artisans and their contributions shall have a tremendous improvement on the national economy at micro and macro levels.
e) A healthy and wealthy nation is an attractive nation to investors, tourists for its serenity and peace. Artisans are into building aesthetics and repairs shall create aesthetic environment for investors, local and foreign.
f) In the comity of nations, nations whose citizens are positively engaged in lucrative jobs from the use of opportunities become world powers that would be treated with respect.
g) There is no more financial cost in the payment of social cost to the unemployed people on the streets!

TO THE CITIZENS

a) The illustrations about how to identify opportunities in the content show that innovations and robots would not send people out of jobs and the fear of losing a job is a thing of the past
b) Families can develop new business owners at homes from little age whose source of income could sustain the families
c) earnings from the youth-entrepreneurs from the young age would later Improve per capita income enhances improve standard of living
d) Inventors and discoverers start to grow in number from each home
e) People would never see a thing as a waste again. The misconception about wastes would be a thing of the past. They develop ability to identify 'wastes' and capability to transform them into wealth
a) Human liabilities are turned into human assets and the nation is free from all the negative effects of the scourge of unemployment.

TOWARDS SUSTAINING THE NEW ENTREPRENEURS AT THE MILK-TEETH STAGE

Government must take these steps:

a) Government agency on employment generation would need the material to communicate how opportunities are created for employment generation for the citizens especially those who have skills to demonstrate. (Ref: '**Artisans**' from the stable of the author)
b) Encourage all who buy into the employment opportunities with the creation of the right business environment in incentives for their operation in order to produce the world standard product with all the aesthetics.
c) Patronize their products and services by using appropriate legislations or legislative tools especially those on the prohibition list of the apex bank. This is a morale booster of the local producers and service providers.
d) Government must endorse the products and services in official launching by the relevant agencies or departments in order to ensure the patronage of home-made commodities.
e) Government could create markets for the products through bilateral pacts with other nations.
f) Create more attractions for artisans for the creation of cottage and small medium enterprises

THE FINAL THOUGHTS

Reading this book and the rest in the series is a great opportunity. By now, lots of jobs opportunities have been unveiled for the readers. Is there any excuse for dearth of jobs in the nations? Would there be publication of percentage of unemployment in nations again? Would nations and the nationals be unable to sustain themselves with the revelations made? Nay! Times without number, opportunities are at your fingertips. Never look for vacancies from the slave-wage payers called employers. Resign from the slave jobs where your freedom and health is jeopardized and programmed like robot. Apply your senses. Take your destiny by your hands. 'The best source of earning is self-employment' according to the noblest among us. Self-employment is self-reliant. Self-reliant is a good path to financial independent and retirement plans. Time resources at your disposal with the proper attention to the opportunities would transform you from Mr. Nothing to Mr. Something within a set target time. Be your own boss. This is an invaluable advice.

PART TWO
How to start a business, where and when

A reader, an engineer by profession, after reading the first book on employment generation '**Jobs with zero capital vol.one**', commented that most of the jobs illustrated in the book with the inputs needed are doable abroad and not in a place like Nigeria. In fact, after different views and illustrations to establish the fact, I deemed it fit to start researching into the environment that is right for a business to thrive. The product of the research is the book '**Understanding Business Environment, right or wrong**'. In the book, it is established that business environment varies with dynamics and several factors within each. A business environment in advanced nations where certain facilities are at the beck and call of the investors can never be comparable with business operating environment in Nigeria where such facilities are lacking. In addition, the people and values of each environment differ. What about their interests, diverse needs and endless wants that are determined by personality ego, status, affiliations, education qualification, the weather and climatic conditions among several other factors? What about the political ideology in operation and economic directions of the governments at the helms of affairs? All these and several others are determinant of how an environment could be.

In view of the above, having showed the readers to different opportunities to start jobs, they must have simple tips on **what**, **when**, **where** and **how** to transform existing opportunities into employment creation in order to their own bosses. These are the tips:

WHAT

a) What is the biggest and most preferred opportunity to work upon?
b) What are the tools needed?
c) What are the facilities at the beck and call for use?
d) What can be done to have access to the right tools, resources and other facilities?
e) What is the potential of attracting customers or clients in the target markets?
f) What should be the first steps for this kind of selected interests to start a job?
g) What are put in place to ensure successful running of the business idea?
h) What are the measures to rate the success running of the business opportunities?

WHEN

a) When should the opportunities start?
b) When should the products from the processed opportunities be officially launch?
c) When can outsource be employed in the course of doing the job?

WHERE

a) Where should the business idea identify start?
b) Where are the manpower and the resources that are inevitable?
c) Where are the supports and incentives needed to run the ideas into fruition?
d) Where can the tools be sourced within and outside?

HOW

a) How do I start?
b) How do I plan for the job?
c) How do I manage the business into success?
d) How do I have firm control over the job?

e) How do I enjoy official recognition for the new business from the identified opportunities?
f) How do I involve people, institution or government agencies to unveil the potentials in the nation?
g) How do I create and increasing generation of clients or customers?
h) How do I strategize the selling and promotion to generate huge patronage and sales within a set time?

With the prompt responses to the posers above, being one's boss may not be a magic after all. Studies show that a new boss must have the following:

a) Passion for the job
b) Belief that the jobs shall impact lives and the business environment
c) Courage and confidence
d) Optimism that the business shall be successful
e) Ability to hire the right persons that share equal passion and interest for the job
f) Time-conscious to achieve the goal of the business
g) Ability and interest to start small
h) Ability to be financial discipline hence such can grow the business gradually
i) Personal discipline to separate owner or manager from the business. Both are different entities
j) Learning new skills and arts that would boost all strategies to run and sustain the business
k) Ability to read and interpret the economic policies of government where the business is operating

In a nation where the operating business environment is inadequate or not available at all, people who desire to be self-bosses should look inward on how to convert the idle assets, unused resources, recyclable materials and available funds to start. We assume that the nation does not have strong financial institutions that can provide funds and the necessary inputs. A dreaming self-boss should be prudent and think outside the box on how to use what is available to start small and grow with dynamics of time.

EPILOGUE

Social and economic opportunities are at the fingertips
Source for them and make the mark
And make the impact felt within the nation
And the nationals are good for it

REFERENCES

Amusa Abdulateef (2017) Jobs with zero capital (vol. One and Two) authorhouse and createspace.com

Idem (2013) Business environment, right or wrong (unpublished)

Idem (2013) Creating new jobs from the existing jobs Iuniverse, Bloomington, IN. United States of America

Idem (2013) Wastes to wealth jobs" createspace.com

AD-COPY

THE AUTHOR

Abdulateef Amusa is the brains behind the outfit, **Addin Resources Ventures** whose foundation is into manpower development and empowerment targeting creating valuable resources for nations across the world through research-based publications.

His profession is creative researching and writing with several successful publications to his credits such as the popular **Jobs with zero-capital** (Vol. 1 & 2). The first volume has become one of the materials in the **British Library** under the categories of Business enterprises and self-employed catalogue. His other works include the first volume of this work titled '**Creating new jobs from the existing jobs**' published under the label of **iuniverse** based in the United States is also a bestseller and one of the collections of IFRA Nigeria. His other books under entrepreneurship are Wastes to wealth jobs; Housewives are prospective entrepreneurs. He had several other works under different issues like sociology, philosophy, economics and finance.

THE BOOK

It is a fact that **opportunities** are limitless and every **opportunity** begets several opportunities hence viable ideas. In the work are **opportunities** to create independent artisans. The book unveils different opportunities knocking on the doors of many casual, domestic and contract staff workers not to talk of idle individuals roaming the streets in search of lucrative jobs opportunities and ideas in different unbelievable dimensions and shapes. Social researches show that all business activities are done with the maximum use of the opportunities by the owners. It exposes how **opportunities** to start lucrative jobs by individuals, institutions, government agencies and associations at different times and places. There is the inevitable need for individuals to identify different sources and types of **opportunities** at different times and climes towards creating lucrative jobs. It is done to create adequate jobs and wealth distribution enhancement from the increase gross domestic products and national income.

www.ingramcontent.com/pod-product-compliance
Lightning Source LLC
Chambersburg PA
CBHW020639220526
45464CB00001B/213